Real Estate Exam Prep
The Authoritative Guide to Preparing for the

Third Edition

John R. Morgan

On-The-Test Publishing
(www.On-the-Test.com)

© 2010-13 by John R. Morgan. All Rights Reserved.

No part of this publication may be reproduced, stored in a retrieval system, or transmitted, in any form or by any means -- electronic, mechanical, photocopying, recording, Internet, or otherwise -- without the prior written permission of the copyright holder or publisher. Please contact the publisher at the address below for information on permissions and licenses.

ISBN-13   978-0-9711941-6-8
ISBN-10   0-9711941-6-5

Published by:

On-The-Test Publishing
   The publishing imprint of Morgan Testing Services
Post Office Box 1982
New London, Connecticut 06320
www.On-the-Test.com
email: Combo@On-the-Test.com

We welcome reader comments and suggestions about our text and test questions.
Please contact the publisher at the email address above regarding either.
Email us about typos, terms, and omissions in this book,
as well as your thoughts on useful inclusions in future printings.
We especially welcome hearing how your understanding of topics was enhanced and your test-confidence -- and success!-- was ensured by anything in this book.

Dedication

This edition is dedicated to the memory of my father, John B. Morgan of Old Saybrook, who, even well into his "retirement," was still active in commercial real estate there, and collected commission checks even after his memorial services in early 2006.

*As a lifelong source of both inspiration and exasperation for me, I am grateful that medical advances gave him an extra six years for us to become even closer friends. And it was a special blessing to watch him hold, sweet-talk, and enjoy his newest namesake, my first-born son,
John A. Morgan, almost to the day of his 1st birthday; I regret he did not get to welcome the newest Charley Morgan to the family in 2007.*

It is also dedicated to my father's commercial colleagues Bob Cancelmo, Ron Lyman, John Jensen, Margie Driscoll, and Bob Russo, who have proven they still honor my father's belief in handshake agreements in real estate transactions. God bless.

Publisher's Foreword

With few exceptions, state real estate licensing agencies contract with a company specializing in examination administration services to administer tests for their licensing candidates. These companies typically offer test development services as well, and have prepared an exam known variously as a "uniform," "national," or "general" exam and follow it with a shorter exam that is state-specific.

General exams are designed to test subject matter that is common across state lines, and to specifically avoid testing terms, concepts, practices, and laws that are either regional or state-specific in nature: those topics are usually tested in the state-specific portion of the exam. This book covers both portions.

Psychological Services, Inc. (PSI), a company based in Burbank, California, has been a provider of real estate licensing examination services for nearly two decades and is becoming increasingly more sensitive to national applicability of specific terms, concepts, and practices as its client roster grows nationwide.

General exams prepared by test vendors are reviewed for adherence to a comprehensive set of guidelines for test development by the Association of Real Estate License Law Officials (ARELLO®). PSI's exams have been repeatedly accredited by ARELLO®'s Examination Accreditation Program.

For more information on ARELLO®, which has links to the Websites of state licensing agencies nationwide, PSI, and other vendors that may have information on a non-PSI-client state of interest to you, especially Candidate Information Brochures with state-specific examination and licensing information, visit the following Websites:

- *www.arello.org* for information about ARELLO® as well as state links
- *www.psiexams.com* for information on PSI and its client states
- *www.goamp.com* for information on *AL, GA, IL, MI, MO, MT, NE, NH, ND, SD, WA, and WY*
- *www.pearsonvue.com* for information on *AK, AZ, AR, DE, DC, FL, ID, IN, KS, ME, MA, RI, UT, and WI*

(Note: states occasionally change exam vendors, so check the other vendor Websites if you cannot find the state you are looking for at the one given.)

The publisher wishes to make these final important clarifications:

Nothing in this publication should be construed as indicating PSI or the Connecticut Real Estate Commission's endorsement of, involvement in, or responsibility for any of the author's interpretations, elaborations, or commentary on the PSI general content outline's list of commonplace real estate topics or the Connecticut state-specific content outline's list of license law topics.

All interpretations of and elaborations on real estate subject matter and state laws are based on close research of standard texts, legal reference works, state-specific curriculum guides, and government Websites, along with editorial recommendations from a nationwide group of reviewers in the fields of real estate regulation, law, practice, and instruction.

All opinions regarding testing practices, policies, or procedures are those of the author based primarily on his professional test development training at the Educational Testing Service (ETS) and subsequent application of that training to real estate licensing programs in over twenty states and the Government of Bermuda. They are not necessarily shared currently by PSI, ARELLO®, the Connecticut Real Estate Commission, or any other organization named in this text.

Author's Introduction to the General Exam Review

As a real estate student or instructor, some of the prelicensing textbook material you study makes you ask yourself that age-old question, "Will this be on the test?"

On-the-Test: Real Estate books address that question through a concentrated, no-nonsense approach that will prepare you more effectively, ***in fewer pages than other exam prep books***, most of which use more than twice the space—and expect you to spend the additional required reading time!

To begin with, consider the PSI exam content outline: It begins where you are, with learning basic real estate terminology and concepts of property ownership, rights, and control in Sections I and II, following these essential basics with terms, concepts, and processes common to valuation in Section III.

Section IV concentrates on the broad range of details involved in financing a property transaction, while Sections V and VI cover those terms, concepts, principles, processes, and requirements applicable to common-law agency relationships as they relate to real estate transactions.

These are followed by Sections VII and VIII, which brings you where most successful real estate transactions go: to contractual relationships between parties, including purchase-and-sale agreements, and a property closing with a host of documents being prepared, explained, signed, and recorded.

Section IX supplements elements of Sections V, VI, and VII by separating out the terminology and requirements specified in federal Fair Housing law as well as advertising requirements found in the federal Truth in Lending Act (Regulation Z) and other important laws, conventions, and practices.

Section X clusters math computation questions commonly performed for various steps in a real estate transaction, and Section XI identifies and discusses several important real estate areas that do not always fit easily in ordinary sales-related transactions.

This book will build on the logical flow of the outline to clarify what you need to know in each of the outline's Topic Areas. As I have considered which terms and concepts are most logically associated with each area, I have addressed them with the following principles in mind.

1. **Exam outline-area organization of key terms and concepts**
   - This means like-terms are clustered where they are most likely to be categorized for test use, regardless of where they may appear in a standard textbook presentation.
2. **Question-count indication of relative importance of each outline Topic Area**
   - This should lessen anxiety about having to know *everything* in a particular Topic Area, since you will know that there may be just a few – perhaps no – questions from it.
3. **Concise, direct definitions and descriptions**
   - This avoids over-explanation, especially where further elaboration could detract from the central, testable content. This book provides a focused review of textbook material. If you want more words, refer to your main textbook.
4. **Synonymous terms are presented together as "extra" terms**
   - This clarifies, as often as possible, that similar terms are, in fact, synonymous, and the way your textbook presented a topic may be tested by PSI with another term.
5. **Bold-faced and italicized identification of terms, definitions, and key phrases**
   - This serves to accentuate the more important content within a description or general statement. These formats will also highlight terms that may be used as <u>*wrong answers*</u>, known as "***distractors***" in the education and testing businesses, so unfamiliar terms will not trick you into thinking, "I should have studied that!"

Author's Introduction to the General Exam Review

6. **Related _nontestable_ information is included, usually boldfaced and/or italicized**
   - This allows you to see more advanced, obscure, or regional information in the cluster of related material that, though inappropriate for testing, may appear as distractors.
7. **Italicized commentary**
   - This allows me to provide occasional conversational asides intended to further clarify a point, reduce potential topic-related anxiety, or stress nontestable topics.
8. **Minimal math emphasis**
   - This low emphasis is based on the less-than 10% emphasis of math on the exam, which makes math-related questions important, but not critical to one's overall score.

     This author is unapologetic about leaving math instruction to your 500+ page textbook: Enough of the math questions on the live exam will be basic enough to be easy. (A test-wise tip for those with weak math skills or high math anxiety is to compensate by becoming stronger in _other_ areas.)
9. **Sufficient, not excessive, numbers of sample questions, and diagnostic chart**
   - The questions presented at the end of this book address central and critical topics adequately rather than exhaustively. The Sample Exam corresponds more closely to PSI's published outline specifications than any you will find by other authors, and the diagnostic chart allows you to check your exam-readiness.

As noted on the cover, this book is designed with **both students and instructors** in mind.

- **Prelicensing students** will find it useful as a concise, comprehensive presentation of textbook principles and practices material in a test-outline format. And, since it distills the key terms and concepts presented in most standard texts, its usefulness will continue once you are licensed by serving as light, handy, quick-reference book!
- **Instructors** will find it a ready-made manual for a highly focused and effectively concentrated end-of-course review.

My only direct experience with PSI's general examination came through taking it in the spring of 1999 to earn my Connecticut real estate salesperson license. Through this exposure, I became convinced that the item pools PSI uses for its exams provide an adequate and well-crafted sampling of the content domain of real estate.

So, sorry: There are no shocking secrets to be revealed about "questions to watch out for." Everything herein is based on well-reasoned consideration and a unique perspective on which real estate terms and concepts are most appropriately suggested by the published outline headings.

Further, my involvement with Assessment Systems, Inc. (ASI)'s fully national Real Estate Job Analysis along with a close review of the follow-up ASI Job Analysis Technical Report (1998), many state-specific prelicensing course outlines, and numerous real estate and legal texts support the inclusion of the key words, topics, and distractors presented in this book.

My confidence that this book is the best one available rests primarily on my belief that the direct, concise presentation and organization of this text is grounded in unparalleled experience with real estate licensing examination subject matter and Subject Matter Experts nationwide.

So, knowing what dozens of committees of Subject Matter Experts have concluded during review sessions does give me a refined sense of what would pass muster. And soon when *you* see a strange term and wonder, "Will this be on the test?" you, too, will know **_exactly_** what to say!

Acknowledgments

Thanks go to the many educators and regulators who have encouraged me to write this book.

By providing a concise reference to both real estate subject matter and how it is tested, I hope it serves their goals of continuing to strengthen and improve both real estate instruction and professional real estate test development programs nationwide.

In addition, many, many thanks to all of the regulators, instructors, and practitioners I've worked with in many high-spirited and highly productive test development meetings nationwide and since going independent, in Bermuda. Every meeting was an adventure and a success. Then, and even more now, I appreciate what Tom Samph, co-founder and longtime president of Assessment Systems, Inc. (ASI), said when I asked him what he missed most about life "after" ASI:

"The clients. They're what it's all about."

So, I would like to thank, at least by reference, everyone who contributed their time to improving their state exams and in doing so helped me hone my skills regarding testable real estate content.

Thanks go to every client and committee member I met with in:
Alaska, Arizona, Arkansas, Colorado, Delaware, the District of Columbia, Hawaii, Illinois, Indiana, Kansas, Kentucky, Massachusetts, Minnesota, New Jersey, Pennsylvania, Rhode Island, South Carolina, Tennessee, Utah, and Washington.

These committees constantly drove home the importance of asking questions drawn from current real estate information, processes, and practices that were both appropriate and relevant for entry-level real estate professionals. The distinction they observed between "need to know versus nice to know" generally weeded out weak, too-advanced, too-detailed, or irrelevant questions during periodic, routine committee reviews of both existing and newly written test questions.

They were painstakingly conscientious in setting expectations for entry-level performance while identifying significant details licensees will learn after entering the business. Further, they duly noted numerous transaction-related topics and details that other professionals, especially lawyers, lenders, appraisers, and accountants, are more appropriately responsible for knowing.

This book aspires to do justice to their example of discussing much more than would be on the test while respecting the line between what is testable and what is also important to know.

This edition incorporates routine updates to the Connecticut State-specific exam based on statute changes along with enhanced treatment of General-exam sections based on PSI's 2009 "expanded" outline, which identifies key sub-topics of the previous one-page "concise" version.

Many general refinements are grounded in elegantly nuanced editorial observations offered by Charlie Wyatt, who founded and still teaches at South Carolina's longest-operating real estate school. I am grateful for his generosity in sharing his sharp-eyed insights and real estate expertise and thank him on behalf of the beneficiaries of his persuasive comments: the readers of this book.

I apologize in advance to the same readers for any deficiencies and oversights that remain—they are solely my doing.

Real Estate Exam: PSI's General Content Outline
Concise Version *(Version with Sub-Topics Begins on Next Page)*
80 questions for both Sales and Broker exams
There are 7 math-related questions; this represents an approximate 9% overall math emphasis.
(Your exam may also include an extra five unscored "pretest" questions for a total of 85.)

I—Property Ownership (6 questions)
    A. Classes of Property
    B. Land Characteristics and Legal Descriptions
    C. Encumbrances
    D. Types of Ownership
    E. Physical Descriptions of Property

II—Land Use Controls and Regulations (5 questions)
    A. Government Rights in Land
    B. Public Controls Based in Police Power
    C. Regulation of Environmental Hazards
    D. Private Controls

III—Valuation and Market Analysis (8 questions)
    A. Value
    B. Methods of Estimating Value/Appraisal Process
    C. Competitive/Comparative Market Analysis (CMA)
    D. When Appraisal by Certified Appraiser is Required

IV—Financing (7 questions)
    A. General Concepts
    B. Types of Loans
    C. Sources of Loan Money
    D. Government Programs
    E. Mortgages/Deeds of Trust
    F. Financing/Credit Laws
    G. Mortgage Fraud, Predatory Lending Practices (Risks to Clients)

V—Laws of Agency (10 questions)
    A. Laws, Definitions, and Nature of Agency Relationships
    B. Creation and Disclosure of Agency and Agency Agreements (General) *[Regulatory Details in State Portion]*
    C. Responsibilities of Agent to Seller, Buyer, Landlord, or Tenant as Principal
    D. Responsibilities of Agent to Customers and Third Parties
    E. Termination of Agency

VI—Mandated Disclosures (7 questions)
    A. Property Condition Disclosure Forms
    B. Warranties
    C. Need for Inspection and Obtaining/Verifying Information
    D. Material Facts Related to Property Condition or Location
    E. Material Facts Related to Public Controls, Statutes, or Public Utilities

VII—Contracts (10 questions)
    A. General Knowledge of Contract Law
    B. Listing Agreements
    C. *Management Agreements [Broker Only]*
    D. Buyer Broker Agreements/Tenant Representation Agreements
    E. Offers/Purchase Agreements
    F. Counteroffers/Multiple Counteroffers
    G. Lease and Lease-Purchase Agreements
    H. Options and Right of First Refusal
    I. Rescission and Cancellation Agreements

VIII—Transfer of Title (4 questions)
    A. Title Insurance
    B. Conveyances After Death
    C. Deeds
    D. Escrow or Closing
    E. Foreclosure, Short Sales
    F. Tax Aspects of Transferring Title to Real Property
    G. *Special Processes [Broker Only]*

IX—Practice of Real Estate (12 questions)
    A. Trust Accounts (General) *[Regulatory Details in State Portion]*
    B. Fair Housing Laws
    C. Advertising
    D. Agent Supervision
    E. Commissions and Fees
    F. General Ethics
    G. Issues in Use of Technology (Electronic Signatures, Document Delivery, Internet Advertising)
    H. Antitrust Laws

X—Real Estate Calculations (7 questions)
    A. General Math Concepts
    B. Property Tax Calculations (not Prorations)
    C. Lending Calculations
    D. Calculations for Transactions
    E. Calculations for Valuation
    F. Mortgage Calculations

XI—Specialty Areas (4 questions)
    A. Property Management and Landlord/Tenant
    B. Common Interest Ownership Properties
    C. Subdivisions
    D. Commercial, Industrial, and Income Property

Note: There may be a few minor differences between the outline Topic Area labels above and those in the current PSI Bulletin. Any such difference in no way affects either the subject matter on the test or its presentation in this book.

Additionally, this outline specifically excludes the occasional one-or-two question difference in questions-per-Section for Broker exams.

Nevertheless, **the material in this book will more than adequately prepare those reviewing for a Broker exam**, which may test some of the terms identified herein as too advanced for Sales-level.

Real Estate Exam: PSI's General Content Outline
Expanded, Published Version Identifying 171 Sub-Topics
80 questions for both Sales and Broker exams
There are 7 math-related questions; this represents an approximate 9% overall math emphasis.

I—Property Ownership   (6 questions)
- A. Classes of Property
    1. *Real versus Personal Property*
    2. *Defining Fixtures*
- B. Land Characteristics and Legal Descriptions
    1. *Physical Characteristics of Land*
    2. *Economic Characteristics of Land*
    3. *Types of Legal Property Descriptions*
    4. *Usage of Legal Property Descriptions*
- C. Encumbrances
    1. *Liens (Types and Priority)*
    2. *Easements and Licenses*
    3. *Encroachments*
- D. Types of Ownership
    1. *Types of Estates*
    2. *Forms of Ownership*
    3. *Leaseholds*
    4. *Common Interest Properties*
    5. *Bundle of Rights*
- E. Physical Descriptions of Property
    1. *Land and Building Area*
    2. *Basic Construction Types and Materials*

II—Land Use Controls and Regulations   (5 questions)
- A. Government Rights in Land
    1. *Property Taxes and Special Assessments*
    2. *Eminent Domain, Condemnation, Escheat*
    3. *Police Power*
- B. Public Controls Based in Police Power
    1. *Zoning and Master Plans*
    2. *Building Codes*
    3. *Environmental Impact Reports*
    4. *Regulation of Special Land Types (floodplain, coastal, etc.)*
- C. Regulation of Environmental Hazards
    1. *Abatement, Mitigation, and Cleanup Requirements*
    2. *Contamination Levels and Restrictions on Sale or Development of Contaminated Property*
    3. *Types of Hazards and Potential for Agent or Seller Liability*
- D. Private Controls
    1. *Deed Conditions or Restrictions*
    2. *Covenants (CC&Rs)*
    3. *HOA Regulations*

III—Valuation and Market Analysis   (8 questions)
- A. Value
    1. *Market Value and Market Price*
    2. *Characteristics of Value*
    3. *Principles of Value*
    4. *Market Cycles and Other Factors Affecting Property Value*
- B. Methods of Estimating Value/Appraisal Process
    1. *Market or Sales Comparison Approach*
    2. *Replacement Cost or Summation Approach*
    3. *Income Approach*
    4. *Basic Appraisal Terminology (Replacement versus Reproduction Cost, Reconciliation, Depreciation, Kinds of Obsolescence)*
- C. Competitive/Comparative Market Analysis (CMA)
    1. *Selecting and Adjusting Comparables*
    2. *Factors to Consider in a CMA*
    3. *Contrast CMA, Broker Opinion of Value (BOV), Appraisal*
    4. *Price/Square Foot*
    5. *Gross Rent and Gross Income Multipliers*
- D. When Appraisal by Certified Appraiser is Required

IV—Financing   (7 questions)
- A. General Concepts
    1. *LTV Ratios, Points, Origination Fees, Discounts, Broker Commissions*
    2. *Mortgage Insurance (PMI)*
    3. *Lender Requirements, Equity, Qualifying Buyers, Loan Application Procedures*
- B. Types of Loans
    1. *Term or Straight Loans*
    2. *Amortized and Partially Amortized (Balloon) Loans*
    3. *Adjustable Rate Loans (ARMs)*
    4. *Conventional versus Insured*
    5. *Reverse Mortgages, Equity Loans, Subprime and Other Nonconforming Loans*
- C. Sources of Loan Money
    1. *Seller/Owner Financing*
    2. *Primary Market*
    3. *Secondary Market*
    4. *Down Payment Assistance Programs*
- D. Government Programs
    1. *FHA*
    2. *VA*
- E. Mortgages/Deeds of Trust
    1. *Mortgage Clauses (Assumption, Due-on-Sale, Alienation, Acceleration, Prepayment, Release)*
    2. *Lien Theory versus Title Theory*
    3. *Mortgage/Deed of Trust and Note as Separate Documents*
- F. Financing/Credit Laws
    1. *Truth in Lending, RESPA, Equal Credit Opportunity*
    2. *Mortgage Loan Disclosure and Seller Financing Disclosure*
- G. Mortgage Fraud, Predatory Lending Practices (Risks to Clients)
    1. *Usury and Predatory Lending Laws*
    2. *Appropriate Cautions to Clients Seeking Financing*

V—Laws of Agency   (10 questions)
- A. Laws, Definitions, and Nature of Agency Relationships
    1. *Types of Agents/Agencies (Special, General, Designated, Subagent, etc.)*
    2. *Possible Agency Relationships in a Single Transaction*
    3. *Fiduciary Responsibilities*

Real Estate Exam: PSI's General Content Outline
Expanded, Published Version Identifying 171 Sub-Topics
80 questions for both Sales and Broker exams
There are 7 math-related questions; this represents an approximate 9% overall math emphasis.

- B. Creation and Disclosure of Agency and Agency Agreements (General) *[Regulatory Details in State Portions]*
  1. *Creation of Agency and Agency Agreements*
  2. *Express and Implied*
  3. *Disclosure of Representation*
  4. *Disclosure of Acting as Principal or other Conflict of Interest*
- C. Responsibilities of Agent to Seller, Buyer, Landlord, or Tenant as Principal
  1. *Traditional Common Law Agency Duties ("COALD")*
  2. *Duties to Client/Principal (Buyer, Seller, Tenant, or Landlord)*
  3. *Effect of Dual Agency on Agent's Duties*
- D. Responsibilities of Agent to Customers and Third Parties
- E. Termination of Agency
  1. *Expiration*
  2. *Completion/Performance*
  3. *Termination by Operation of Law*
  4. *Destruction of Property/Death of Principal*
  5. *Termination by Acts of Parties*

VI—Mandated Disclosures   (7 questions)
- A. Property Condition Disclosure Forms
  1. *Agent's Role in Preparation*
  2. *When Seller's Disclosure Misrepresents Property Condition*
- B. Warranties
  1. *Types of Available Warranties*
  2. *Coverages Provided*
- C. Need for Inspection and Obtaining/Verifying Information
  1. *Agent Responsibility to Verify Statements Included in Marketing Information*
  2. *Agent Responsibility to Inquire About "Red Flag" Issues*
  3. *Responding to Non-Client Inquiries*
- D. Material Facts Related to Property Condition or Location
  1. *Land/Soil Conditions*
  2. *Accuracy of Representation of Lot or Improvement Size, Encroachments or Easements Affecting Use*
  3. *Pest Infestation, Toxic Mold, and other Interior Environmental Hazards*
  4. *Structural Issues, Including Roof, Gutters, Downspouts, Doors, Windows, Foundation*
  5. *Condition of Electrical and Plumbing Systems, and of Equipment or Appliances that are Fixtures*
  6. *Location within Natural Hazard or Specially Regulated Area, Potentially Uninsurable Property*
  7. *Known Alterations or Additions*
- E. Material Facts Related to Public Controls, Statutes, or Public Utilities
  1. *Local Zoning and Planning Information*
  2. *Boundaries of School/Utility/Taxation Districts, Flight Paths*
  3. *Local Taxes and Special Assessments, Other Liens*
  4. *External Environmental Hazards (Lead, Radon, Asbestos, Formaldehyde Foam Insulation, High-Voltage Power Lines, Waste Disposal Sites, Underground Storage Tanks, Soil or Groundwater Contamination, Hazardous Waste)*
  5. *Stigmatized/Psychologically Impacted Property, Megan's Law Issues*

VII—Contracts   (10 questions)
- A. General Knowledge of Contract Law
  1. *Requirements for Validity*
  2. *Types of Invalid Contracts*
  3. *When Contract is Considered Performed/ Discharged*
  4. *Assignment and Novation*
  5. *Breach of Contract and Remedies for Breach*
  6. *Contract Clauses (Acceleration, etc.)*
- B. Listing Agreements
  1. *General Requirements for Valid Listing*
  2. *Exclusive Listings*
  3. *Non-Exclusive Listings*
- C. Management Agreements *[Broker Only]*
- D. Buyer Broker Agreements/Tenant Representation Agreements
- E. Offers/Purchase Agreements
  1. *General Requirements*
  2. *When Offer Becomes Binding (Notification)*
  3. *Contingencies*
  4. *Time is of the Essence*
- F. Counteroffers/Multiple Counteroffers
  1. *Counteroffer Cancels Original Offer*
  2. *Priority of Multiple Counteroffers*
- G. Lease and Lease-Purchase Agreements
- H. Options and Right of First Refusal
- I. Rescission and Cancellation Agreements

VIII—Transfer of Title   (4 questions)
- A. Title Insurance
  1. *What is Insured Against*
  2. *Title Searches/Title Abstracts/Chain of Title*
  3. *Cloud on Title/Suit to Quiet Title*
- B. Conveyances After Death
  1. *Types of Wills*
  2. *Testate versus Intestate Succession*
- C. Deeds
  1. *Purpose of Deed, when Title Passes*
  2. *Types of Deeds (General Warranty, Special Warranty, Quitclaim) and When Used*
  3. *Essential Elements of Deeds*
  4. *Importance of Recording*
- D. Escrow or Closing
  1. *Responsibilities of Escrow Agent*
  2. *Prorated Items*
  3. *Closing Statements/HUD-1*
  4. *Estimating Closing Costs*
- E. Foreclosure, Short Sales
- F. Tax Aspects of Transferring Title to Real Property
- G. Special Processes *[Broker Only]*

Real Estate Exam: PSI's General Content Outline
Expanded, Published Version Identifying 171 Sub-Topics
80 questions for both Sales and Broker exams
There are 7 math-related questions; this represents an approximate 9% overall math emphasis.

IX—Practice of Real Estate   (12 questions)
- A. Trust Accounts (General) *[Regulatory Details in State Portions]*
  1. *Purpose and Definition of Trust Accounts*
  2. *Responsibility for Trust Monies*
  3. *Commingling/Conversion*
  4. *Monies Held in Trust Accounts*
- B. Fair Housing Laws
  1. *Protected Classes*
  2. *Covered Transactions*
  3. *Specific Laws and their Effects*
  4. *Exceptions*
  5. *Compliance*
  6. *Types of Violations and Enforcement*
  7. *Fair Housing Issues in Advertising*
- C. Advertising
  1. *Incorrect "Factual" Statements versus "Puffing"*
  2. *Uninformed Misrepresentation versus Deliberate Misrepresentation (Fraud)*
  3. *Truth in Advertising*
- D. Agent Supervision
  1. *Liability/Responsibility for Acts of Associated Agents*
  2. *Responsibility to Train and Supervise*
  3. *Independent Contractors*
  4. *Employees*
- E. Commissions and Fees
  1. *Procuring Cause/Protection Clauses*
  2. *Referrals and Finder Fees*
- F. General Ethics
  1. *Practicing Within Area of Competence*
  2. *Avoiding Unauthorized Practice of Law*
- G. Issues in Use of Technology (Electronic Signatures, Document Delivery, Internet Advertising)
- H. Antitrust Laws
  1. *Antitrust Laws and Purpose*
  2. *Antitrust Violations in Real Estate*

X—Real Estate Calculations   (7 questions)
- A. General Math Concepts
  1. *Addition, Subtraction, Multiplication, and Division*
  2. *Percentages/Decimals/Fractions*
  3. *Areas, including Acreage*
- B. Property Tax Calculations (not Prorations)
- C. Lending Calculations
  1. *Loan-to-Value Ratios*
  2. *Discount Points*
  3. *Equity*
  4. *Qualifying Buyers*
- D. Calculations for Transactions
  1. *Prorations (Utilities, Rent, Property Taxes, Insurance, etc.)*
  2. *Commissions and Commission Splits*
  3. *Seller's Proceeds of Sale*
  4. *Total Money Needed by Buyer at Closing*
  5. *Transfer Tax/Conveyance Tax/Revenue Stamps*
- E. Calculations for Valuation
  1. *Comparative Market Analyses (CMA)*
  2. *Net Operating Income*
  3. *Depreciation*
  4. *Capitalization Rate*
  5. *Gross Rent and Gross Income Multipliers (GIM, GRM)*
- F. Mortgage Calculations
  1. *Down Payment/Amount to be Financed*
  2. *Amortization*
  3. *Interest Rates*
  4. *Interest Amounts*
  5. *Monthly Installment Payments*

XI—Specialty Areas   (4 questions)
- A. Property Management and Landlord/Tenant
- B. Common Interest Ownership Properties
- C. Subdivisions
- D. Commercial, Industrial, and Income Property

Note: There may be a few minor differences between the outline Topic Area or Subtopic labels above and those in the current PSI Bulletin. Any such difference in no way affects either the subject matter on the test or its presentation in this book.

Additionally, this outline specifically excludes the occasional difference of one or two questions per Section for Broker exams.

Nevertheless, *the material in this book will more than adequately prepare those reviewing for a Broker exam*, which may test some of the terms identified herein as too advanced for Sales-level.

Comments on PSI's 2009 "Expanded" Outline

Since mid-2009, PSI has been publishing an "expanded" outline in its Candidate Information Bulletins (CIBs) that reflects some minor changes to its major Section Area question-counts and some additions and "crafting" to its Topic Area headings.

Most notably, though, the outline provides 171 sub-topics, which makes it substantially longer than all previous PSI outlines—it is now six columns spread over three pages compared to one-and-a-half columns that typically fit on the same page.

At first blush, this makes the exam seem massively altered. But taking a step back shows that PSI's design has been to present an outline that illustrates and reinforces the real estate industry's belief that the profession requires robust, ever-changing applications of an enormous knowledge base to an extensive variety of both routine and innovative tasks.

Unavoidably, such detail risks looking like it is exhaustive in itemizing what is 'in-bounds' for testing, and that if a term or topic is not found here, it cannot be fair game for use on the test.

However, this is just not so: the sub-topics do not definitively limit the scope of content coverage.

For example, in Topic Area IV-F, Financing/Credit Laws, TILA, RESPA, and ECOA are listed while the Fair Credit Reporting Act and the Private Mortgage Insurance (PMI) Act are not.

It would be remiss of any testing company to send the message that these are either unimportant laws or off-limits for testing, and I am confident that PSI not only recognizes their importance, but assembles some exams using questions on these topics rather than testing solely on the others.

This expanded outline is a progressive, instruction-friendly step for PSI, which in its own CIBs' "Tips for Preparing for Your Licensing Examination," specifically states that students should "use the examination content outline as the basis of your study."

In finally making some of the essential sub-topics explicit for students, PSI is attempting to help facilitate, not frustrate, pre-examination review of textbook and other pre-license course material.

Now when students—and instructors—wonder "What do they mean by 'Financing/Credit Laws,'" PSI provides at least a partial reply that offers _some_ guidance about what to study.

As previously noted, PSI's examinations routinely undergo review by the ARELLO® Examination Accreditation Program, which has standards for determining what is testable and how test vendors can stay in-bounds. The following excerpts from its guidelines will support many of the comments you will find throughout this book regarding subject matter or terms that are either too-advanced, obscure, or insignificant, and are therefore not fair game for testing.

> Among ARELLO®'s question-writing guidelines are standards that for each question, the "subject matter being tested . . . must be **relevant and appropriate**" and "must be based on an **important** point, idea, or skill that reflects an appropriate level of competency in knowledge or skill related to tasks shown to be needed for entry level" *(ARELLO®'s emphasis)*.

So, despite the appearance of complexity presented by the overwhelmingly extensive array of sub-topics, PSI's expanded outline—and this book—simply helps students stay on-track while using "the examination content outline as the basis of . . . study."

Now it's time to begin the adventure!

Table of Contents

	Dedication		*iii*
	Publisher's Foreword		*iv*
	Author's Introduction to the General Exam Review		*v*
	Acknowledgments		*vii*
	PSI Content Outline—Concise Version		*viii*
	PSI Content Outline—Expanded, Bulletin Version		*ix*
	Comments on PSI's 2009 "Expanded" Outline		*xii*
General Section I	Property Ownership	(6 questions)	1
General Section II	Land Use Controls and Regulations	(5 questions)	18
General Section III	Valuation and Market Analysis	(8 questions)	26
General Section IV	Financing	(7 questions)	38
General Section V	Laws of Agency	(10 questions)	54
General Section VI	Mandated Disclosures	(7 questions)	63
General Section VII	Contracts	(10 questions)	70
General Section VIII	Transfer of Title	(4 questions)	81
General Section IX	Practice of Real Estate	(12 questions)	94
General Section X	Real Estate Calculations	(7 questions)	108
General Section XI	Specialty Areas	(4 questions)	116
Transition Page	Preface to Connecticut Rules & Regs Exam Prep		125
State Outline Page	Connecticut State-Specific Content Outline		126
State Section I	Connecticut Real Estate Commission and Licensing Requirements	(5 questions)	127
State Section II	Connecticut Laws Governing the Activities of Licensees	(10 questions)	139
State Section III	Connecticut Real Estate Agency	(8 questions)	153
State Section IV	Connecticut-Specific Real Estate Principles and Practices	(7 questions)	166
Appendix A	Sample General Real Estate Exam		189
Appendix B	Sample Connecticut State-Specific Exam		203
Appendix C	Answer Key and Diagnostic Chart for General Exam		210
Appendix D	Answer Key and Diagnostic Chart for State Exam		211
Appendix E	Statutes, Commission Regulations and Policies (SCRAP): Commission Interpretations and Statutory Forms		212
E-1 →	SCRAP 1: Commission Agency Memorandum—10/31/1997		213
E-2 →	SCRAP 2: The Connecticut Real Estate Commission Policy on Agency—1/6/2000		214
E-3 →	SCRAP 3: REAL ESTATE AGENCY DISCLOSURE NOTICE		221
E-4 →	SCRAP 4: DUAL AGENCY CONSENT AGREEMENT		223
E-5 →	SCRAP 5: DUAL AGENCY/DESIGNATED AGENCY DISCLOSURE		224

[This page intentionally left blank]

I. General: Property Ownership (6 questions)
(5 Topic Areas; 16 Sub-Topics—each will be covered in its respective Topic Area)

I-A. Classes of Property (Expect 1-2 questions from this area)

Real property, or ***realty***, is **land along with its improvements**, things attached to it, and the benefits, rights, and interests included in its ownership.

> ***Real property*** and ***real estate*** *are well acknowledged as synonymous terms. However, "**real property**" is generally the preferred usage whenever it helps distinguish specific types of property as **real** instead of **personal** by avoiding the word "**estate**," which, in its broadest sense, means everything one owns, including both real and personal property.*

> As will be noted in Section I-B, **land** includes the **earth's surface, subsurface to the center of the earth, the space overhead**, and **the rights to each**.

> ***Improvements*** are generally seen as additions to the property that increase its value or enhance its appearance and may include attached property, such as a house, garage, or fixtures like sinks or built-in bookcases, as well as trees and landscaping improvements.

>> *The opposite of improvements is **waste**, which is the legal term for property deterioration, abuse, or destruction, generally by a negligent tenant.*

> ***Personal property***, also known as ***personalty*** or ***chattel***, is generally considered anything that is **unattached and moveable**, such as furniture, housewares, lawn mowers, and throw rugs.

>> *Personal property also includes various **intangible assets**, like **bank accounts**, **stocks**, and many other **securities and financial instruments**.*

> ***Fixtures*** are ***once-moveable items that have been attached to real property***. Since attaching the object *may* change its status from personal to real property, as with a sink, a ceiling fan, or even a coat hook screwed to the back of a door, tenants and those selling their property must be careful about how they install items they may want to take away with them.

>> ***Trade fixtures*** are fixtures used by a business tenant, such as display cases or supermarket freezers, that are generally considered the tenant's removable personal property.

>> ***Annexation*** is the term for how, by attachment, something that was formerly personal property becomes real property. Also referred to as ***accession***, which includes additions to property from natural causes, such as a riverfront property that benefits from a shift in the river's path.

>> ***Severance*** refers to the process of separating a fixture from the real property, thereby changing it ***from real to personal*** property.

> ***The legal tests for a fixture*** include considering the total circumstances of these four elements to determine whether or not the fixture is real or removable property
> 1. ***intention*** of the person who attached the item to make it permanent
> 2. ***method of attachment***, or ***annexation***, generally meaning the degree of permanence
> 3. ***adaptation*** of the item to the use of the property, as in a custom-made bookshelf that

I. General: Property Ownership (6 questions)
(5 Topic Areas; 16 Sub-Topics—each will be covered in its respective Topic Area)

      fits precisely into a recessed area and is attached with bolts
4. ***relationship and general understanding*** between parties, as in whether the owner paid for and installed the fixture, or a tenant has done so at the tenant's expense with the owner's permission to remove it later

Appurtenances are those things that "belong" to something else, generally by ***attachment***, and in real estate generally include any number of rights that "***run with the land***," which means the rights do not end when a new owner takes title. Examples of these are gardens, buildings, and certain ***easements***, such as deeded rights-of-way. *(More in Section I-C.)*

Emblements are crops that a tenant generally owns as personal property and may return to harvest even after a lease expires.

*Growing crops are technically referred to as **fructus industriales** ("fruits of industry"), which distinguishes them from other plants, **fructus naturales** ("fruits of nature"), such as trees and brush, which are generally considered real property.*

*These terms are popular <u>**distractors**</u> – the testing industry's term for "wrong answers," but ones that will distract the less-prepared -- and way too advanced for entry-level. You are more likely to have a personal encounter with a living American president than with these terms during the course of a lengthy real estate career.*

Additional "distractor" terms related to classes and characteristics of property include
- ***tangible*** (or ***corporeal***) ***property***, which means **physically touchable, material** property, most notably **land and its improvements**, and
- ***intangible***, (or ***incorporeal***) ***property***, which means such abstract, "untouchable," yet very real elements as **mortgages, rights**, and **other encumbrances, as well as assets such as bank accounts and most financial instruments, like stocks and retirement accounts.**

*Though these terms <u>**occasionally**</u> appear in prelicensing curriculum outlines and textbooks, do NOT expect to be tested on definitions or examples of tangible, intangible, corporeal, and incorporeal property, since these terms, though they provide useful distinctions, are more legally refined than is appropriate for an entry-level exam.*

I-B. Land Characteristics and Legal Descriptions (Expect 1-2 questions from this area)

Land includes the ***earth's surface, subsurface to the center of the earth, the space overhead, and the rights to each***. Some broad categories identifying the most ***common rights in land*** include ***surface rights, subsurface rights, mineral rights, water rights***, and ***air rights***.

An owner is entitled to handle each of these rights separately and may, for example, lease out the right to farm the land, drill for oil, or erect a billboard to three different tenants.

Three commonly recognized ***physical characteristics of land*** are its ***immobility, permanence*** (or ***indestructibility***), and ***uniqueness***.

I. General: Property Ownership (6 questions)
(5 Topic Areas; 16 Sub-Topics—each will be covered in its respective Topic Area)

*All three of these characteristics can be illustrated by the simple example of a **global positioning system (GPS)** reading at a particular spot: **the latitude and longitude reading for that spot cannot be moved, destroyed, or duplicated.***

Four commonly recognized **economic characteristics of land**, or factors that bear on a property's particular value, are **scarcity**, **improvements**, **permanence of investment**, and **area preference**.

*The fact that land is permanent and unique does not mean the land itself is desirable, or that there aren't similar properties available if it is. So, the elements identified above as **economic characteristics** are what add up to making a particular property valuable.*

Property descriptions may be **legal descriptions**, such as **metes and bounds**, **lot and block**, or in certain regions of the country, **rectangular survey**, or less formal, such as a **street address**.

*In some areas, street addresses will suffice to identify properties on listing agreements, but a **full legal description**, meaning one that would not only keep one property from being confused with another but could be precisely traced by a surveyor, **is required for a deed to be valid**.*

Metes and bounds is the widely used system of property description that "walks" the property boundaries by first identifying a physical **point of beginning (POB)** and then describing the distance and directions along the property line, generally, but not always, following a clockwise direction back to the point of beginning.

A **monument** is any of a number of landmarks that provides a stable point of reference for surveys. They can be natural, such as trees, rivers, or "the northwest corner of the pasture lot near the house in which I live" (from an 1881 New England deed), or artificial, such as **surveyors' stakes**, metal markers, or **"pins,"** stone boundary markers (a.k.a. **merestones**), or a government **benchmark** (see below).

*With advances in technology, **GPS coordinate readings** of latitude and longitude are appearing more frequently in surveys—and deeds—to fix the location of monuments and other points where the boundary line changes direction.*

Lot and block, or **lot, block, and tract**, system of property description is generally used for **subdivisions**. Also known as the **recorded plat system**, it identifies properties according to a **plat map**, or sometimes even an **assessor's map**, of the subdivision, which in turn shows the specific dimensions of each lot, the access roads, and easements. (**Assessor's maps** almost always have a disclaimer statement that they are "**for tax purposes only**.")

Government rectangular survey, or **rectangular survey**, or even **rectangular**, property descriptions are used in over thirty states, mostly in the Midwest and the West. It is a grid system that starts measuring from the axis where a **baseline**, an east-west line, and a **principal meridian**, or north-south line, intersect.

*Six-mile by six-mile squares are known as **townships** and are identified by where the **township line** (east-west) and **range line** (north-south) are in relation to the principal meridian and*

I. General: Property Ownership (6 questions)
(5 Topic Areas; 16 Sub-Topics—each will be covered in its respective Topic Area)

baseline. Each township contains 36 one-mile squares, or **sections**, each of which in turn is ordered and numbered. Four townships add up to a **quadrant**.

Property descriptions using this method are commonly presented in terms like, **the SW 1/4 of the SW 1/4 of Section 22, Township 15 South, Range 13 East, Gila and Salt River Base and Meridian, Arizona**.

Since the rectangular system is **NOT** in national use, many state licensing agencies prohibit testing on this method within the general portion of the exam used in their state.

This method is definitely NOT used in Connecticut, which makes it a 'nice to know' not a 'need to know' topic for Connecticut licensees, especially since it does nothing more to help protect the in-state public than knowing the capital city of Canada; it should NOT be on the test.

Some of the above terms in boldface **MAY**, however, appear on tests as distractors, or be tested as part of the state-specific portion of the exam in states where applicable.

Vertical land descriptions are necessary for defining air rights, as in specifying the floor-to-ceiling sale of ***air lots*** in multistory condominiums or cooperatives (which are generally governed by state-specific ***horizontal property acts***), as well as subsurface rights for mining and drilling. Terms related to vertical descriptions include

- ***geodetic survey system*** refers to the U. S. Coast and Geodetic Survey System, which established a series of markers nationwide that serve as permanent reference points for orienting accurate surveys
  - ***benchmarks***, the name for these permanent markers, are typically brass disks set in concrete and/or stone that identify the latitude, longitude, and elevation of the marker
- ***datum***, which is a term for the point, line, or surface from which elevations are measured; there are local and national datum for reference in establishing local and national benchmarks for surveys

I-C. Encumbrances (Expect 1-3 questions from this area)

Encumbrances are non-ownership interests, ***monetary*** and ***non-monetary***, that represent ***a restriction on the use and/or transfer of real property.***

Three broad types of encumbrances are ***liens, easements,*** and ***encroachments.***

A ***lien*** is a ***monetary encumbrance*** that asserts the ***lienholder*** has a creditor's claim to a specific monetary interest in the property's value. A lien may be satisfied by the property owner through simply paying the debt directly or by paying the debt out of the proceeds of a property sale.

Liens can be categorized as ***voluntary***, which means the debt was approved by and acceptable to the owner, such as a mortgage, or ***involuntary***, which means they have been placed against the owner's will, such as a tax lien, judgment, or other claims against a property for equity interest.

I. General: Property Ownership (6 questions)
(5 Topic Areas; 16 Sub-Topics—each will be covered in its respective Topic Area)

Voluntary and involuntary liens may be further classified as **general**, which **affects all of a debtor's property and assets**, as in a bankruptcy proceeding or IRS tax lien, or **specific**, (or **special**), which means it **is limited to a specified item controlled by the debtor**, such as a mortgage on a house or loan on a car.

> *You may also see references to* **statutory liens**, *which are created automatically by statute, as with tax liens, and* **equitable liens**, *which are created by a court order, as in a judgment lien. These are too specialized for test use except as distractors.*

A short list of common types of liens and their broad categories includes
- **mortgage liens**, which result from property financing, are <u>voluntary, specific</u> liens
- **mechanic's liens**, which result from non-payment of claims by those who worked on a property, are <u>involuntary, specific</u> liens
    - **materialman's liens**, a category of mechanic's lien, which may result from non-payment of claims by those who provided materials for a property, are <u>involuntary, specific</u> liens
- **special assessment liens**, when they result <u>from an owner's request</u> for the improvement, are <u>voluntary, specific</u> liens
    - **special assessment liens**, when they result <u>from a municipality-initiated improvement</u>, are <u>involuntary, specific</u> liens
- **municipal property tax liens**, which result from unpaid taxes, are <u>involuntary, specific</u> liens
- **federal (IRS) tax liens**, which result from unpaid taxes, are <u>involuntary, general</u> liens
- **judgment liens**, which result from a court order to pay a certain amount to a creditor, are <u>involuntary, general</u> liens

Liens are generally effective the day they are **recorded**, or officially filed, in the appropriate office of public records.

> **In Connecticut, this means town or city hall**, *depending on the municipality, since* **we are one of a very few states that does not observe a county system for recording land records**. *Exam questions* **may** *refer to* <u>counties</u>: *Oops! Think* **town** *or* **city** *instead.*

In the event more than one lien is recorded, the **priority of liens** for payment after a voluntary or forced property sale typically goes by **date of recordation** from the first to the most recent. However, the government is a line-jumper, and **property tax liens are always superior to other liens**, regardless of when they became effective.

> *Note:* **mechanic/materialman's liens follow state-specific rules** *for time limits on recording the lien, such as within one year of the project, as well as determination of the lien's effective date.* **Commonly, though, they are effective as of the date work began**, *not the date of recording, and represent an enforceable lien for a statutory period after recording, generally a year, unless satisfied or renewed.*

Non-monetary encumbrances include such physical and legal restrictions as **easements** and **encroachments**, both of which may restrict the use and/or transfer of property. *They also include* **subdivision covenants, conditions, and restrictions (CC&Rs)**, *and* **owners' association rules** *for*

I. General: Property Ownership (6 questions)
(5 Topic Areas; 16 Sub-Topics—each will be covered in its respective Topic Area)

most common-interest ownership arrangements; these will be outlined in greater detail in Section II-D, Private Controls.

Easements are interests in land that give a nonowner the right to use a property for a specific purpose, generally to cross over it. Easements affording access are commonly distinguished as either ***appurtenant*** or ***in gross***.

An ***easement appurtenant***, or ***appurtenant easement***, is the right to use one property for the benefit of another one. The most common example is a ***right-of-way*** across someone else's land to get to one that has no other access. The rights to enter, exit, and reenter are sometimes referred to as ***ingress***, ***egress***, and ***regress***, respectively.

An ***easement by necessity***, or ***easement of necessity***, is a special, but common, type of appurtenant easement that arises automatically in cases where an owner sells a ***landlocked parcel*** of a larger property.

In these situations, the property that provides, and must allow, the access is referred to as the ***servient tenement***, or ***servient estate***, since that property is a 'servant' to the interest of the one that requires it. The land that 'commands' the benefits of this use is referred to as the ***dominant tenement***, or ***dominant estate***.

Appurtenant rights and interests such as those above are said to ***run with the land***, which means they typically remain in full force even if omitted from the language of a deed during a property transfer.

Future sales of properties with an easement appurtenant should include clear reference to the easement in all applicable documents to not only clarify the scope and limits of the easement, but to help assert and ensure its continued existence.

An ***easement in gross*** differs from an easement appurtenant in that ***there is only a servient tenement***. For example, a ***utilities easement***, or ***utilities pass-through***, for sewer pipes and telephone lines do not benefit a utility company's physical property, so there is no neighboring dominant tenement, but ***the servient tenement owner must allow access for maintenance and repairs***.

Other common examples of ***easements in gross*** are ***those for personal use***, as when an owner lets a neighbor or friend cross a property as a shortcut or to get to a waterway. Such ***personal-use easements*** are typically not transferable, and terminate with the death of either party or the sale of the property.

However, owners that allow others to use their land without a specific arrangement may lose the right to stop that use if it becomes protected by law through an ***easement by prescription***, or ***prescriptive easement***.

Prescriptive easements must meet several legal tests, most notably, that the use of the property has occurred regularly for the minimum ***statutory period*** required by state law.

I. General: Property Ownership (6 questions)
(5 Topic Areas; 16 Sub-Topics—each will be covered in its respective Topic Area)

This period of ***adverse use***, meaning that ***the use may have adverse consequences on the owner's unencumbered property rights***, may be fewer than ten years or longer than twenty, depending on the state. ***In Connecticut it is fifteen years.***

Other conditions for acquiring an easement by prescription include several particulars about ***the pattern of use***. Typically, the use must be characterized as ***open***, ***notorious***, and ***hostile*** in the legal meaning of these terms.

Similar terms arise in different real estate textbook and legal dictionary definitions of prescriptive easements. The following terms may be understood as incorporated into the legal meaning of their closest match above: ***visible, continuous, exclusive,*** *and* ***adverse.***

Also, such property use is more likely to entitle the user to an easement by prescription if the owner is unaware through years of neglect than if the owner has knowingly allowed the use to occur.

> *Some legal authorities recommend posting a sign indicating "Private Property: Use by Permission" or "Walkers Welcome" on a subject property to* ***thwart prescriptive claims by providing open, public notice of permissive use.***
>
>> *Consult a lawyer regarding these matters: a landowner may need to record a notice of 'interruption of use' within the statutory period to ensure that the owner's rights are legally protected. Also note that new neighbors **may** be entitled to go back to claim the time of a previous owners' use through **tacking**.*
>>
>>> *According to* <u>Black's Law Dictionary</u>, ***tacking*** *may allow an owner to meet the statutory requirement quite quickly by* ***"adding one's own period of land possession to that of a prior possessor."***
>>>
>>> *This all means that simply changing ownership of either the potential servient or dominant tenement does not necessarily reset the statutory clock.*
>>>
>>> *Complicated stuff, since a current owner's legal entitlement to tack on prior periods would almost surely require a judge's ruling and depend on clearly demonstrating a relay-race style of the same "open, notorious, and hostile" use by current and immediate past owners.*
>>>
>>> *For* ***test purposes****, just remember that **tacking** is the principle by which **a new owner may be able to claim a previous owner's period of similar adverse use to satisfy a statutory minimum-period requirement.***
>>>
>>> *Though this term is unlikely to appear on a test, except as a distractor, it is a good example of how seemingly simple terms could suddenly open a world of complications in specific real estate transactions.*

I. General: Property Ownership (6 questions)
(5 Topic Areas; 16 Sub-Topics—each will be covered in its respective Topic Area)

It also illustrates how learning about such wrinkles might not only be professionally valuable by helping clients anticipate and address property problems, but have direct application for yourself as a property owner.

*In some more public cases, such as when a private entity owns a road or gathering place used by the public, that entity may publish a notice and/or block off the private property one day a year to formally assert its continued right to do so. (See also **property dedication** in Section VIII-G.)*

***Prescriptive easements are often confused with "adverse possession,"** a second type of adverse use; it is **a form of involuntary alienation**. With adverse possession of a property, actual title is transferred** based on demonstrated use similar to that needed for a prescriptive easement's right to continue a specific use.*

Party wall easements are just what the name suggests: a common building wall or a stand-alone wall either on or at a property line, and therefore involves both owners in ownership, maintenance, and/or access issues.

Creation and termination of easements represents a longer, more detailed list than is worth itemizing here, given their relatively self-evident nature, legal technicalities, and low importance for entry-level testing. However, a few of the most common categories include
- *creation of easements* may arise through
  - ***mutual agreement*** of the parties, either in writing (***express***) or through behavior (***implied***)
  - ***necessity***, as with certain landlocked properties
  - ***longtime use***, as in a prescriptive easement
- *termination of easements* may occur through
  - ***abandonment*** of use
  - ***release of easement*** by the owner of the dominant estate
  - ***conclusion of the reason*** for the easement
  - ***merger of the dominant and servient estates*** through purchase of one property by the owner of the other

A ***license*** is a personal, revocable right or privilege granted by an owner to someone else to use the property, typically in a brief, limited way. ***A license***, which is often simply a verbal approval, ***can be seen as changing a trespasser into a visitor***. It is ***not considered a type of easement*** and may or may not include compensation. Examples include tickets to use a parking lot, attend an event, or watch a movie in a theater.

Encroachments are a special type of encumbrance that involve ***some form of overlapping use of one property by another***, as when a portion of a building actually crosses the line, known technically as ***trespass***, or tree limbs or a roofline extend across a property boundary, known technically as ***nuisance***.

Whether or not such close calls as those above are encroachments are often resolved by either a ***visual inspection*** or a ***property survey***, which determines ***the accurate location***

I. General: Property Ownership (6 questions)
(5 Topic Areas; 16 Sub-Topics—each will be covered in its respective Topic Area)

and dimensions of property boundary lines. Surveys are also used to *discover unrecognized encroachments.*

Encroachments are legally categorized as **unauthorized and/or illegal infringements that can affect a title's marketability**, but they may arise and exist with the knowledge and consent of the owners.

An encroachment **may affect the marketability of title for both properties** unless it is adequately addressed. Depending on the situation, some simple encroachments may be removed by
- *selling the property* in question to the encroaching property owner
- *deeding the use as an easement*

Another property encumbrance that affects the marketability of a property's title is a ***lis pendens***, which is Latin for "*pending lawsuit.*"
- If a *lis pendens* has been recorded against a property, it means that *some form of litigation against the property is pending* that *may become the responsibility of a new owner* to address.
  - *This term also appears in upcoming Topic Areas as a defect in title or a title insurance issue; it may be categorized and tallied for testing in those areas if the question relates more to a title defect or title insurance than a type of recorded property encumbrance.*

I-D. Types of Ownership (Expect 1-3 questions from this area)

Title refers to both the *ownership* of something as well as to the *legal evidence of ownership*, such as a *deed*.

The degree and type of ownership gives rise to a variety of *types of title*, such as the following ones that are often mentioned in the marketing and transfer of ownership
- *clear title*, or *good title*, which refers to a title *free of restrictions that would limit its transfer*
- *marketable title*, which refers to a title that *a reasonable buyer would accept as a clear title*
- *equitable title*, which refers to *the holder's right to acquire ownership and formal legal title*, as when a *prospective buyer has entered into a valid, enforceable contract* to purchase a property; *this title interest may be sold, assigned, or transferred by the prospective buyer*
- *legal title*, or *bare legal title*, or *naked title*, refers to the holder having **apparent ownership but not full title**, as when a seller has entered into a binding sales contract, thereby relinquishing equitable rights to the buyer, or when a lender requires the right to hold legal title during the loan period

> **NOTE:** *The last two types of title,* **legal** *and* **equitable**, *represent the primary pair regarding basic legal rights of lenders and borrowers. Though too legally involved for entry level testing,* **legal theories about who holds and controls <u>legal title</u> and subsequent rights are at the heart of mortgage lending and foreclosure laws nationwide** *and will be described briefly in Section IV-E, Mortgages/Deeds of Trust.*

I. General: Property Ownership (6 questions)
(5 Topic Areas; 16 Sub-Topics—each will be covered in its respective Topic Area)

*You may also encounter the term **color of title**, which is defined as anything that **appears to give title**, but does not—the proverbial deed to the Brooklyn Bridge is an obvious example. Also known as **apparent title**, the appearance can be fostered by forged, inaccurate, or outdated deeds, or other legally insufficient ownership/transfer documents regardless of whether the holder knows about or is unaware of the flaw.*

*Color of title and apparent title are too legally refined for any licensee to "need to know," but **could easily appear as distractors**.*

Forms of ownership: Ways to "take title," or "hold title"

Sole ownership, or ***tenancy in severalty***, or simply ***severalty***, means that an individual is the sole owner of a property.

Concurrent ownership, or ***co-ownership***, refers to ownership by two or more parties at the same time. Among the types of concurrent ownership are

- ***tenancy in common***, under which the parties, or ***tenants in common***, hold an ***undivided fractional interest in the property***. For example, three family members may own a house together as equal one-third owners, or two may own 25% each and the third owns the remaining 50%. In either case, the fractional interest does not convey either the use or ownership of separate thirds, quarters, or halves of the house itself or other physical property to any of them. *Also*, ***each tenant may hold a deed that does not name any of the other owners***; compare with ***unity of title*** below.
- ***joint tenancy***, under which the parties, or ***joint tenants***, hold an ***undivided*** rather than uneven shares. The following considerations apply to this form of ownership
    - the ***four unities***, which refers to the following ***set of legal requirements for creating a joint tenancy***
        - ***unity of title***, which means all parties are ***named on the same deed***
        - ***unity of time***, which means all parties ***took title at the same time***
        - ***unity of possession***, which means all parties have ***undivided possession and use rights***
        - ***unity of interest***, which means all parties have an ***equal interest***
            - *this is a basic concept and **general questions will assume interests must be equal** despite at least one state, **Connecticut**, allowing unequal interests (**Connecticut note**: this difference will be tested in the state section—**for general questions, think equal**); **Alaska has gone even further by abolishing joint tenancy altogether as a method of property conveyance**, following the lead of Ohio and Oregon*
    - the ***right of survivorship****, meaning that as each individual joint tenant passes away, the remaining tenants' interest would increase until ***the last remaining person becomes the sole owner***; this condition is ***historically an assumed part*** of a joint tenancy, and ***some older deeds will specify "as joint tenants and not as tenants in common"***
        - **state laws and court rulings** *in some states have interpreted* **some joint tenancy arrangements** *as being* **the same as a tenancy in common**, *and do not consider the right of survivorship as automatic*

I. General: Property Ownership   (6 questions)
(5 Topic Areas; 16 Sub-Topics—each will be covered in its respective Topic Area)

- *joint tenancy with right of survivorship*, under which the objection noted immediately above is removed **by specifically including "with right of survivorship"** in the language of the deed; sometimes seen abbreviated on forms and financial instruments as **JTWROS** or **JTRS**
  - *Non-testable note*: some textbooks illustrate this concept by referring to joint tenancy ownership of any asset as *"a poor man's (or person's) will,"* since ownership automatically transfers from a deceased owner to the remaining one(s) by operation of law without requiring either a written will or probate approval; a properly drafted legal notice should be recorded, though, to ensure clear title for the survivor(s)
- *marital property ownership rights*, which **do not exist in over a dozen states, including Connecticut**, and **vary from state to state where they do**, include
  - *tenancy by the entireties*, or *tenancy by the entirety*, which has the same unities as a joint tenancy, but adds the concept that the couple owns the property as one indivisible legal unit, which provides broad property protection against creditors; it exists in some form in over twenty states, including our Western neighbor, New York
  - *community property*, which is generally understood to mean that property acquired by married people during the marriage is owned by both, unless it is exempted by one party acquiring it as separate property through gift, inheritance, or separate funds; there are nine community property states
    - AZ, CA, ID, LA, NV, NM, TX, and WA are the eight "traditional" states; WI recognizes community property rights by a state Uniform Marital Property Act
  - *community property with right of survivorship*, which strengthens the estate transfer and tax benefits of the survivorship right of the remaining spouse, has become applicable in most of the above nine states within the past ten years

Common interest ownership is a type of ownership that refers to multiple owners having an overlapping, inseparable interest in a property complex; **condominiums**, **townhouses**, **coops**, and **timeshares** are the most common examples and will be discussed below.

Condominium ownership grants the owner (1) **fee simple title to the unit <u>and</u> (2) an undivided interest in the jointly owned common areas as tenants in common** with the other association members.

The **condominium** form of community ownership also has several components that go by various similar names, depending on the state. In general, though, condominiums are created through some form of state-approved **horizontal property act** that allows ownership of the unit's airspace.

Condominium status is achieved when a developer's organizational plans, widely known as the **declaration**, are recorded. The declaration typically includes a copy of the **bylaws**, **legal descriptions and surveys**, which identifies common areas as well as units, and a list of **restrictive covenants**, also known as the **covenants, conditions, and restrictions (CC&Rs)**.

In addition, the developer typically creates a **condominium owners' association** for the self-governing of the property by the unit owners. This association is responsible for ongoing upkeep and maintenance of common areas, which it funds by assessing and collecting each unit's proportionate share of cost through **association fees**.

I. General: Property Ownership (6 questions)
(5 Topic Areas; 16 Sub-Topics—each will be covered in its respective Topic Area)

The municipal tax authority taxes the unit owner directly for the assessed value of the unit. Like an owner of a detached residence, **the unit owner is directly and solely responsible for taxes**: the association has no liability for unpaid unit taxes.

A *townhouse*, or *townhome*, or *row home*, is one of a row of homes sharing a **common wall**, or party wall, **with a neighbor on either side (except for end units)** and **no units above or below**. Although there may be common elements, such as a central courtyard, ***townhouses differ from condominiums in that there is actual ownership of land from the ground up, sometimes with a small private yard***. Typically they are constructed with multiple stories; three-story townhouses are often called "trinities."

Cooperative ownership, or a *co-op*, or *coop*, looks similar to a condominium to the general public, but the unit occupant does not own the unit like the condo owner does. Instead, the occupant is a **shareholder** who owns **stock** in the company that owns the complex, and in exchange for agreeing to **obey the bylaws** and **pay the co-op's fee**, generally billed monthly, is granted a *proprietary lease* interest to occupy the specific unit.

Put simply, **the unit "owner" owns stock, not real estate**; the stock entitles the stockholder to a *leasehold interest* in a specific unit's possession and use.

Unlike the condominium form of ownership, the **cooperative corporation is liable for the entire building's property taxes** and **collects them from the owners through the co-op fees** that are prorated for each unit's proportionate size and value within the complex. These **prorated fees** are also the way the corporation collects other operating expenses and assessments.

Timeshare ownership is typically characterized by **fee simple ownership** of **interval occupancy of a specified unit**, although it may take the legal form of a right-to-use contract that simply conveys **a contractual fixed-year, recurring-use** of a specific unit.

Either way, the unit, generally an apartment unit at a resort property, is **available to the owner for the specified period every year**, such as the first week of June. **It may also involve being able to "bank" the week** and exchange it for a **"floating use"** week at a different participating timeshare site.

Corporate and business ownership structures are generally more intricate than those sketched above; they will be touched on briefly in Section XI-D, Commercial, Industrial, and Income Property.

As noted above, in its broadest sense, *estate* simply means everything one owns, **including both real and personal property**.

Estates in real property can be either *freehold estates*, which means owned property, or *nonfreehold estates*, also known as *leasehold estates*, which means leased property.

I. General: Property Ownership (6 questions)
(5 Topic Areas; 16 Sub-Topics—each will be covered in its respective Topic Area)

***Leasehold estates**, including why they are classified as **personal property**, will be covered in Sections VII-G and XI-A, which concentrate on leases, leasehold estates, and property management topics.*

*The **bundle of rights**, or **bundle of legal rights**, is a common illustration of property ownership that compares the entire set of ownership rights to a bundle of sticks. (The bundle contains private rights; the government reserves additional rights to itself.)*

Each stick represents a separate, distinct ownership right, such as the right to possess and use it, exclude others from it, and rent, sell, or mortgage it.

As any stick is given over to someone else, the absolute and complete ownership is increasingly limited by those who now control a "stick."

Freehold estates commonly imply **fee simple**, or **absolute and complete ownership of real property**. The key distinctions for testing are that a freehold estate may or may not include conditions on its use and/or transfer.

If there are **no conditions on its use and/or transfer**, it may be known by any of these interchangeable terms: **fee**, **fee simple**, **fee simple absolute**, or **estate in fee simple**.

Note: This is one of the first of many cases to come in this book in which <u>Black's Law Dictionary</u> (8th ed. 2004) confirms that different terms are synonymous. As noted in the Introduction, the purpose of "extra" terms where applicable throughout this book is to show you some of the alternate ways "your" term may appear on the test.

If there are conditions on its use and/or transfer, they may take a variety of forms with long, elegant, impressive, and often interchangeable names. Those most commonly mentioned in textbooks and used for **distractors on tests** include
- **fee simple defeasible**, or **defeasible fee**, or **qualified fee**, which means that the deed or title has some sort of qualification of its use that makes it subject to being annulled or voided and reverting to the original owner or some third party. Two types include
  - **fee simple determinable**, also known as **qualified fee**, or **determinable fee**, which means that should a stated condition occur, the estate automatically ends and grantor has a **possibility of reverter**, or a **reversionary interest** in or **reversionary right** to the property.
    For example, someone may deed a property to a religious organization with the condition that if the organization no longer uses the property as intended, the deed reverts back to the grantor, or to the grantor's heirs or assigns as **reversioners**.
  - **fee simple subject to a condition subsequent**, which means that should a stated condition occur, the grantor, heirs, or assigns must take action to exercise a right to terminate the estate under the **power of termination**, or **right of entry**, or **right of reentry**. If no one exercises this right, the estate remains under the control of the grantee.

I. General: Property Ownership   (6 questions)
(5 Topic Areas; 16 Sub-Topics—each will be covered in its respective Topic Area)

Phew! How about that "fee simple subject to a condition subsequent"! Think you'll get a question trying to find out if you know how it differs from "fee simple determinable"?

Relax – if you do, shame on the test!

Information like that above is presented throughout this book primarily to expose you briefly to terms and concepts in the very content area where they might appropriately be used as distractors.

Remember, some hard-looking choices taken from the same Topic Area as the correct answer will distract less confident test-takers, who will think, "I knew I should have studied harder – I'll bet the one I don't know is a slightly better answer than the one I think is right."

Bingo! They take the bait! But by seeing it here, you will avoid waffling and recognize it for what it is: a term you've seen, are not afraid of, and know enough about to find when you need it, probably a long time after you've been selling property.

The terms above also demonstrate how quickly a subject area that will only get at most three questions on the actual test can look like a mini-course in legal minutia.

This area, and a few others to come, have enough terms and complexity to give rise to some delightful charts in real estate textbooks, as well as earnest contention among their authors about which of several interchangeable terms is the more correct.

In fairness to the more advanced and/or obscure material presented both in textbooks and here, it is part of the professional language you are learning to speak, so you should be no stranger to it.

Remember, though, that while this is an important area to understand in general, this section, like most others, will only contribute a few questions to the test.

And those questions on the test are MOST likely to be testing the more common and important topics, not the obscure, 'weird,' or 'tricky' ones.

So relax: you're not studying for the legal bar exam. Plus, you get to miss a few and still pass. Now, back to the "real" subject . . .

A **life estate** is another category of estates in property, one that conveys an estate for the duration of the life of the **life tenant**. For example, a parent may deed the family home to an heir but retain the right to use the property for life. Or a husband may will his wife a life estate in a house they share for the duration of her life with it going to his children from a previous marriage upon her death. Unless specifically restricted, a life tenant may move out and use the property as a rental for life.

Other situations include such circumstances as a university buying—or being "gifted"—a house adjacent to campus under the condition of allowing a life estate use for the sellers. So, life goes on as usual for the occupants, often plus extra cash from the transaction, and the university eventually gets possession and full control.

I. General: Property Ownership (6 questions)
(5 Topic Areas; 16 Sub-Topics—each will be covered in its respective Topic Area)

There are a few related terms for life estates, including
- ***conventional life estates***, which arise by intentional arrangements among the interested parties, as in the situation above
    - ***life estate pur autre vie***, which means a life estate "for the life of another" in French, measures its duration by the life of someone other than the life tenant, as when a caregiver or companion is allowed to live in a property until the death of the specified other person
- ***future interests***, which refer to the right to acquire the estate upon its termination as a life estate. They typically take one of the following two forms
    - ***remainder***, or ***remainder interest***, which means the grantor of the life estate has named someone else to take title; such an individual is referred to as a **remainderman**; this would be the case in the situation above about a parent leaving a spouse a life estate—the heir(s) would be remainderman/**remaindermen**
    - ***reversion***, or ***reversionary interest***, which means the estate reverts to, or is returned to, the grantor of the life estate, who is known as a **reversioner**; this would be the case in the situation above about a university purchasing a property and granting a life estate
- ***dower*** and ***curtesy***, which are once-common terms now used in fewer and fewer states to refer to the property inheritance rights of widows and widowers, respectively; some states, **including Connecticut**, have statutes that address rights of a surviving spouse

*Note: as noted above about other terms, entry-level licensees do not <u>need</u> to know about "**life estate pur autre vie**" arrangements at time of licensure -- these estates are rare enough that many seasoned brokers—and many lawyers—may never have encountered one.*

*Plus, an attorney would draft any such estate document. So, while the term is common textbook fare, it is rarely, if ever, tested. It is, however, like the terms **dower** and **curtesy**, a favorite term for use as a distractor.*

While you should have a general familiarity with all of the terms above, the more intimate details and nuances of all of these types of estates, as well as those of the upcoming section, exceed the professional expectations of real estate licensees and are properly left to real estate attorneys.

*In fact, to offer opinions or interpretations, or to prepare documents, on these matters could subject you to a suit for **practicing law without a license**. **Always tell clients to get a legal opinion on legal details from a practicing attorney.***
- **This point will be further emphasized—and tested**—in Sections related to Agency Relationships, Responsibilities, and Ethics in business practices; see Sections V-A, V-C, and IX-F, respectively.

But knowing more than you need to pass the test can be a handy thing for later on: a listing licensee in South Carolina was recently sued by a would-have-been buyer for not having discovered that the "seller" only had a life estate interest in the property.

I. General: Property Ownership (6 questions)
(5 Topic Areas; 16 Sub-Topics—each will be covered in its respective Topic Area)

Speaking of specific states, there are two Louisiana-unique encumbrances of general interest here that are definitely off-limits for testing, except, perhaps, in Louisiana
- **usufruct** *refers to a Louisiana-only term for a type of estate similar to a life estate, though it may be for a less-than-life period; a usufruct grants the right to use a property, including renting it out and keeping the rent monies*
  - *the **usufructuary** is the owner of the usufruct*
  - *the **naked owner** is the one who actually owns the property and has what is referred to as **naked ownership**; a **naked owner** is similar to a **remainderman** (or sometimes a reversioner) in a life estate.*
- *Louisiana also recognizes a **right of habitation**, which is when a person has not been granted a full usufruct but does receive **a nontransferable real right to dwell in the house of another**.*

I-E. Physical Descriptions of Property (Expect 0-1 question from this area)

This Topic Area will tally questions that may actually be introduced and discussed in other areas but are written to provide scenarios and applications of those principles, especially as they apply to definitions of lots and property particulars used in listing or previewing property for a client.

For example, a question might focus on the description or size of a particular lot, or other site or construction considerations. The following should be useful in understanding these basics:

A *lot,* or *site*, is the parcel of land under consideration. *Lot size* is a crucial element in describing a property and determining its possible uses, especially regarding the area available for buildings and other improvements. It can be determined **by computing the area defined by the legal description in the property's deed** or **by reviewing the** taxing authority's **assessor's data**, often found in a printout known by such names as a property's *field card*; assessor's data generally gives the lot size in acres.

*Neither of these methods is foolproof, and depending on the particular property, it may be prudent, even necessary, at some point in the transaction to have the boundaries and lot size confirmed through a professional property **survey**, which will determine **the accurate location and dimensions of property boundary lines**.*

*It is worth noting that while acreage is a unit of area commonly computed according to the **conventional acre**, also known as a **survey acre**, which is **43,560 square feet**, in some areas, assessors may use an **assessor's acre**, which is **40,000 square feet**. So use caution when using acreage data, and remember this distinction if you find conflicting data once you are a practicing licensee—it may be the reason for the difference.*

For test purposes, the survey acre of 43,560 square feet will be the standard size, unless specifically noted as otherwise.

Important property-specific details for listing and marketing property include determining the *physical dimensions* of the primary structure and any outbuildings along with the *basic type of construction* for each, such as masonry/stucco, brick, or framed with siding.

I. General: Property Ownership (6 questions)
(5 Topic Areas; 16 Sub-Topics—each will be covered in its respective Topic Area)

Further, a physical property description should identify **utilities**, **such as availability and hookups**, **type of heating and cooling**, whether there is **private or public access to water and sewer**, and if the property is in compliance with building codes that govern its construction and occupancy.

In the course of gathering data from the public records regarding a subject property, a licensee should research the **tax assessor's records**. These will generally identify the property acreage along with the physical dimensions, square footage, and construction type of any buildings on the property, as well as **the zoning code** for the property.

*In **determining the square footage** of a building, the conventional standard among appraisers, and certainly municipal assessors, is to **use the exterior dimensions** of each floor, even though more and more appraisers also include interior living space dimensions using laser rulers.*

The zoning code will identify such basic property-use classification, such as whether the property is residential, commercial, or industrial, the minimum lot size required for new construction, and other basic usage restrictions and minimum setbacks from the lot lines for the placement of building construction and other improvements.

*In one municipality, for example, a lot that is zoned **R-40**, or **"one-acre zoning,"** is classified as **"Low Density Residential**,*" *and requires a minimum of 40,000 square feet in order to build a residence, which cannot occupy more than 35% of the property's total lot size.*

Zoning codes, classifications, and requirements, despite many basic similarities, can vary widely from one municipality to another, and are tied to each one's planning documents.

As noted at the beginning of this Topic Area, many of the terms and principles relevant to this Area will be more appropriately defined and discussed elsewhere, though a question drawing on those particulars may be tallied here for test purposes.

This ends the presentation of key terms and concepts likely to be either tested or used as distractors in this Content Outline Section.

II. General: Land Use Controls and Regulations (5 questions)
(4 Topic Areas; 13 Sub-Topics—each will be covered in its respective Topic Area)

II-A. Government Rights in Land (Expect 1-2 questions from this area)

The *four government powers* are *police power, taxation, eminent domain,* and *escheat.*

Police power refers to the State's authority to provide for the general welfare of the community through legislation and a range of *enabling acts*, or *enabling statutes*, that authorize agencies to organize and both implement and enforce their obligations.

Zoning, which will be covered in more detail in the next Topic Area, is a primary mechanism for municipalities to implement their police power by establishing regulations controlling how land is used.

Taxation is a government power necessary to raise revenue for municipal expenses, like schools and roads; the governmental right to set taxes allows a municipality to assess properties, levy taxes, and sell the property if the taxes go unpaid.

Typically, real property is assigned an *assessed value* by the municipal government's assessor's office that is then used as the basis for annual taxation for *general assessments*, which raise funds for the entire municipality.

These *general real estate taxes* are also called *ad valorem* taxes, which means they are taxed **"at value,"** so that properties with a higher assessed value pay proportionately more than those with a lesser value.

Practical note: assessed values for tax purposes rarely match, or even intend to match, a property's actual, current, fair market value, although the two are commonly confused by the general public. One reason for this is that the assessment values may remain unchanged for years, whereas current market values are subject to constant change.

A property may also be subject to **special assessment** taxes if there are certain improvements, such as neighborhood sidewalk construction or streetlight installation, that benefit the immediate area only.

The governmental *power of taxation includes the power to place liens* on property in the event of an outstanding special assessment or unpaid general taxes. These include *special assessment liens*, *municipal property tax liens*, and *federal (IRS) tax liens*, all of which were previously listed as types of encumbrances in Section I-C, Encumbrances.

Note: taxation issues span multiple content outline Topic Areas, including details regarding tax liens in Section I-C, Encumbrances; and both details and calculations of tax math in Section X-B, Property Tax Calculations.

Eminent domain is another government power. It refers to the *taking* of title to real property for some use, public or private, that has been judged by the appropriately authorized governmental entity to be beneficial to the community's interest, as with certain utility or industrial expansions. It is most commonly exercised, though, for civic improvements such as road or school construction projects.

II. General: Land Use Controls and Regulations (5 questions)
(4 Topic Areas; 13 Sub-Topics—each will be covered in its respective Topic Area)

Eminent domain represents a type of ***involuntary alienation of property*** *(more on **alienation** in Section VIII-G Special Processes)* and involves (1) the process of ***condemnation*** and (2) ***payment of just compensation*** to the displaced owner.

Eminent domain proceedings generally begin with an attempt to negotiate the purchase of the subject property, which, ***if the owner rejects the offer***, typically leads to the government or authorized entity to ***file a notice of condemnation in the land records***.

This action sets the stage for ***court hearings*** on the matter during which the owner gets to respond to the attempt to take the property. ***If the government prevails, proceedings are held to establish a fair market value for the property***, which can be accepted or disputed by the property owner. Ultimately, the owner gets money and the government takes title.

*Eminent domain is a power granted by the Fifth Amendment to the Constitution of the United States (1791) in what is referred to as **the "takings clause": "nor shall private property be taken for public use, without just compensation."***

In practice, the determination of what constitutes "just compensation" is subject to court battles, and is rarely as simple as it looks.

Also, condemnation under eminent domain is entirely different from the condemnation of property under safety or health codes.

Escheat is also one of the four government powers. It refers to the transfer of property ownership from an individual to the State when the individual dies ***intestate***, or without a will, and ***with no known heirs***. The transfer is often phrased as ***reverting*** to the State.

Escheat also transfers certain types of property to the State at the end of a statutory period of inactivity, as with dormant bank accounts or abandoned property.

Property, such as land or bank accounts, that escheats to the State may be available to be claimed by heirs or owners once they make their interest in the property known.

Most states hold such property as custodians under a state-specific Unclaimed Property Act, and have an "unclaimed property" area on their Website to help owners or their heirs reclaim abandoned property – have a look!

II-B. Public Controls Based in Police Power (Expect 1-2 questions from this area)

Zoning is a type of ***police power*** under which municipalities can regulate land use. This begins with a ***master plan***, or ***comprehensive plan***, or ***general plan***, that identifies the broad economic objectives and goals and seeks to achieve them through classifying certain areas or buildings as usable for specific purposes, such as residential, retail, industrial, and agricultural.

Nonconforming use in zoning refers to a property ***continuing a prior use after a zoning change***. For example, a commercial area that has been rezoned residential may include a building that has a

II. General: Land Use Controls and Regulations   (5 questions)
(4 Topic Areas; 13 Sub-Topics—each will be covered in its respective Topic Area)

corner grocery. It may continue to sell groceries, though if it closes, it may have to be converted into residential space.

A common residential example of nonconforming use would be **an existing house on a small lot in a neighborhood that has been rezoned** to require at least one acre for new construction. The house will generally be **"grandfathered"** and allowed to remain on its now "substandard" lot; typically it can be rebuilt if destroyed. *Rebuilding or home improvement plans are generally prohibited from expanding* **"the footprint"** *of the grandfathered structure's existing foundation or assessor's external dimensions.*

A *variance* also allows for a use other than the primary zoning category, and may be ***granted after review by the zoning authorities***. Examples include a restaurant in a residential area or a hairdressing salon in a renovated portion of a family residence.

A *conditional use*, or *special use*, is similar to a variance, but differs primarily in that it is typically more restrictive, and therefore governed by a ***permit*** that can be revoked if the holder does anything not specifically allowed.

Spot zoning is also similar to a variance, but differs in that the parcel or small ***area in question is actually rezoned*** to allow it to coexist within an area of different zoning requirements.

Other common zoning terms include
- *setback*, or the specified distance a building must be from a property line
- *buffer zone*, or area that serves to separate one use from another, as when an open stretch is required to separate a new industrial park and an existing school
- *zoning ordinances*, which are simply municipal regulations governing zoning and land-use requirements
  - *building codes*, or *housing codes*, which are governed by zoning ordinances and outline the local requirements for construction standards
  - *building permits* are typically required to begin new construction or significant renovations; they serve to notify the municipality of intended improvements and allow the municipality to review the plans for conformity with codes
  - *certificate of occupancy*, or *CO*, is typically required in order for residents to move into a newly constructed building or return to a renovated one

Special study zones are areas that contain ***one or more natural hazard, such as flooding, earthquake, landslide, coastal management, or another geological hazard specific to that area***. These zones can be identified and defined for closer review by any combination of federal, state, and local governments.

Special study zones may have applicability to specific listed properties, and there are a variety of *requirements that MAY apply* to property sales in special study zones.

For example, both coastal and inland areas nationwide fall within a **"Special Flood Hazard Area"** according to the **Federal Emergency Management Agency (FEMA) Flood Insurance Rate Map** that indicate whether **special property insurance is required**.

II. General: Land Use Controls and Regulations (5 questions)
(4 Topic Areas; 13 Sub-Topics—each will be covered in its respective Topic Area)

*And California legislated the **Alquist-Priolo Special Studies Zone Act** that **requires disclosure** to homebuyers that a property is in an area with one or more active earthquake faults that may be hazardous to structures.*

As part of working for clients, licensees should be familiar enough with their market territory to know if any properties they will be showing—or listing—are within a special study zone.

Also, licensees should ensure that they are aware of whether the property is subject to restrictions due to being **in or near a designated wetland area** or serving as **a habitat for an endangered species**.

*If so, the **licensee should perform the due diligence** of **identifying the implications of a study zone or other restriction on property ownership**, such as whether it requires mandatory flood insurance or zoning approval for property improvements, **and then both disclosing and explaining these factors** to buyers.*

Licensees and owners who demonstrate **willful negligence** in discovering and/or disclosing any of the above environmental problems that might reasonably be associated with a property may be subject to legal action.

These environmental hazards will be repeated, and perhaps tested and tallied, in Sections VI-D/E, Material Facts; they are presented here to illustrate the scope of Police Powers.

The area of **water rights** is one that also demonstrates the exercise by government authorities of police power. These rights are especially full of twists, turns, terms, and statutory controls, so will get some extended attention here.

Water rights come in many forms, both above and below ground, and may include such terms and concepts as
- *riparian rights*, which are the rights of an owner to the use of a flowing watercourse, such as a river, pond, or lake that borders the property or a stream that crosses one's land. This term is generally understood to refer to a *commercially nonnavigable waterway*, and gives an owner who borders on it *ownership to its middle*.
- *littoral rights*, which are those an owner has to the use of frontage on an ocean, sea, or large lake. This term is generally understood to refer to *commercially navigable waterways*, and gives an owner who borders on it *ownership to the high-water mark*.

Property may be added or removed by water's action due to floods, droughts, storms, tidal action, currents, sediment deposits, or changes in the course of a river or stream as described by
- *terms of addition*, such as *accession, accretion, alluvial, alluvium,* or *alluvion, reliction,* and *dereliction*
- *terms of reduction*, such as *erosion, avulsion,* or *deliction*

While the terms above are important to owners, some are about as obscure and special-interest as they come. Nevertheless, it is good to have a basic-recognition awareness of water-related terms, and they may turn up as distractors.

II. General: Land Use Controls and Regulations (5 questions)
(4 Topic Areas; 13 Sub-Topics—each will be covered in its respective Topic Area)

*A water right of great significance in some of the more arid Western and Southwestern states is the **prior-appropriation doctrine**, or **doctrine of prior appropriation**.*

> *This doctrine asserts that those along a waterway may take all they want regardless of those downstream. This is commonly summarized as **"first in time, first in right**," and generally assumes that the water will be taken for reasonable and beneficial uses.*
>
> *However, in some states and/or counties where this doctrine prevails, the government may reserve that right and allow others to use **surface water** as well as **groundwater**, or water that is in the ground and tapped by drilling, by **permit**.*
>
> *This doctrine and subsequent government control is critical in areas where water is limited yet necessary for irrigation, industry, and/or residential use.*
>
> *The opposing doctrine for water use is the **riparian-rights doctrine**, which rules that all owners benefiting from bordering a river or stream have equal rights to use the water passing by or through the property. So, owners upstream cannot deprive those who own property downstream by damming or redirecting the watercourse.*
>
> *These doctrines and their local applications may be tested on state-specific portions of those states' state-specific exams; the terms themselves may appear as distractors.*

An additional public control based in police power is a ***judgment lien*** on real property, which ***results from a court order*** to pay a certain amount to a creditor; *this term appeared and was defined earlier as a type of encumbrance.*

II-C. Regulation of Environmental Hazards (Expect 1-2 questions from this area)

Environmental regulations, both federal and state, are public controls grounded in the government's ***exercise of police power***.

> Each of the following types of hazard has its own set of requirements for acceptable levels as well as ***abatement, mitigation, and cleanup requirements***.
>
> > *Though a licensee needs to be aware of each hazard and be able to explain its general treatment considerations, certified professionals will generally be required to identify, document, and then address the actual presence of any environmental hazard. This would include determining contamination levels and making legally acceptable decisions regarding how to proceed with any proposed property sale or development.*
>
> On the federal level, the ***Environmental Protection Agency (EPA)*** has primary responsibility for most environmental ***regulations*** and ***enforcement*** for environmental Acts such as
> - ***Comprehensive Environmental Response, Compensation, and Liability Act (CERCLA)*** (1980), or the ***Superfund Act***, which established prohibitions, requirements, and liabilities concerning closed and abandoned hazardous waste sites, and established a trust fund to provide for cleanup when no responsible party could be identified. It was amended by the

II. General: Land Use Controls and Regulations (5 questions)
(4 Topic Areas; 13 Sub-Topics—each will be covered in its respective Topic Area)

- *Superfund Amendments and Reauthorizations Act* (1986), which, among other things, stressed the importance of permanent remedies and innovative treatment technologies in cleaning up hazardous waste sites, and provided new enforcement authorities and settlement tools
- *Resource Conservation and Recovery Act (RCRA)*, which is a 1976 amendment to the *Solid Waste Disposal Act* and also regulates the hazards involved with municipal and industrial waste generated nationwide
    - the *Underground Storage Tank (UST)* program was a 1984 amendment
    - the *Leaking Underground Storage Tan (LUST) Trust Fund* for some UST sites was a 1986 amendment
- *Oil Pollution Act (OPA)*, which is part of the *Clean Water Act*, and regulates responses and responsibilities for oil contamination

The particulars of Superfund, RCRA, and OPA are too subject to funding and legislative changes to provide stable testing material, except for distractors, and perhaps a few very broad questions based on the information above.

*Also, the **National Environmental Policy Act** (1969) requires certain federally funded projects to submit an **Environmental Impact Statement (EIS)**. This is a highly complex document, not entry-level information, so will not get elaboration here.*

*However, you **MAY** see a question that makes reference to it as a document required for special sales; any such question is MOST likely to be tallied in Topic Area VI-E, Material Facts.*

Further, the following *environmental conditions and hazardous materials are governed by discovery and disclosure requirements*
- *lead-based paint*, which was banned in 1978, so sales contracts and leases for residential properties built *prior to 1978*, are, because of the *Residential Lead-Based Paint Hazard Reduction Act of 1992*, required to include a federally approved *disclosure notice*
- *asbestos*, which was widely used for insulation and causes lung problems; *abatement*, which means to reduce or end, is a term commonly linked with professional asbestos treatments, and generally takes the form of containment by *encapsulation*, or sealing off, or actual *removal* of materials containing asbestos
- *radon gas*, which is a colorless, odorless gas that the Surgeon General has warned is the second leading cause of lung cancer, arises from the decay of radioactive minerals in the ground and can collect in a basement or other closed areas
- *toxic mold*, which has become a major health hazard in homes nationwide; it often infests humid wall spaces and generally spreads unseen
- *drinking water problems*, such as finding unacceptable levels of coliform or e-coli bacteria and/or adverse chemicals in tap water; generally this applies to properties with their own deep or shallow well rather than municipal water
- *urea formaldehyde foam insulation (UFFI)*, which was used extensively in the late 1970's for wall insulation, and may continue to exude formaldehyde gas, is an irritant and potential cancer-causing agent; its use was discontinued in 1980, but its presence in a property must be disclosed

II. General: Land Use Controls and Regulations (5 questions)
(4 Topic Areas; 13 Sub-Topics—each will be covered in its respective Topic Area)

- *property environmental problems (external)*, such as the on-site or nearby presence and effects of
    - *contaminated soil and/or groundwater*, from faulty septic systems, landfills, chemical discharges, spills, or toxic disposal
    - *underground storage tanks*, particularly **buried and/or abandoned home heating oil tanks**, which may be deteriorating and/or leaking, and contaminating groundwater supplies
    - *protected species*, such as certain endangered shore birds, fish, or nesting turtles, may present limitations on property development that needs to be discovered prior to finalizing a property transfer
- *additional toxic problems* that could arise in property inspections, but **should not appear on the test**, include
    - *polychlorinated biphenyls (PCBs)*, which are long-banned, were used as coolants and insulators; they are slow to break down and are known to cause liver damage
    - *polybrominated diphenyl ethers (PBDEs)*, which are used in appliances as a flame retardant

All of the above hazardous situations should be discovered or indicated by a thorough, professional *property inspection*, **which may require additional inspections by a specialist** wherever there are suggestions of problems beyond the standard property inspection.

As noted previously, licensees and owners who demonstrate **willful negligence** in discovering and/or disclosing any of the above environmental problems that might reasonably be associated with a property may be subject to legal action.

II-D. Private Controls (Expect 1-2 questions from this area)

Private controls on property include *encumbrances*, such as certain types of *liens*, *easements*, and *encroachments*, which were all defined in Section I-C, Encumbrances.

But they also extend to other controls on land use including *private restrictions* such as *subdivision covenants, conditions, and restrictions (CC&Rs)*, and *owners' association rules*. These are *non-monetary encumbrances* that encumber the use and/or transfer of property.

Private restrictions, regardless of their label, generally seek to accomplish similar ends, such as allow or disallow pets in a subdivision or complex, or clarify where to put trash and recyclables. Depending on the property type and local conventions for terminology, they may be referred to as
- *deed restrictions*
- *restrictive covenants*
- *covenants, conditions (or codes), and restrictions (CC&Rs)*
- *condominium owners' association rules* for condominium-specific restrictions
- *homeowners' association (HOA) rules* for subdivision-specific restrictions

II. General: Land Use Controls and Regulations (5 questions)
(4 Topic Areas; 13 Sub-Topics—each will be covered in its respective Topic Area)

Private controls and restrictions are often more restrictive than local zoning ordinances, which means they may either *enhance or detract from property values*, and *in a conflict between CC&Rs and zoning ordinances, generally the more restrictive will prevail*.

Private restrictions on land use are *contractual rather than statutory* and are prepared by *subdivision developers* as well as *individual property owners* to limit the use of a property by future owners. For example, a *developer* may sell lots with restrictions on building styles or property uses, and *property owners* may later decide to restrict the height of shrubs and trees or the colors allowed for exterior house use.

CC&Rs, as well as most other enforceable deed restrictions, *are generally available in the public record*; in the event a resident violates a restriction, another lot owner can seek a *court injunction to stop violators* and enforce compliance.

Note, however, that *illegal restrictions, such as those that violate federal Fair Housing laws, are not enforceable*.

Exam Note: test questions about non-government property encumbrances that focus on their effect on land use rather than being a type of encumbrance may be tallied in this Topic Area.

This ends the presentation of key terms and concepts likely to be either tested or used as distractors in this Content Outline Section.

III. General: Valuation and Market Analysis (8 questions)
(4 Topic Areas; 13 Sub-Topics—each will be covered in its respective Topic Area)

III-A. Value (Expect 1-2 questions from this area)

Value is a broad term for the monetary worth or price of something, or whatever else it might bring in exchange.

There are a variety of *types of value*, including
- *market value*, or *fair market value (FMV)*, which is best understood in real estate to mean *the most probable price a property would bring in a competitive, fair, and open market*, in other words, the *price an informed seller is willing to accept* and *an informed buyer is willing to pay*
- *appraised value* is generally intended to <u>estimate</u> market value
- *assessed value*, which means *the value a taxing authority has placed on a property* for purposes of tax computations, and *NOT a current, actual market value*, even if the tax documents assign the label "Fair Market Value" to a property value
- *loan value*, or *mortgage value*, which is the maximum amount a lender will lend
- *insurable value*, which is the maximum amount an insurance company will insure
- *Insured value*, or *agreed value*, which is generally the face value of an insurance policy coverage
- *actual cash value*, which is an insurance determination of the *depreciated value* of a property, or *replacement cost minus accrued depreciation* *(see the end of the next Topic Area for more on the complex appraisal principle of depreciation)*
- *condemnation value*, which identifies what the property is worth to the condemning authority *in an eminent domain proceeding*
- *estate value*, which is the value given on the probated asset list for the real property of a deceased owner; *estate appraisals typically assess the property's value adjusted to match the exact date the owner died, regardless of when the appraisal is performed*

All property values include some commonly understood *elements of value*, which are
- *utility*, which means that it is useful for something
- *scarcity*, which refers to the available supply
- *demand*, which is a combination of *the desire to own it* and *the ability to purchase it*
- *transferability*, which means that *it can be sold or exchanged*

Further, the term *"value"* is *not directly interchangeable* with either *price* or *cost*, since circumstances may create significant differences. For example, the *cost* of a $20,000 addition to a house generally does not add the same amount of resale *value* to the property.

Similarly, the *market price*, which is *the price a property actually sells for*, may vary considerably from its *appraised value* or *market value* depending on factors an appraisal or comparable sales do not consider, such as *the motivation of either party to depart from an estimate of fair market value.*

For example, an owner might sell a property for considerably less than market value to a family member, or a buyer may pay more for either sentimental or investment reasons.

III. General: Valuation and Market Analysis (8 questions)
(4 Topic Areas; 13 Sub-Topics—each will be covered in its respective Topic Area)

General influences on property value include applications of the principles of value identified throughout this Section, often in combination with other considerations, such as *overall market conditions*, especially *market cycles of ups-and-downs*, which take into account *the economic climate and the supply of properties that are in demand.*

However, the real estate adage that *"the three most important considerations in property value are location, location, and location"* leads us to list of some *factors that make location* so important; *location is often considered the single most important element in property value*. The value of a particular location, though, involves national, regional, local, and neighborhood considerations of how the following elements apply to a property:
- *economic trends and circumstances*, which include elements such as
    - local business and employment opportunities
    - labor force composition and diversity
    - availability of private utilities, such as phone service and cable
- *government controls, regulations, and services*, such as
    - taxation
    - zoning restrictions
    - anticipation of the exercise of eminent domain
    - availability of public utilities, e.g., water and sewer
    - schools and other municipal services
- *physical/environmental conditions*, such as
    - annual weather patterns
    - natural resources, such as mountains, lakes, or seashore
    - topographical elements, such as soil types and wetland, swamp, or desert
    - possible hazards, such as hurricanes, flooding, or mudslides
    - recreation areas and outlets
    - local industries and potential air, soil, and water pollution
- *social trends*, such as
    - region and municipality demographic makeup
    - neighborhood cycles and population changes

Property-specific considerations are generally at the center of all value considerations. Some of the property-specific factors to consider may include, but are not limited to
- *overall condition*, such as whether it is new construction or a "handyman special"
    - *property depreciation* is a critical term associated with property condition and value, and is discussed in detail as an appraisal principle in the next Topic Area; it is defined as **the loss of value resulting from any cause**
- *construction type*, meaning both design style and materials
- *amenities*, which could be *internal*, such as an indoor Jacuzzi, *or external*, such as a better view of some attractive sight than the neighboring properties offer
- *site improvements*, which means *additions to the raw land* such as a residential or commercial building, detached garage and other outbuildings, landscaping, gardens, wells, septic, or connections to public utilities
- *defects*, such as structural problems or negative actions of past owners that have made it a *stigmatized property*, or *psychologically impacted property*

III. General: Valuation and Market Analysis (8 questions)
(4 Topic Areas; 13 Sub-Topics—each will be covered in its respective Topic Area)

- ***historic value***, if any, such as being on the National Register of Historic Properties or being near an historic site
- ***aesthetic factors***, such as a unique architectural design, attractive appearance, or "curb appeal"
- ***distance from, and access to, population centers, work, shopping, and major roads***
- proximity to ***special study zones***, such as ***earthquake, flood,*** and other ***geological or environmental concerns,*** such as ***wetlands, mudslides, and volcano activity***

*Questions based on **principles of value** are identified by PSI's expanded outline as being tallied in this Topic Area; however, most of the key terms and concepts of appraisal principles are listed as being treated in the next Topic Area. To keep them all together, they are clustered below, so get ready—here they come!*

III-B. Methods of Estimating Value/Appraisal Process
(Expect 3-4 questions from this area)

The most basic definition of an ***appraisal*** is ***an estimate of value***, and it is critical to remember that ***appraisals do not <u>determine</u> value, sales do***—appraisals merely estimate property value.

Generally speaking, people commonly "appraise" a property's value while simply driving by, tossing off remarks like, "That place could go for a million bucks, easy."

However, within the real estate profession, a licensee learns how to perform a closer review and prepare a ***competitive market analysis (CMA)*** based on the professional appraisal methods and principles below; a CMA would provide a more probable estimate of a property's value than the simple drive-by. ***Usage note: in some areas or real estate firms, "CMA" is short for "<u>comparative market analysis</u>"—the meanings are synonymous.*** *(CMAs are the subject of the next Topic Area.)*

Except for a very few states, appraisals must be prepared by a licensed appraiser rather than by a real estate licensee. So, the term "appraiser" will be used in this book when referring to appraisals and the appraisal process and "licensee" will be used when referring to the party preparing a CMA or noting other differences between a CMA and an appraisal.

The ***purpose of an appraisal*** is, in most cases, to provide ***an estimate*** of a property's specific type of value ***as of a specified date***, which may differ from the date of the report, that will in turn ***support the use intended by the person who ordered the appraisal***.

*Appraisals are commonly used for special purposes, such as defending against a municipal over-assessment for taxes or setting a date-of-death value for estate purposes. So, **both the purpose and the effective date vary** depending on its intended use.*

Since the value of a property can change suddenly and dramatically due to disasters, accidents, or other events, ***the appraisal value***, though generally unaffected for some time, ***cannot be guaranteed as accurate for any other time than the specified effective date***.

To grasp this concept, simply consider the value of most New Orleans properties the month before and the day after Hurricane Katrina raged through in 2005.

III. General: Valuation and Market Analysis (8 questions)
(4 Topic Areas; 13 Sub-Topics—each will be covered in its respective Topic Area)

In the course of a full-scope appraisal, an appraiser will analyze a property based on considering each of the following *three approaches to value*, though only one will have primary applicability to determining the final appraisal value of any particular property.

> *The three approaches are (1) the **direct sales comparison (market data) approach**, (2) the **cost approach**, and (3) the **income approach**. Each one will be laid out after the following basic elements of the appraisal process and principles are covered.*

The **appraisal process** can be defined as an **orderly, concise, and systematic procedure for reaching an estimate of value**. It generally follows a common sequence of procedures, which can be summarized by the following check-list
- *define, or state, the problem*, which means clarifying the purpose and scope of the appraisal
- *determine the data needed* and *collect it*
- *determine the highest and best use* of the land and the improvements
- *estimate the property value* using the three approaches to value
- *reconcile the data*, which means to analyze it and settle on a final value estimate
- *prepare the final report* of the value estimate

The **appraisal report** prepared in the final step of the process will follow a format appropriate to the purpose of the report, from a detailed narrative to a simple two-page Uniform Residential Appraisal Report.

Regardless of length, the report will present, analyze, and summarize the data supporting the appraiser's **reconciliation** of data and **final determination-of-value estimate**.

In performing an appraisal, an appraiser will collect and interpret a wide range of data. Some of the common **principles of property value** used by appraisers and real estate licensees alike include the principles of
- **substitution**, which looks at the maximum amount it would *cost to buy an alternate property* that is the same as the subject property, *either by a comparable replacement or an exact reproduction*; this principle is *central to the first two of the three approaches to value* described later in this Topic Area
- **anticipation**, which estimates value based on *looking ahead at the value, positive or negative*, on a property *due to possibility of future changes* to either the property or its surroundings, such as changes in zoning, local economy and businesses, or the character of the neighborhood; this principle is *primarily used in the income approach to value*
  - **plottage**, or **plottage value**, which refers to *combining adjoining properties into a single property* with a total value greater than the sum of their separate plot values due to a more profitable use for the larger property. The *process of assembling* these properties is known as **assemblage**.
- **highest and best use**, which determines *the use that will produce the greatest current value, or the most profitable return on investment*, as exemplified by a developer converting a vacant urban industrial building into profitable residential condo units
- **balance**, which refers to *the mix of land uses that maximizes value* for all of the properties involved, as when the proportion of residential, commercial, recreational, industrial, and other uses make *a general area or building complex* attractive to both residents and businesses

III. General: Valuation and Market Analysis (8 questions)
(4 Topic Areas; 13 Sub-Topics—each will be covered in its respective Topic Area)

- *supply and demand*, which simply applies this common economic principle to real estate. It can be readily seen by **considering the supply, demand, and cost for an acre of land in central Manhattan versus an acre of land in many Southwestern desert areas**.
- *competition*, which means that **if a particular property is yielding high profits, similar ones are likely to follow** and try to get in on the action
- *conformity*, which means that all **properties in a given area are likely to benefit from being similar to the others**, as in a subdivision of new homes. When conformity is ignored, it can affect property values in either of the following directions
  - *progression*, which is the **benefit a smaller property receives** from being among larger, more valuable ones; *unfortunately, the value increases from progression may backfire on current owners through higher assessments, and taxes!*
  - *regression*, which is **the negative impact on the value of an large and/or expensive property** when it is in an area of smaller, lower-priced, or run-down properties
- *contribution*, or *increasing and diminishing returns*, which makes a cost/benefit analysis of **the actual increase in property value based on the cost of an improvement**, as in how much more a house will sell for after a $7,000 kitchen renovation. If the $7,000 kitchen only adds $2,000 to the property's market value, it would be considered an *overimprovement*.
- *depreciation*, which in an appraisal valuation refers to **the loss of value resulting from any cause**. Two key terms associated with depreciation are
  - *deterioration*, which applies to **physical factors**, such as normal **wear and tear** as well as poor and/or **deferred maintenance** or **prolonged neglect**
  - *obsolescence*, which applies to **outdated functionality** or **non-property influences**

The **three types of depreciation** used in valuations/appraisals, plus whether or not they are **curable**, meaning they can be remedied, or **incurable**, meaning they are not cost-effective or feasible to fix, are

- *physical deterioration,* which refers to **any downturn from the original condition** of the property, such as an old roof, weathered paint, or broken windows
  - *curable* physical deterioration includes **economically feasible repairs**, such as new exterior paint job
  - *incurable* physical deterioration includes **excessive, cost-prohibitive repairs**, such as correcting a seriously damaged foundation after a landslide or other natural disaster
- *functional obsolescence*, which refers to **outdated design or safety standards**, such as a two-story, three-bedroom house built in the 1920's that still has its original wiring and a single bathroom on the second floor
  - *curable* functional obsolescence would generally include wiring upgrades and new plumbing in the house noted above
  - *incurable* functional obsolescence is generally identified after **weighing the value added** to the property **by the cost of any upgrades and finding the "cure" cost-prohibitive**, sometimes even in comparison to tearing down a property and starting over altogether
- *external obsolescence*, or *economic obsolescence*, or *locational obsolescence*, which refers to **surrounding influences on a subject property**, such as the discovery that a nearby factory has contaminated the groundwater supply, or a pig farm is located just

III. General: Valuation and Market Analysis (8 questions)
(4 Topic Areas; 13 Sub-Topics—each will be covered in its respective Topic Area)

upwind of the subject property—*style note: for clarity, test questions often refer to this as **external (economic) obsolescence***

- ***curable** external obsolescence* – <u>**no such thing**</u>, since it arises from factors "external" to the owner's direct control, and someone else must cure it
- ***incurable** external obsolescence **is the only kind**,* since ***spending money on the subject property cannot reverse the actual problem***

For appraisal purposes, ***only improvements can be depreciated. Land simply loses value***, and even when it does lose value, as it typically does when the property suffers from external (economic) obsolescence, in the process of determining overall property value, ***this loss is categorized separately from the loss of depreciated improvements***.

Estimates of property value, according to appraisal standards, require an analysis of a property based on each of the following ***three approaches to value***; as noted previously, only one will have primary applicability to any particular property.

#1: The ***first approach***, the ***direct sales comparison (market data) approach***, compares the ***subject property***, or ***subject***, which is the one being appraised, to similar properties, or ***comparable properties***, or ***comparables***, or "***comps***," *that have recently <u>sold</u>* in the local market, *generally within the past six months to a year.*

> *Style note: the above term for this approach is a common testing convention, since it combines the terms **direct sales comparison**, **sales comparison**, and **market data**, all of which represent regional and local usage to identify this actual **"sales data" research, compilation, and comparison** approach to value. **Be prepared to see any of these synonymous terms used separately on the PSI exam.***

This comparison is used to estimate the subject property's ***relative value in the same market*** that produced ***the sale*** of the comparables. This means that ***the sale of a comparable must be fair and open*** rather than a foreclosure, tax, auction, estate, forced, special-interest, or insider sale.

This approach to value is ***an application of the principle of substitution***, since it assumes that similar properties are similarly desirable and may be substituted for each other. This approach is widely and ***extensively used for residential properties***.

When available, ***three or more comparables are reviewed*** and analyzed to provide a balanced estimate.

> The ***price of a comparable gets adjusted up or down*** based on valuable differences between it and the subject property – ***the final figure is applied to the subject***.
>
> > For example, if the subject and the comparable houses ***were identical except one has an extra bay in its garage***, the value of the extra bay would be used to adjust for price comparisons.
> > - ***If the comparable has the extra bay***, the value would be ***subtracted from the comparable's sales price*** to estimate the market value of the subject property.

III. General: Valuation and Market Analysis (8 questions)
(4 Topic Areas; 13 Sub-Topics—each will be covered in its respective Topic Area)

- *If the subject property has the bay*, the value would be **added to the comparable's sales price** to estimate the market value of the subject.

All relevant property conditions, including influences from **depreciation**, are factored into the final estimate of value using the direct sales comparison (market data) approach.

The ***direct sales comparison (market data) approach*** is also commonly, though more loosely, used by appraisal companies in preparing **assessments for municipal taxation**, often referred to as **mass appraisals**, as well as by licensees in preparing a **CMA**. *(As previously noted, see the next Topic Area for more on CMAs.)*

#2: The *second approach*, the *cost approach*, estimates value based on **what it would cost to buy the land and build comparable replacements** for all of the property improvements.

*This approach was once also known as the **summation approach**, since it "summed-up" the value of the land and all individual improvements on it. This term, though obsolete, may appear on your test—it is simply an old synonym for the cost approach.*

The ***cost approach is also based on the principle of substitution***, since it assumes that no rational person will pay more for a property than the amount it would cost to purchase a comparable site and construct a comparable building without any undue delays.

The cost approach is commonly **used for commercial properties, as well as for special-use properties** that do not have many comparables, such as **churches, schools, and municipal buildings**.

In order to adjust for the difference between new construction and existing improvements, the **current structures are evaluated for depreciation, which is then subtracted from the new construction cost**.

There are *five steps* in the preparation of a cost approach analysis. These are
1. *estimate the value of the land only*, as if vacant
2. *estimate the new construction cost* of all improvements
3. *determine the accrued, or combined, depreciation* from the three types of depreciation (see the end of this Topic Area) as they affect the current improvements
4. *subtract the accrued depreciation* of the improvements from the estimate of new construction to get the estimated value of the current improvements
5. *add the value of the land to the value of the improvements*

The completion of the last step will produce the ***estimated property value by the cost approach***; because **the cost approach** "sums-up" individual elements, it is occasionally *referred to as **the summation approach**, so watch for that on the test!*

There are **two methods for determining the new construction costs** of improvements needed for the steps above: **replacement cost** and **reproduction cost**.
- ***Replacement cost*** determines ***the current cost of an acceptably similar copy***, often somewhat more contemporary in functionality and construction.

III. General: Valuation and Market Analysis   (8 questions)
(4 Topic Areas; 13 Sub-Topics—each will be covered in its respective Topic Area)

- *Reproduction cost* determines *the current cost of an exact copy* of the improvements, flaws and all, such as outdated features or construction materials of older buildings; *this is often seen in estimating costs for recreating historical buildings or building similar properties for aesthetic purposes.*

There are several ways to estimate the above construction costs, including the *square-foot method*, the *unit-in-place method*, the *quantity survey method*, and the *index method*. *Details of these appraisal methods are best left to appraiser exams.*

However, the *square-foot method* is so commonly used in practice for estimating a wide variety of new-construction that it may appear in math questions.

To compute construction costs using the square-foot method, simply *multiply the cost-per-square-foot of building a comparable property by the square footage of a new building*.

So, if a 10,000 square foot warehouse were built for $397,500, or $39.75/square foot, a 12,000 square foot warehouse would cost $477,000.

#3: The *third approach*, the *income approach*, estimates the present value of future net income of income-producing properties through the process of *capitalization*, which converts *future income projections into current value*.

The *income approach* is *based on the principle of anticipation*, which asserts that value is created by the expectation of benefits to be derived from *return on investment* during ownership as well as any capital gain realized at resale.

The *capitalization rate*, or *cap rate*, is the term for the *rate of return* on the cost of the investment.

To *compute the capitalization rate* for a particular property, simply *divide the property's net operating income by its price*.
- For example, a $200,000 property that has a $20,000/year net operating income has a capitalization rate of 10 percent.

The following *three categories of income* are important to remember for rentals and other investment properties. *(All of these will be repeated and used in Section XI-D, Commercial, Industrial, and Income Property.) **The last of these is the one to use for computing cap rates.***
- *potential gross income*, or *projected gross income*, or *scheduled gross income*, which means the *maximum rental income* at 100 percent occupancy
- *effective gross income*, which means the *actual income* after subtracting vacancies and rent collection losses
- *net operating income (NOI)*, which is *what's left of the effective gross income after subtracting all of the property's operating expenses*, such as maintenance, taxes, insurance, reserves for replacements, and other recurring expenses (but not debt service, such as mortgage interest)

III. General: Valuation and Market Analysis (8 questions)
(4 Topic Areas; 13 Sub-Topics—each will be covered in its respective Topic Area)

To *estimate a property value from a cap rate*, an appraiser, licensee, or investor may analyze several recent comparable sales to determine their cap rates, develop an appropriate composite cap rate for the subject property, then *divide the subject property's NOI by the cap rate*.

- For example, if the appraiser determines that a cap rate of 5 percent is what the area market is currently supporting, and the NOI for a property is $10,000, the estimated property value would be $200,000.

Another income approach method of estimating value is the *gross rent multiplier (GRM)*, or *gross income multiplier (GIM)* method. This is a simple, informal rule-of-thumb technique that is often used for one-to-four unit residential rentals or small commercial and industrial sites.

Using recent sales, the appraiser *divides each comparable property's sales price by its gross income, either monthly or annual*, using the same time-period standard for all, to determine their respective GRMs.

Then, after developing a representative GRM from a reconciliation of the collective GRMs, the appraiser *multiplies the subject property's income by the GRM* to arrive at a general estimate of value.

- For example, if the appraiser develops a GRM of 135 for monthly rents in an area, and is analyzing a property with a monthly rent of $1,200, the property's value would be expected to be around $162,000.

In practice, the income approach is very sensitive to property differences and complexities, highly specialized analysis techniques, and disagreements among appraisers about applications.

The above explanation of the income approach is intentionally very basic, and is presented more to expose you to a few terms you may see on the test than to provide a short-course in this appraisal method.

III-C. Competitive/Comparative Market Analysis (CMA)
(Expect 1-2 questions from this area)

The above broad definition of an appraisal does not adequately distinguish between an *appraisal* performed by a professional appraiser and a real estate licensee's *competitive (or comparative) market analysis (CMA)*.

The following additional description helps define the role of an appraiser's appraisal in property valuation compared to a CMA

- *an appraiser's* appraisal is performed by a licensed appraiser or, in some states, a state-approved real estate licensee, and is a *more extensive analysis* than a CMA because it *follows a set of comprehensive guidelines* outlined in the *Uniform Standards of Professional Appraisal Practice (USPAP)* and results in one of several standard-format *appraisal reports*
- a formal appraisal report, rather than a CMA, is typically *required by lenders or insurers* to support *a property value that has been more rigorously researched in support of the accuracy and legal accountability of the actual risk they are assuming*

III. General: Valuation and Market Analysis (8 questions)
(4 Topic Areas; 13 Sub-Topics—each will be covered in its respective Topic Area)

So, the role of an appraiser in property valuation is to prepare a *formal appraisal*, which provides *stronger documentation* in support of its estimate of value for use by others, such as lenders, insurers, and tax assessors.

Nevertheless, the less rigorously researched licensee's *CMA* is still useful for estimating property value, typically using *three or more comps that have sold within the past year.* Though a CMA is not as "official" as an appraisal and is generally compiled using "rule of thumb" approximations rather than precisely researched data, if carefully prepared, it will often result in a final figure that is roughly the same as that of a formal appraisal.

> *A broker's price opinion (BPO) or broker's opinion of value (BOV) are terms used in some areas for what are sometimes an even more informal valuation than a CMA. Often no more than an oral "educated guesstimate" or a one-paragraph letter in response to a 'general value' inquiry from a financial institution or curious individual, they are often subject to both state regulations and company policies.*
>
>> *In Connecticut, for example, it is legally prohibited to accept compensation for a BPO unless the BPO is intended to result in a listing, and even then, the fee must be credited back as an advance on earned commission if the listing leads to a closing.*

A licensee's CMA is typically used to establish a *reasonable listing price* for sellers and a *reasonable offering price* for buyers.

Despite the figures in a licensee's CMA estimate, *it is the seller's responsibility to set a list price* and *the buyer's responsibility to determine an offering price.*

A licensee's role in preparing a CMA involves *gathering, interpreting, and computing the value of comparable properties* as well as performing other *property-related math*. Therefore, some of the appraisal topics raised above may be directly applicable within this Topic Area, including non-math questions about preparing a CMA for income properties by using comparable Gross Rent Multipliers or Gross Income Multipliers.

> However, if a question involves a computation instead of an interpretation, it will most likely be tallied in the Section X-E, Calculations for Valuation.
>
> *This area will include appraisal-type questions, but from the perspective of a licensee who is preparing a CMA; watch for the use of "licensee," "broker," or "agent" rather than "appraiser" in CMA questions.*
>
> *The emphasis in this area may include scenario-type questions that have examples of how a licensee reviews a property for age, condition, and defects, and then discusses and/or explains these factors and their effect on the property's value with the owner or prospective buyer.*

Some of the property conditions that might be used in these examples include
- *general property information* for the listing, such as age, condition, or zoning
- *material defects*, which are defects that would affect a potential buyer's decision on either buying the property or how much to pay

III. General: Valuation and Market Analysis (8 questions)
(4 Topic Areas; 13 Sub-Topics—each will be covered in its respective Topic Area)

- *internal environmental problems*, such as the existence of lead paint, asbestos, radon, or toxic mold
- *external environmental problems*, such as contamination or pollution
- *stigmatizing conditions*, or *psychologically impacted properties*, such as a history of illegal activity, death, suicide, or health information about either a seller or past residents
- *adjustments to comparable properties*, such as extra amenities and features that make the subject property different from particular comps
- *depreciation considerations* as they apply to the subject property's final value

III-D. When Appraisal by Certified Appraiser is Required
(Expect 0-1 question from this area)

Widespread, often fraudulent, overvaluation of real estate led to bank failures nationwide in the mid-to-late 1980s.

In response, the federal government mandated the establishment of professional standards and licensing for appraisers, and required lenders making **federally backed residential loans** to support their values **with an appraisal by a certified appraiser**.

The Appraisal Foundation was established in 1987 by Congress to foster professionalism through establishing generally accepted professional valuation standards and licensing qualifications, the former through the Appraisal Standards Board (ASB) and the latter through the Appraiser Qualifications Board (AQB).

Under AQB guidelines there are two broad categories of appraisers: **certified general appraisers**, *who are qualified to appraise all types of real estate, and* **certified residential appraisers**, *who are qualified to appraise all residential real estate.*

Every state has its own licensing requirements for appraisers, and generally implement AQB's guidelines for classroom education, field experience, and examinations for each category of appraiser.

Though lenders and insurers may require a formal appraisal on any property, it may be a **company policy rather than a legal requirement <u>unless</u> government funding is involved**.

Ever since the last half of 2007, the residential real estate market, the financing industry, and the stock market have been hit hard by widespread defaults and foreclosures stemming from subprime borrowers failing to keep up with their mortgage payments, notably those that were structured as Adjustable Rate Mortgages (ARMs) and had reached a scheduled rate increase (see Sections IV-A and IV-B in the upcoming Outline Area for more).

Since much of this has been attributed to lenders accepting a combination of "optimistic" appraisal figures, often ones that anticipated property appreciation, and a similarly optimistic assessment of a borrower's ability to pay, expect to see more changes in both government regulations and lender requirements for conservative appraisals. (Also watch for more stringent requirements, including licensing, for mortgage lenders and brokers.)

III. General: Valuation and Market Analysis (8 questions)
(4 Topic Areas; 13 Sub-Topics—each will be covered in its respective Topic Area)

Questions on this situation, as important as it is, are unlikely to appear on your test. However, if you are familiar with the trend to hold appraisal professionals accountable for appraisals that are neither tailored to nor influenced by lender or borrower objectives, you should be able to answer any that might pop up.

This ends the presentation of key terms and concepts likely to be either tested or used as distractors in this Content Outline Section.

IV. General: Financing (7 questions)
(7 Topic Areas; 21 Sub-Topics—each will be covered in its respective Topic Area)

IV-A. General Concepts (Expect 1-2 questions from this area)

There is an extensive list of terms for *general concepts* related to financing, since *financing instruments can be intricately tailored to the particular situation*, and involve a lot of time-honored as well as new and creative concepts.

Some of the more common terms in property financing include
- an *instrument*, which is a written legal document or contract defining rights, duties, and other obligations
    - a *secured instrument* is one that has some form of *collateral* identified as *alternate compensation* in the event the borrower *defaults*, or fails to perform, according to the instrument, or contract.
- *equity*, which refers to *the amount of principal, or after-debt money, a property owner has in the property*; for example, if a property worth $250,000 has a $200,000 loan balance against it, the owner has $50,000 of property equity
- *liquidity*, which refers to an asset's being readily convertible to cash; *real estate is generally not considered a highly liquid asset, at least at fair market pricing, since it takes time to market property and close on a sale*
- *points* refer to a measurement unit for loan costs -- *one point* equals *one percent of the face value of the loan*
- *yield* is the term for the *return* or *profit* a lender makes on a transaction, *generally expressed as a percentage of the amount invested*
- *loan-to-value ratio (LTV, or L/V)* is a ratio *obtained by dividing the loan amount by the property value*, which is taken from *the lesser of the appraised value or the sales price*. For example, a loan of $80,000 on a property valued at $100,000 has an LTV of 80 percent. Clearly, *the lower the LTV, the lower the risk of loss for the lender* in the event a borrower defaults and the lender has to sell the property.
- *leverage*, which refers to *the amount of money borrowed in relation to the property's value – high leverage*, or a *high LTV*, equates to a <u>*large loan amount*</u> coupled with a <u>*low downpayment*</u>
- *private mortgage insurance (PMI)* typically refers to *policies that cover the "top" portion of the loan amount, generally no more than 30 percent*, against early default, since the property's value might not cover the entire remaining loan balance due after other foreclosure costs. Lenders making *high LTV conventional loans* commonly require the borrower to protect the lender against default by purchasing PMI, which *thereby lowers a lender's risk and sometimes allows them to lend upwards of 95 percent LTV*.
- *buy-downs* refer to an *up-front sum paid by a borrower specifically to reduce the interest rate and thereby bring down the monthly payment*. The reduced rate may be temporary or permanent, depending on the arrangement.
- *lock-in commitment* is *a lender's charge* that prospective borrowers may elect to pay in exchange for the lender's promise to fund the loan at a quoted interest rate even if the lender's rates change before the loan is funded at closing
- *annual percentage rate (APR)* is the term for the *effective* annual percentage rate, or *true annual cost of borrowing*; it allows more accurate consumer comparisons of lenders and financing offers by taking into account all loan charges and fees, such as points and prepaid interest, rather than just identifying the interest rate applied to the loan balance.

IV. General: Financing (7 questions)
(7 Topic Areas; 21 Sub-Topics—each will be covered in its respective Topic Area)

- *APR details are defined and regulated by the **Truth in Landing Act (Regulation Z)** – see Sections IV-F and IX-B for more on TILA and Regulation Z.*
- ***conforming loans*** refer to loans that ***conform to a set of lending specifications, especially standard maximum limits on property values*** or requirements for borrower credit worthiness
  - ***nonconforming loans*** typically involve greater risk on the part of the lender by relaxing the standards for property values, LTV, and/or borrower credit history
- ***prime interest rate, prime rate,*** or often simply ***prime***, refers to ***the rate charged by banks to their most creditworthy customers***, generally large corporations, and are generally the same or very close to those of other banks; the Wall Street Journal defines it as "The base rate on corporate loans posted by at least 75% of the nation's 30 largest banks." ***It also commonly refers to the rate the Federal Reserve System charges for its loans to banks***. Prime rates do not adjust at any regular interval.
- ***prime*** may ***also refer to borrowers*** considered to be of high quality, meaning low risk of default; prime borrowers are typically offered attractively low interest rates
- ***subprime*** or ***non-prime*** refers to the ***credit status of borrowers*** with poor, limited, or no credit history, and are therefore unable to qualify for a conventional or conforming mortgage due to the greater risk of default; ***credit scores*** *generally range between 300 and 900, and many lenders consider scores lower than 660, 620, or 600, depending on the lender, as subprime*
- ***usury*** refers to ***a lender's charging an illegally high rate of interest***. Usury laws vary from state to state, and do not apply at all in some states.
  - *The term originally applied to charging **any** interest on loans and is still **commonly defined as charging exorbitantly high interest**; in legal terms it refers to charging a rate in excess of legal limits. **Though your state may not have a usury law (many do not, and thereby serve as "home-base" for credit card companies), this financially relevant concept is still valid for testing**.*
- ***predatory lending*** is a term closely associated with usury, though it refers to a wide array of practices by which borrowers are taken unfair advantage of, such as extremely severe penalty fees and interest rate hikes after a late payment
  - *This term is finding widespread use in reference to the problems within the mortgage industry based on subprime borrowers' inability to make continued payments and then lose and/or owe money after a property foreclosure sale; many of these foreclosures are triggered by an adjustable interest rate adjusting upward at the end of an introductory period.*

Lenders may also require some of the following additional charges and conditions as part of the processing and funding of certain loans

- ***discount points***, often simply called ***points***, are ***a lender's up-front charge*** for making a loan; ***points are typically charged to increase the lender's yield when funding a loan at below-market interest rates***; as noted above, one point equals ***one percent of the loan***
- ***origination fee*** is a lender's ***charge for preparing and processing a loan***
- ***document preparation***, or ***"doc prep,"*** is a lender's ***charge for preparing and copying loan-related documents***
- ***funding fee*** is also a lender's processing charge, most commonly associated with VA loans
- ***impound,*** or ***reserve account***, which is an ***account for the funds held by the lender to pay recurring expenses, such as property taxes and insurance, during the life of the loan***; known in some areas as an ***escrow account***

IV. General: Financing (7 questions)
(7 Topic Areas; 21 Sub-Topics—each will be covered in its respective Topic Area)

- *satisfaction of mortgage certificate*, or, for deeds of trust, a *release deed*, or *deed of release*, required of the seller's lender(s) to confirm that funds have been applied to pay off the seller's loans
- *estoppel certificates*, or confirmation notices from interested parties, such as getting a lender's signature attesting to the exact remaining principal balance or a tenant's signature attesting to the amount of security deposit held by the seller

General **IRS tax issues** regarding the costs, benefits, and tax implications of property financing include the following borrower-related items
- *interest payments* on mortgage loans *are deductible* if the homeowner itemizes deductions, though *for homeowners with low-balance loans and few other deductions, the standard deduction may be better than itemizing*; in practice this is best addressed by tax professionals
- *real estate taxes* are deductible
- *certain costs* of financing and refinancing may be deductible, such as *origination fees*, *discount points*, and loan *prepayment penalties*

The process of reviewing an applicant for a loan typically includes the following components and considerations
- *prequalification* generally refers to a lender, or even a licensee, determining the probable maximum loan amount the borrower can repay by collecting preliminary information about the borrower's financial circumstances, generally during a brief interview. It is a nonbinding preliminary assessment.
  - *The terms **prequalified** or **preapproved** are sometimes applied to a fully qualified buyer who is looking for property, as in, "My client has been prequalified by a lender for the amount of financing given in this offer."*
- *qualification* refers to the process a lender goes through of more closely reviewing a buyer's credit and financial status to determine the actual maximum loan amount the lender would fund. Once approved for funding, the applicant becomes known as a *qualified buyer*, or *approved buyer*.
- *credit report* from a major credit reporting agency will be requested by the lender to determine the official status of an applicant's financial history in order to qualify or approve the buyer

When a prospective buyer, qualified or not, finds a property and approaches the lender for funding, *the lender will perform a property review prior to fully approving the loan*. The process of reviewing a property for a loan typically includes the following components and considerations
- *property appraisal,* or *Certificate of Reasonable Value (CRV)* for VA funding, for a current estimate of value
- *title search* or *attorney's opinion of title*, to confirm that the title is unencumbered
- *title insurance policy*, to transfer the risk of loss in the event of undiscovered flaws in the chain of title
- *property survey*, if there are any questions about the exact boundaries and possible encroachments or physical encumbrances
- *zoning* codes and ordinances that govern the use and future of the property

IV. General: Financing (7 questions)
(7 Topic Areas; 21 Sub-Topics—each will be covered in its respective Topic Area)

IV-B. Types of Loans (Expect 1-2 questions from this area)

There are a host of ordinary, special, and creative financing options in lending. For the sake of broad categorizations here, *loan types can be distinguished by three primary elements*: *repayment options*, *interest rates,* and *loan purpose*. Clearly, all three categories are present in every loan, but one tends to be more evident in the loan's name.

> Note: The term *"mortgage"* may be substituted for *"loan"* as soon as it is clear that *the loan is, or will be, secured by real property*. However, *"loan"* is used here as the default term *to keep the primary focus on the basic financing arrangements*. The test questions may use the terms interchangeably as appropriate to the topic being tested.

Types of loans with names that suggest their *repayment options* include
- *amortized loans*, which are those that are paid off over time, usually through equal monthly payments for a set number of years
    - *fully amortized loans*, or *level-payment loans*, are structured to pay down the *loan amount*, or *principal*, plus interest, in *equal payments*, generally paid monthly until the balance is zero. These loans begin with a higher portion of each installment going toward the interest, and end with most of the loan payment being applied directly to the remaining principal.
    - *partially amortized loans* can be structured any number of ways, but typically mean that the principal is paid down according to an agreed-upon schedule, with a final payment that is larger than the others
        - *balloon payment* is the term applied to this sort of large final payment
- *growing equity mortgages* have payments that increase over time with the additional amount applied directly to principal, which brings down the interest payments and overall repayment period of the loan
- *graduated payment loans* are fixed-rate, scheduled payment loans that allow the borrower to make lower payments initially, and increase them to make up for the difference. Similar to growing equity mortgages, they both are structured in anticipation of the borrower's income rising along with the payments due.
- *term loans*, or *straight loans*, or *straight note*, or *interest-only loans*, look similar to a partially amortized loan in that they have single, level payments for the life of the loan with a much larger final payment. However, under a term loan, the *payments are interest-only*, and *the entire principal amount is due* at the end of the loan's *term*, or time period for the borrower to use the capital.
    - since there is no reduction in principal, these are classified as *nonamortized loans*

Types of loans with names that identify their *interest rate structure* include
- *fixed rate loans*, which have *an interest rate that remains the same for the life of the loan*
- *adjustable-rate mortgages (ARMs)*, which have a fluctuating interest rate that gets adjusted at periodic intervals. They typically allow a borrower to pay a *lower rate for the first few years*, which keeps their initial expenses low, then *adjusts either to a preset interest rate or a rate based on market conditions at a scheduled, contract-based adjustment interval*.
- *interest-only*, which is essentially the more currently used name for many term loans, and *may be structured to allow lenders to adjust the interest rates periodically* according to

IV. General: Financing (7 questions)
(7 Topic Areas; 21 Sub-Topics—each will be covered in its respective Topic Area)

preset conditions, such as changes in prime interest rates; *these loans require a balloon payment of the entire principal at a contractually set date*

- *variable rate mortgages (VRMs)*, which allow the rate to vary over the life of the loan, generally based on an appropriate index; they are often structured to adjust at six-month intervals with a ½ percent per year cap on increases, and a 2-1/2 percent increase cap over the life of the loan
- *renegotiated, or renegotiable, rate mortgages (RRMs)*, which are loans in which the interest rate is adjusted periodically, general every three to five years, to remain in line with current market rates. *This is a popular financing instrument in Canada, where the Canadian Rollover mortgage is structured to include renegotiated rates every five years.*

Types of loans with names that suggest their *loan purpose or primary characteristic* include

- *construction loans*, or *interim loans*, are loans that are generally paid to the borrower in installments during the course of a construction project. They typically require the borrower to make interest-only payments and arrange for *permanent financing*, called an *end loan*, or *take-out loan*, of some sort at the end of the construction period
- *blanket loans* 'cover' more than one lot, parcel, or property; they are common in subdivision developments, and typically include a *partial release clause*, which allows the borrower to *pay off and release separate parcels* as they get sold
- *package loans* include *funding to purchase personal as well as real property*, as in the sale of a furnished condo
- *wraparound loans* allow a borrower to take out *a second loan*, make a payment *large enough to cover both loans* to the new lender, and have *the new lender make the payments on the original loan*
- *open-end loans* offer a line of credit secured by a property, and are usually created for improvements that will be done in stages, so the borrower's monthly indebtedness keeps pace with actual outlays
- *home equity* loans are typically made on an agreed amount of a homeowner's equity in the property, either in a lump sum or a line of credit. They are often referred to as *second mortgages*, or *junior mortgages*, and typically have a lien priority below any other existing mortgages.
- *reverse mortgages*, or *reverse annuity mortgages (RAMs)*, provide payments from a bank to the homeowner, who generally has already paid off any original loans. This is an increasingly popular form of financing among retirement-aged homeowners who want to have access to their equity and leave repayment to their estate or heirs.
- *bridge loans*, or *swing loans*, both often referred to as *gap financing*, are short-term loans made to cover a temporary shortfall or period prior to the funding of the permanent loan
- *nonrecourse loans* are secured loans that allow the lender to attach only the collateral, leaving all other borrower assets judgment-proof in the event of borrower default
- *conventional loans* and *insured loans* are very broad categories that generally refer to *basic loans between an individual and a lender* and *loans that are made with government backing after satisfying certain specific government guidelines*, respectively; *these will be treated in greater detail in the next two Topic Areas*
- *seller-financing* is a type of loan that provides funding for a buyer, and property-secured income for the seller. (There is more on seller-financing, especially *contract for deed (land contract)*, in Topic Areas IV-C, Sources of Loan Money, and IV-E, Mortgages/Deeds of Trust.)

IV. General: Financing (7 questions)
(7 Topic Areas; 21 Sub-Topics—each will be covered in its respective Topic Area)

- *sale/leaseback* financing is a method used by some businesses **to free up equity** in a business property by **selling it to an investor who in turn leases it back** to the business
- **subprime mortgages** refer to **mortgage loans arranged for subprime borrowers**, also known as **non-conforming loans** since they have no set guidelines; due to strong growth in subprime mortgage lending over the past five-to-ten years and subsequent, recent high default and foreclosure rates, you will undoubtedly become very familiar with this category of loans, lenders, and borrowers once you are licensed
  - **the subprime lending crisis** has been fueled by abuse of underwriting standards, mostly by mortgage brokers and lenders either inflating a borrower's actual income or falsifying income entirely to make a borrower look capable of making mortgage payments that are, in fact, too high

IV-C. Sources of Loan Money (Expect 1-2 questions from this area)

Financing sources for buyers who either cannot or simply prefer not to pay cash include *lending institutions*, *the seller*, and, of course, family, friends, and personal contacts.

In most cases, though, buyers will make arrangements with *a local bank* for property financing. *The local bank or financial institution that originates the loan* represents what is known as the *primary mortgage market*, or *primary market*.

Sometimes buyers are introduced to a lender by a *mortgage broker*, who operates as a middleman between the public and lenders. Mortgage brokers assess the individual's credit worthiness and then try to match that party with a suitable lender, which could be a local bank, or it could be an institution or investment group in some other part of the country that do not deal directly with the public.

In turn, the local bank, or other lending source, will simultaneously be making, or *originating*, loans to other buyers, and eventually have a collection, or *portfolio*, of loans, which it *warehouses*, or holds, until they can be packaged and sold as a group.

These loans, as a group, may look attractive to a larger financial institution as a *secured investment*. Once a loan is sold as part of a package like this, it has been *securitized* as component of a *mortgage-backed security*, and enters into what is known as the *secondary mortgage market*, or *secondary market*.

If the bank sells its portfolio of loans to a financial investor, the bank regains its capital while shifting the ownership, and risk of default, to the institution in the secondary market. The local bank now has the funds available to make new loans, create a new portfolio, and sell it off. And so the cycle goes.

*The widespread infusion of subprime loans into the secondary mortgage market has resulted in widely publicized financial disasters, largely since investors were not aware of the actual risk of some of these securitized mortgages or the dazzlingly confusing array of **derivative products** tied to **toxic assets**, such as **subprime-mortgage-backed securities**.*

IV. General: Financing (7 questions)
(7 Topic Areas; 21 Sub-Topics—each will be covered in its respective Topic Area)

As noted earlier, these problems are affecting the real estate industry by, at a minimum, tightening access to mortgage money and instigating more stringent requirements, including licensing, for mortgage lenders and brokers. During your real estate career, you will certainly have Continuing Education courses on the complexities of this mess.

Conventional financing is one of the three most common financing methods available to ***institutional lenders.*** The other two are made through the ***Federal Housing Administration (FHA)***, and the ***Department of Veterans Affairs (VA)***, both of which are discussed more fully in the next Section, IV-D, Government Programs.

Conventional loans are loans made by lending institutions without following any particular government program's requirements. ***These loans typically charge somewhat higher interest rates and require a greater down payment than FHA or VA loans***.

Seller financing may take the form of a ***purchase-money mortgage***, or seller ***carryback***, in which the seller generally provides ***a supplementary loan*** to the buyer that makes up the difference between the purchase price and the total of the buyer's other loans and cash.

Or, ***it may take the form of primary financing*** under a ***contract for deed (land contract)***, which is a type of two-party mortgage between the seller and the buyer and is discussed in greater detail in Section IV-E, Mortgages/Deeds of Trust.

Seller financing is ***attractive in situations where lenders are reluctant to lend***, such as on raw land, or when the seller wants to ***'play bank' and collect the interest*** or ***spread out the receipt of proceeds*** for tax benefits or some other personal financial reason.

Often, though, the seller elects this option simply to help ***close the gap*** on a sale where the buyer's other financing and available cash fall short of the purchase price.

The ***terms of repayment*** and the ***creation of a security instrument*** may be structured in a variety of ways for both ***purchase-money mortgages*** and a ***contract for deed (land contract)***, depending on negotiations between the seller and the buyer.

Sale and leaseback, ***sale/leaseback***, or simply ***leaseback*** is an arrangement by which a property owner, usually commercial, sells the property to an investor with the understanding that the seller may lease the property from the buyer immediately. This arrangement is often ***made to free up capital for use by the former owner***, now the lessee.

Also, in some markets there may be ***down payment assistance programs*** for certain buyers. Questions linked to this area are most likely to be broad, and simply concentrate on the fact that ***first time home buyers***, meaning ***those who have not had an ownership interest in a residence within the last three years***, may be eligible for a ***home-buyer grant*** to help with a down payment.

There are a host of programs and charities that provide this assistance; you should research the ones available in your area in order to better serve both buyers who can use some help and sellers who may expand the prospective buyer pool by sharing this assistance information with them.

IV. General: Financing (7 questions)
(7 Topic Areas; 21 Sub-Topics—each will be covered in its respective Topic Area)

IV-D. Government Programs (Expect 1-2 questions from this area)

Two of the three most common financing methods for institutional lenders are made through the ***Federal Housing Administration (FHA)***, and the ***Department of Veterans Affairs (VA)***.

FHA loans are residential loans ***funded by FHA-approved lenders*** but <u>***insured by the FHA***</u>. Both ***the borrower*** and ***the property*** must meet FHA guidelines.

FHA loans have a ***maximum loan amount*** that is ***adjusted periodically for <u>local markets</u>***, require a very ***low down payment***, often as low as three percent, and are ***insured*** by an up-front ***mortgage insurance premium (MIP)*** and periodic ***renewal premiums***.

Lenders providing funds for ***FHA-insured loans*** must follow FHA guidelines in order to ensure that the loan qualifies for FHA approval and backing. Some of these include
- ***FHA-approved appraisal***, or ***conditional commitment***, on the property, typically requiring that the appraisal be performed by an ***FHA-approved appraiser***
- ***standards for property condition,*** such as construction type and pre-sale repair of property defects
- payment of ***an up-front mortgage insurance premium (MIP)***, plus ***an annual renewal premium*** of one-half of one percent (.5%) of the loan balance; <u>***often the up-front MIP is rolled into the loan total***</u>

Historically, ***FHA loans have been assumable***, and most still are, though the rules for assumption have become increasingly stringent.

VA loans are also residential loans ***funded by a VA-approved lender*** but <u>***a portion of the loan amount is guaranteed by the government***</u>. Like FHA loans, they have guidelines for both the borrower and the property
- VA loans are available for military and ex-military borrowers who qualify for a ***certificate of eligibility*** from the VA
- the property has to be appraised by the VA and receive a ***certificate of reasonable value (CRV)***, which serves as the VA's counterpart to a standard appraisal

Lenders providing funds for ***VA-guaranteed loans*** must follow VA guidelines in order to ensure that the loan qualifies for VA approval and backing. Some of these include
- use of the ***Certificate of Reasonable Value (CRV)***, or 'VA appraisal' for property valuation
- ***no prepayment penalty*** is allowed
- ***assumption rights*** -- historically, VA loans have been ***assumable***, and most still are, though the rules for assumption have become increasingly stringent

*Also, unless the original borrower has received **a release of liability** from the VA and the lender has accepted it, **the borrower remains financially liable** to the lender for the loan in the event a subsequent buyer defaults.*

*The original borrower may also qualify for a **restoration of entitlement**, allowing full entitlement use on future purchases, if the person assuming the loan is a veteran and*

IV. General: Financing (7 questions)
(7 Topic Areas; 21 Sub-Topics—each will be covered in its respective Topic Area)

substitutes their entitlement for the seller's, or whenever the loan is paid off by either an assuming buyer or the original borrower.

The **Farm Service Agency (FSA)**, formerly the **Farmers Home Administration (FmHA)**, represents another source of ***funding for rural, farming, and ranching communities***. FSA provides programs for beginning farmers and ranchers who do not qualify for conventional loans as well as loans to established farmers who have suffered setbacks from natural disasters. ***FSA makes direct and guaranteed farm ownership along with business operating loans*** to qualified applicants.

If you are planning to enter the real estate business in a rural, farming, or ranching area, you should become familiar with FSA guidelines for qualifying borrowers; however, the particulars are too regional to merit specific questions on the general portion of the exam.

In addition to the government programs above, the following ***three major government programs*** are involved in the ***secondary mortgage market***:
- *Fannie Mae*, the commonly used name for the **Federal National Mortgage Association (FNMA)**,
- *Ginnie Mae*, the commonly used name for the **Government National Mortgage Association (GNMA)**, and
- *Freddie Mac*, the commonly used name for the **Federal Home Loan Mortgage Corporation (FHLMC)**.

Fannie Mae is a corporation chartered by the government to purchase and sell conventional, FHA and VA mortgages in the secondary market; it converts some of its mortgage loans into mortgage-backed securities. It has a set of requirements for the loans it will buy, and has been influential in making mid-range residential mortgages available.

Ginnie Mae is a federally owned corporation that is a division of the **Department of Housing and Urban Development (HUD)**; it works with Fannie Mae to provide a government guarantee for mortgage-backed securities, and underwrites FHA, VA, and certain farmer's home administration loans.

Freddie Mac is the newest of the three, and is a corporation created by Congress to increase the availability of residential financing. It deals primarily in conventional loans, and has strict standardized qualification standards.

IV-E. Mortgages/Deeds of Trust (Expect 1-2 questions from this area)

Secured instruments for real estate property loans are broadly termed ***mortgages***.

A mortgage typically has a ***note***, or ***promissory note***, which is ***the financing instrument*** that serves as ***evidence of the debt*** and ***details the terms of repayment***, and the ***mortgage***, which is ***the security instrument that creates a lien*** on the property ***as security for the loan***.

A common way of expressing this is that a ***borrower secures the note by signing the mortgage***.

IV. General: Financing (7 questions)
(7 Topic Areas; 21 Sub-Topics—each will be covered in its respective Topic Area)

The note and the mortgage are two separate documents; **the mortgage is typically recorded** *to assert the encumbrance on the property and is released when the loan is paid off per the terms of the note.*

Two key terms for mortgage instruments are
- *hypothecate*, which is *to pledge property as security* for a debt *while retaining possession and use of the property*
- *pledge*, which is to *provide something as security* for a debt, *generally by surrendering possession but not full title*; commonly illustrated by a pawn shop's holding of personal property in exchange for a short-term loan

The two most common ways of structuring mortgages are
- the ordinary ***mortgage***, which is a ***two-party instrument*** between a borrower and an institutional lender. Typically, ***the borrower***, or ***mortgagor***, pledges the property as security against default and retains the title, and ***the lender***, or ***mortgagee***, gives the agreed-upon financing for the borrower to acquire the property in exchange for the legal right to force the sale of the property in the event of default.
- a ***deed of trust***, or ***trust deed***, which is a ***three-party instrument*** under which a borrower, known as the ***trustor***, and an institutional lender, known as the ***beneficiary***, have a third party, known as the ***trustee***, hold ***the property's legal title "in trust" until the debt is repaid*** at which time it is conveyed to the property owner; during the repayment period, ***the "owner" holds equitable title***
  - in the event of default, ***lender foreclosure rights*** under a deed of trust ***are generally nonjudicial***, or operate without the courts but rather are governed by the financing contract provisions, ***so are more direct*** than under most two-party mortgages, which typically create lien rights requiring court enforcement, ***especially in lien theory states*** *(see below)*
  - since deeds of trust are not in common, conventional use nationwide, they are not likely to be tested in detail, though the terms related to this type of security instrument are quite likely to appear as distractors

A third common instrument used to provide security in certain seller-financing situations is the ***contract for deed***, whereby the seller's security is title retention
- a ***contract for deed***, or ***land contract***, or ***installment contract***, is a ***two-party instrument***, typically between the buyer and the seller, under which the seller agrees to accept payments until the purchase price, plus interest, is satisfied, and then to deliver the deed.

  Style note: it is a testing convention to present this as ***contract for deed (land contract)***, though it may appear under any of the terms given above.

The following broad differences between mortgages governed by **lien theory**, **title theory**, and **intermediary theory** property laws are presented for information and are not likely to be tested; however, since **most states have lending and foreclosure laws that favor one over the others**, the basic concepts are worth noting here.
- **Lien theory states**, which are in the majority nationwide, favor lending and foreclosure laws that presume a mortgagor retains both legal and equitable title while the lender simply has a lien interest in the property. In the event of loan default, the lender needs to force a

IV. General: Financing (7 questions)
(7 Topic Areas; 21 Sub-Topics—each will be covered in its respective Topic Area)

foreclosure sale in order to recover the remaining loan amount; the lender rarely acquires any title interest in the property.

- **Title theory states** base their lender's rights in the principle that the lender acquires legal title when the mortgage is executed, but is obligated to return it to the borrower upon full loan repayment. This generally allows for a fairly rapid property possession and foreclosure process in the event of mortgage default; in some cases it even legally entitles the lender to full title rights, including all equity, thereby denying the borrower any share in property improvements or appreciation.
- **Intermediate**, or **hybrid**, or **modified title theory states** take a **modified** position whereby legal title is held by the borrower barring loan default, which allows it to shift to the lender. Once the lender acquires a title interest, the lender also gains other state-determined title rights, such as the right to sell and/or take possession of the property.
  - **Connecticut is a "modified title theory" state**; see page 84 for how this affects **foreclosures** here and page 80 for the title-theory based **mortgage deed**.

Another critical area for **general mortgage concepts and terms** has to do some of the more **common clauses or provisions in a financing agreement** that relate to the method, timing, or other details regarding what is required or allowed in a loan repayment. These include

- *alienation clause*, also known as a *due-on-sale clause*, which allows the lender to call the entire **balance of the loan due-and-payable upon the transfer of the property**
- *acceleration clause,* which allows **the lender to call the entire remaining debt due on default**, or after a certain number of consecutive late payments
  - *nonrecourse clause*, or *nonrecourse provision*, which allows the lender to attach only the collateral in the event of default, *leaving all other borrower assets judgment-proof*; this clearly helps protect the borrower's overall interests by **making the loan a specific rather than general lien**
- *defeasance clause*, which requires the lender to provide a *release of mortgage*, or *satisfaction of mortgage*, document when the loan has been repaid; this document can be recorded in the public record to assert that the lien has been removed.
    In the case of financing by a deed of trust, this document is known as a *release deed*, or *deed of reconveyance*.
- *assumption clause,* which may be included in a loan document to *either prohibit or allow a borrower to pass along the loan obligation to a subsequent buyer.* In some cases, the original borrower remains liable for the loan in the event the new owner defaults. **But a lender may release the original borrower through**
    - *novation*, which means *substituting one party to a contract for another*, thus releasing the first party from further obligation while shifting that obligation to the new party alone
- *prepayment clause*, or *prepayment penalty clause*, which helps lenders increase their return when a borrower pays off a loan ahead of schedule by charging a fee for early payoffs. *Once quite common*, they are now often subject to regulatory limits, and *are prohibited in some loans*, such as FHA and VA loans.
- *subordination clause*, which serves to clarify that *a loan will accept a subordinate*, or *junior, position* and remain *behind another loan in the priority order of liens*. It is a common clause in second mortgages, although some commercial lenders require borrowers to get existing loan holders to allow their loans to be made secondary to the new loan through a *subordination agreement*.

IV. General: Financing (7 questions)
(7 Topic Areas; 21 Sub-Topics—each will be covered in its respective Topic Area)

- *subrogation*, an insurance term regarding an insurance company's right to pay a claim and then collect directly from the responsible party (see Section VIII-A, Title Insurance), may appear as a similar-looking-word type of **distractor for "subordination"**

Other clauses and provisions that arise in financing, and may appear as distractors, include
- *partial release clause*, or *release clause (also noted in Section IV-B, Types of Loans, under blanket mortgages)*, which allows a borrower with a single loan covering several properties to sell one, pay off its share to the lender, and receive a release of its property description in the lien from the lender; commonly used by developers when building out a subdivision so they can sell unencumbered properties to purchasers
- *escalation clause,* or *escalator clause,* which may be included in a loan document to **allow the lender to increase the interest rate in the event the borrower makes late payments** or is in default
  - *an escalator clause* may also refer to *a clause in leases* that allows rent changes based on inflation or changing market conditions, such as taxes or operating expenses; when applicable to leases, it will be tested in either Section VII-G, Leases, or XI-A, Property Management and Landlord/Tenant
- *nondisturbance clause,* which may be in a mortgage for properties that are rented, and states that the lender will not terminate leases in the event of foreclosure
  - an *assignment of rents clause* may also be included in mortgages on rental properties to give the lender the right to collect rents directly in the event of borrower default; this assures a lender that a borrower in default does not have long to simply pocket rent money that should be going toward the mortgage

IV-F. Financing/Credit Laws (Expect 1-2 questions from this area)

There are several federal financing and credit laws that apply to real estate transactions backed by certain government loans.

While it is important for real estate licensees to be familiar with the main provisions of the following laws, the more intricate details are better left to tests for professional lenders than those for entry-level real estate licensees. Also note that there are mandatory disclosures involved with each one and that these are testable material, especially since you should be familiar with what lenders are supposed to provide to your clients.

Remember as you read through the details of the following five federal laws, you should expect to see <u>at most</u> three questions on all of this material, and the questions should test the most relevant and appropriate facts that an entry level licensee ought to know.

The primary financing and credit laws include
- **Truth-in-Lending Act (TILA)** and **Regulation Z**
- **Real Estate Settlement Procedures Act (RESPA)**
- **Equal Credit Opportunity Act (ECOA)**
- **Fair Credit Reporting Act**
- **Homeowner's Protection Act of 1998,** also known as the **Private Mortgage Insurance (PMI) Act**

IV. General: Financing   (7 questions)
(7 Topic Areas; 21 Sub-Topics—each will be covered in its respective Topic Area)

The federal **Truth in Lending Act (TILA)**, a part of the **Consumer Credit Protection Act**, has a detailed set of loan **disclosure** and **advertising** requirements for lenders who originate residential loans. **Regulation Z** is the regulation that implements TILA and explains how lenders are to comply with those parts of TILA that bear on consumer credit.

> *Since TILA and Regulation Z relate primarily to loan advertisements and disclosures, they will be presented more fully in Section IX-C, Advertising.*

The **Real Estate Settlement Procedures Act (RESPA)** is a critical federal law that governs lender practices, often in connection with the **Truth in Lending Act (Regulation Z)**.

> **RESPA requirements apply to most loans on one-to-four family residential properties**, specifically when they involve a **federally related residential mortgage loan in any lien position**, including home purchase loans, refinances, lender-approved assumptions, property improvement loans, equity lines of credit, and reverse mortgages.

First passed in 1974, RESPA is a consumer protection statute **enforced by** the **Department of Housing and Urban Development (HUD)**.

The purposes of RESPA are
- *to help consumers become better shoppers* for **settlement services**
- *to eliminate kickbacks and referral fees* that unnecessarily increase the costs of certain settlement services

Further, the lender must also provide, **upon the borrower's request**, a completed **HUD-1 Settlement Statement**, or **HUD-1**, **one day before the actual settlement**, as well as **at the actual settlement** with the final, accurate charges for all parties.

> **HUD-1 is a standard form that clearly shows all charges imposed on borrowers and sellers in connection with the settlement**. *It is used nationwide for loan transactions covered by RESPA to make loan information uniform for ease in the secondary market, and is often used for other transactions as well due to its acceptability as a standard form for recording closing costs and proceeds.*

RESPA requires that borrowers receive certain specific **disclosures** at various times in the loan process. These include
- *costs* associated with settlement
- *lender practices* in loan servicing and **impound/escrow accounts**
    - **impound/escrow accounts** for paying taxes, insurance, and other routine charges **are limited** to a 'cushion' of funds equivalent to **approximately two months' worth of prorated annual expenses**
- **business relationships** between **settlement service providers (SSPs)**, formerly referred to as **Controlled Business Arrangements (CBAs)**, more recently revised to **Affiliated Business Arrangements (AfBAs)**

IV. General: Financing (7 questions)
(7 Topic Areas; 21 Sub-Topics—each will be covered in its respective Topic Area)

For example, at the time of loan application, a lender must give an applicant for financing to purchase a RESPA-covered residential property with the following documents

- ***Good Faith Estimate (GFE) of settlement costs***, which lists the charges the buyer is likely to pay at settlement; ***this is only an estimate and the actual charges may differ***
- ***Mortgage Servicing Disclosure Statement***, which discloses to the borrower whether the lender intends to service the loan or transfer it to another lender
- ***Special Information Booklet***, which contains consumer information regarding various real estate settlement services

If these are not given at the time of application, the lender must mail them within three days unless the loan is turned down within that time.

The federal ***Equal Credit Opportunity Act (ECOA) requires lenders to ignore the following factors about an applicant*** when reviewing a credit application

- *race*
- *color*
- *religion*
- *national origin*
- *sex*
- *marital status*
- *age (over the age of majority)*
- *receipt of income from public assistance programs, such as food stamps*

This list has many of the same protected groups as those in federal Fair Housing law, but ***the last three*** *categories are unique ECOA protected groups* for borrowers.

The federal ***Fair Credit Reporting Act (1970)*** is designed to protect consumers from inaccurate credit reporting by ensuring the right of consumers to ***inspect their credit reports*** and ***make corrections or attach explanations*** where necessary.

The Act also requires lenders to ***notify an applicant which reporting agency's report it used*** in the event a lender's review of a credit report prompted the lender to decide ***to deny credit***.

The ***Homeowner's Protection Act of 1998***, or the ***Private Mortgage Insurance (PMI) Act*** is a federal act that applies to many ***high LTV*** loans originated after July 29, 1999. According to the PMI Act, since PMI only covers the 'top' of the loan, it generally does not even apply once the loan's balance drops below an LTV of 80 percent. Therefore the PMI Act requires

- ***PMI coverage and payments to terminate automatically once the mortgage has amortized to 78 percent of the original value of the property*** if the borrower is current on all mortgage payments and does not have a government-defined "high-risk" loan
- ***the lender must tell the borrower at closing when the mortgage will hit that mark***

*The **PMI Act** was enacted in response to abuse in the PMI market. Historically, and still, lenders making high LTV **conventional loans** typically require the borrower to protect the lender against default by purchasing **PMI**.*

IV. General: Financing (7 questions)
(7 Topic Areas; 21 Sub-Topics—each will be covered in its respective Topic Area)

***PMI policies cover the portion of the loan amount that is at greatest risk for the lender**, and **generally cover no more than the top 30 percent of the loan amount** against default, thereby lowering the lender's risk and allowing them to lend upwards of 95 percent LTV.*

Unfortunately, since PMI premiums are relatively small and most borrowers are unaware of PMI's limited coverage, it long went unnoticed when unscrupulous lenders collected them for the life of the loan, even though the coverage ceased to apply after the first few years.

This too-widespread practice prompted the development of the PMI Act as a federal protection for homeowners.

*Also, though **some state and regional conventions use MIP and PMI interchangeably**, generally **MIP refers to FHA's up-front mortgage insurance** requirements and **PMI** refers to insurance required by other lenders **that is billed as a line-item, like taxes, in the monthly payment for PITI**.*

IV-G. Mortgage Fraud, Predatory Lending Practices (Risks to Clients)
(Expect 0-1 questions from this area)

As was noted previously and is amply apparent in the current economic news, ***mortgage fraud*** has had a massive impact on the real estate industry.

Broadly defined, ***mortgage fraud*** refers to the many unscrupulous lending practices that allowed home-loan applicants to receive loans based on such weak information as self-reported income rather than income supported by their most recent two or three tax returns.

Other such creative yet unsupported "documentation" proving credit-worthiness led to funding loans that the borrowers could not repay for very long, and ultimately resulted in quite predictable default.

Due to the global problems these too-widespread practices created, perhaps more than ever, the following terms are worth repeating, and committing to memory
- ***usury***, which refers to ***a lender's charging an illegally high rate of interest***. Usury laws vary from state to state, and do not apply at all in some states.
  - *The term originally applied to charging **any** interest on loans and is still **commonly defined as charging exorbitantly high interest**; in legal terms it refers to charging a rate in excess of legal limits. **Though your state may not have a usury law, this financially relevant concept is still valid for testing**.*
- ***predatory lending*** is a term closely associated with usury, though it refers to a wide array of practices by which borrowers are taken unfair advantage of, such as extremely severe penalty fees and interest rate hikes after a late payment
  - *This term is finding widespread use in reference to the problems within the mortgage industry based on subprime borrowers' inability to make continued payments and then lose and/or owe money after a property foreclosure sale; many of these foreclosures are triggered by an adjustable interest rate adjusting upward at the end of an introductory period.*

These concepts are critical when guiding clients through the financing process; you should encourage them to read the fine print and grill their lender on the particulars of loans.

IV. General: Financing (7 questions)
(7 Topic Areas; 21 Sub-Topics—each will be covered in its respective Topic Area)

This applies especially to the "hidden" costs of borrowing, such as points, loan origination costs, prepayment penalties, interest rate adjustments, and anything else that will either be an up-front cost or surprise later on.

<u>This ends the presentation of key terms and concepts likely to be either tested or used as distractors in this Content Outline Section.</u>

V. General: Laws of Agency (10 questions)
(5 Topic Areas; 15 Sub-Topics—each will be covered in its respective Topic Area)

V-A. Laws, Definitions, and Nature of Agency Relationships
(Expect 2-3 questions from this area)

Common law broadly refers to the body of "general" laws that are based on custom, conventions, and case law rather than statutory or civil law. The ***common law of agency*** refers to the category of common law that applies to relationships and responsibilities created when one person acts as a representative for another.

> ***Agency relationships and terminology*** have been the subject of great discussion and state-specific legislation nationwide for over fifteen years.
>
> This entire Content Outline Section provides a broad treatment of agency relationships based on the ***common law of agency***. Many of the terms and definitions found in common law have been adopted by many jurisdictions in their statutes and administrative policies.
>
> ***State-specific terms, definitions, and applications of agency may also be tested on the state portion of the exam***. Further, if some terms below do not appear in your state's agency law, or are defined differently there, they still represent basic, general knowledge that may be presented and tested on the general portion of the exam as common law.
>
> ***Because so many states have adopted agency statutes, you may see essentially the same questions on both the general and the state-specific portion of the exam.*** It is important to remember that when that happens, it often means that a state's statutes or policies were enacted to allow licensing officials to act directly, swiftly, and often quite severely to punish licensees who violate agency responsibilities.
>
>> Therefore, the Sample Exam at the end of this book will include the qualifying phrase ***"according to the common law of agency"*** wherever necessary to clarify that the intent of the question draws on common law for its answer.
>>
>> However, PSI may not yet be doing the same, so ***think of that phrase whenever you see an agency question on the general portion of the licensing exam.***
>>
>> ***While taking the test***, set aside legal nitpicking and ***assume that the principles of common law are implicit in <u>general</u> questions,*** and that they remain valid despite state-specific differences in terminology, definitions, or application. After all, you are in "the testing state," NOT your home state, so think past the border.
>>
>> And keep this thought firmly in mind, too: Your ticket to passing the test lies in remembering that despite whether or not you like a particular question, one of the four choices will give you one more point toward a passing grade – so find it!

Under the common law of agency, which serves as a starting point for state-specific agency laws and regulations, the definitions of the primary terms that identify the ***parties*** and ***their functions in agency relationships*** include

V. General: Laws of Agency (10 questions)
(5 Topic Areas; 15 Sub-Topics—each will be covered in its respective Topic Area)

- *an agent*, who is authorized to act on behalf of another (generally the principal) and bind them by the agent's decisions and actions; also known as a *fiduciary*, or *person in a position of trust*
- *a principal*, who grants the authority for another to act on their behalf
- *a subagent*, who acts as an agent of an agent
- *a customer*, who is not in an agency relationship with a licensee
- *a client*, who is in an agency relationship with a licensee, generally as a principal
- *an attorney-in-fact*, who is any person, not necessarily a lawyer, who has been granted a *power of attorney (POA)* to act on behalf of someone else
- *a proxy*, who is a stand-in for another and has limited, generally very temporary authority; can be loosely used to mean agent

The nature of agency relationships, regardless of whether an agent is working for one or both parties in a transaction, requires adhering to a variety of *professional and ethical expectations* which are typically guided by a set of *fiduciary responsibilities*.

Fiduciary is the term for the position of *trust* that marks an agent/principal relationship: the principal trusts the agent to 'do right.' But 'doing right' involves some common legal requirements and obligations, most notably adhering to *basic fiduciary duties* such as *loyalty*, *obedience*, *accounting*, *disclosure*, and *confidence*.

> *Each of these terms has a specific meaning under the common law of agency; some also go by other legally synonymous names. And many respected lawyers, textbook authors, and classroom instructors would supplement this list. These terms will be explained in Section V-C, Agency Duties.*

Though licensees acting as agents have specific fiduciary duties to a client, **they always owe** the obligations of **honesty and fair dealing** to all parties, **including customers**.

Types of agency differ depending on the **extent of an agent's authority**, which ranges from being **specific to one issue or transaction** right **up to being unlimited**. The following are three broad categories of agent authority within agency relationships

- *universal*, which grants the agent the authority to **represent the principal in all matters**; this may be exemplified by the authority given someone who has been granted an unlimited power of attorney in both personal and business matters
- *general*, which grants the agent **broad authority to act continuously on behalf of the principal in all authorized business matters**, such as **a licensee affiliated with a broker/agent** or **a property manager acting on behalf of a landlord**
  Note: Though <u>Black's Law Dictionary</u> *identifies this term as synonymous with universal agency, many real estate textbooks distinguish between them, limiting general agency to the range of ongoing responsibilities and authority contained in a particular employer/employee relationship, so look for this distinction in test questions.*
- *special*, which means the agent's authority to represent the principal is more restricted than general agency, and typically is **limited to a particular transaction**, such as **a listing**

Types of agency relationships vary depending on who the agent represents in a transaction; the most

V. General: Laws of Agency (10 questions)
(5 Topic Areas; 15 Sub-Topics—each will be covered in its respective Topic Area)

common *types of agency representation* and *terms for the agent* include
- **single agency**, which means that the agent is representing only one party, buyer or seller, in a transaction
  - **seller's broker**, or **seller's agent**, which means the type of single agency in which the agent is representing the seller, *typically as a listing agent*
  - **buyer's broker**, or **buyer's agent**, which means the type of single agency in which the agent is representing the buyer
- **dual agency**, which means the agent is a **dual agent**, and **represents both parties**
  Note: <u>disclosure</u> of dual agency status has always been a good idea, but is becoming a requirement in an increasing number of states.
- **subagency**, which means anyone who is authorized to act as an agent for the agent of a principal, in other words, 'below' the primary agent as a **subagent**

   *Note: for many decades, many licensees who were working with buyers were <u>technically</u> working <u>for</u> the seller as a subagent of listing brokers through membership in a **multiple listing service (MLS)**.*

   *To avoid genuine and perceived **conflicts of interest**, the vast majority of states have legislated state-specific applications of agency law. Some have gone so far as to leave the terms 'subagency/subagent' out of their list of agency relationships to avoid linking it with its former 'automatic' creation. The concept and basic relationship, though, still survive.*

   *In many states, there are now **restrictions on the automatic subagency** of the primary broker and affiliated licensees, and the broker may assign a **designated agent**, or **transaction agent**, to be the only one in the office who is working for a particular client.*

   *Other states recognize **transaction brokers**, or **intermediaries**, or **facilitators**, who are not agent-advocates for either party, but act in a professionally prudent manner for both parties while performing **ministerial**, or administrative, tasks in the course of a transaction.*

   As you can see from comparing the above to your state-specific prelicensing study materials, agency issues, though rooted in the common law of agency, vary considerably in definition and application from state to state.

   Once you are licensed, you will undoubtedly be expected to keep up with your state's agency terms, definitions, relationships, disclosure policies and forms, and changes through taking continuing education courses for license renewal.

V-B. Creation and Disclosure of Agency and Agency Agreements (General)
[Regulatory Details in State Portions] (Expect 2-4 questions from this area)

The *creation of agency relationships* occurs in a variety of ways: they may be created by *express* agreements, either written or oral, or *implied* by the actions of the parties.

V. General: Laws of Agency (10 questions)
(5 Topic Areas; 15 Sub-Topics—each will be covered in its respective Topic Area)

An express relationship means that the parties have a *definite oral or actual written mutual understanding* of their representation relationship
- *listing agreements* and *property management agreements* represent the most common examples of *express agency contracts*, since they clearly identify the principal and the agent, and their mutual obligations and responsibilities

An implied relationship means that *the actions of the parties suggest there is a representation understanding between them*, as when a licensee and a potential buyer have visited several properties together but have not yet discussed or executed an agency representation agreement
- *family members, former clients,* and *friends* represent three categories of potential clients that may have *an automatic implied agency with a licensee*, so are subject to creating *misunderstandings about actual agency representation – these people are likely to show up in test questions*, and *in practice are best handled with a written representation agreement*

In cases where a licensee is representing a family member in a real estate transaction, the most ethical course is to inform all parties, preferably in writing, of the family relationship. This will also serve to protect the licensee against legal action for ***nondisclosure of a potential conflict of interest*** *should other parties in the transaction find out later and feel they were mistreated.*

*Terms like **ostensible agency**, or **agency by ratification**, or **agency by estoppel** are related to the above terms and **may show up as distractors**, but are too legally technical for entry-level testing, or quick explanation here.*

Agency employment contract is the increasingly widespread term for the most common **agency agreement**, the time-honored **listing agreement**, since this term encompasses other, newer representation arrangements such as **buyer representation** and **dual representation**. It also clarifies the agreement's status as an **employment contract that specifies the licensee's duties, obligations, agency relationship, and compensation arrangements**.

As indicated in the Topic Area heading, details of agency disclosure requirements are almost exclusively governed by state-specific statutes.

*Questions in this area will rely on information provided in the other Topic Areas in this Section, and probably include scenario-type questions **illustrating or exploring issues related to the explanation and disclosure of agency relationships** as well as any **licensee disclosure of pre-contract-signing interest in a property**, such as buying or selling a property for a relative, friend, business associate, or the licensee personally.*

State-specific regulations often define events that create agency relationships, e.g., "upon signing an employment contract," or trigger mandatory disclosure of agency relationships, e.g., "at first substantive contact." These phrases and similar language are now common in state agency laws, but state-specific language should not appear on this portion of the test.

Remember that questions from this Topic Area need to be correct based on either common law of agency or basic contract law.

V. General: Laws of Agency (10 questions)
(5 Topic Areas; 15 Sub-Topics—each will be covered in its respective Topic Area)

So, as noted in other Topic Areas for Agency, if the focus of information in those Topic Areas is disclosure, it will most likely be tallied here even though it was discussed elsewhere within the Content Outline.

However, this Topic Area may include **application questions** that **illustrate or explore issues related to the types of agency and fiduciary obligations** defined above, as well as **examples of licensee and agent conduct and obligation to various parties in real estate transactions.**

Some questions are likely to present **examples of licensee conduct** in relation to **principals, clients, customers,** and **members of the public.**

Agency duties would include questions about licensees' **disclosure of any conflict of interest**, such as informing a principal of an agent's personal interest before buying or selling something for themselves, their family, their friends, or their business associates.

> *Self-dealing* is a term that describes a situation in which an agent breaches a fiduciary trust while pursuing the agent's own personal interest at the expense of the principal's best interests.
>
> *One of the many, many examples of self-dealing would be for a licensee to take a listing, convince the principal to sell for a below-market price either to the agent personally or an associate, and soon thereafter resell the property at its actual value and pocket the profit.*

V-C. Responsibilities of Agent to Seller, Buyer, Landlord, or Tenant as Principal
(Expect 2-4 questions from this area)

An agent acting as a fiduciary and an agent's basic fiduciary duties were noted above in Section V-A, Laws, Definitions, and Nature of Agency Relationships; they will be explained in more detail below and most likely be tallied for testing in this Topic Area.

The nature of agency relationships, regardless of whether an agent is working for either or both parties in a transaction, requires adhering to a variety of **professional and ethical expectations** which are typically guided by common law **fiduciary responsibilities**.

> *Fiduciary* is the term for the position of **trust** that marks an agent/principal relationship: the principal trusts the agent to 'do right.' But 'doing right' involves some common legal requirements and obligations, most notably
> - *loyalty*, or *allegiance*, which means to steadfastly work for, never against, the best interests of the principal while applying expected, **reasonable care, skill, and diligence** in the performance of all transaction-related matters
> - *obedience*, which means to adhere to the principal's instructions, but **does NOT include illegal actions**
> - *accounting*, which means to give a fair and accurate accounting of all funds that are transaction-related, **even if that means after the transaction is over and the agency relationship has been terminated**
> - *disclosure*, which means to disclose all pertinent information **to the principal**

V. General: Laws of Agency (10 questions)
(5 Topic Areas; 15 Sub-Topics—each will be covered in its respective Topic Area)

- *confidence*, which means to keep confidential all information that might weaken the principal's interests, such as lowest acceptable price or unusual/extenuating circumstances. ***Note, though, these conditions regarding confidentiality:***
  - confidential information *may* be revealed *with the principal's permission only*
  - this obligation *does NOT apply to illegal information*, such as material property conditions, which **MUST be disclosed** to other parties
  - *confidentiality outlives the termination of the agency relationship*, which means an agent is bound to maintain indefinitely the confidentiality of information acquired in the course of the transaction; *some states allow licensees to disclose confidential information without legal liability for breaching a fiduciary duty when necessary in the course of a real estate commission investigation into complaints against the licensee*

PSI's sub-topic list identifies the above duties with the textbook memory aid **"COALD"**; *some publishers use* **"COLAD"** *instead, but both refer to* **Confidentiality, Obedience, Accounting, Loyalty,** *and* **Disclosure**. *Use whichever one you like, or learned in class.*

As noted above, the fiduciary responsibility of *confidentiality outlives the termination of an agency relationship*, as does *final accounting* for funds – this Topic Area is the most likely place to find questions on which responsibilities outlast the termination of agency.

As a fiduciary, the agent who accepts earnest money has an obligation of *accounting*, which means the agent is obligated to avoid either of the following situations with transaction-related funds

- *commingling*, which means mingling, or combining, transaction funds with other funds that are required to be maintained separately; this could result from putting the funds in the wrong account, either business or personal
- *conversion*, which refers to **converting funds to another use than the one intended by the principal**, or **misappropriating them**, as in using earnest money to pay office expenses *or for any personal use*; conversion is generally preceded by commingling

Additional particulars regarding the **handling of earnest money**, *such as* **to whom it is given, into which account it gets deposited,** *the* **time period within which it must be deposited,** *and* **method(s) of disbursal, especially when there is a dispute,** *are all state-specific and may be tested on the state portion of the exam.*

Remember that even though licensees have specific fiduciary duties to a client, they owe the obligations of **honesty and fair dealing** to all parties, **including customers**.

Conflict of interest is an especially delicate—and litigious—prospect within any ***dual agency relationship***, since a licensee representing both parties has unusual restrictions on every fiduciary duty, most notably *loyalty, confidence,* and *disclosure*.

In general, dual agency imposes obvious **constraints on disclosures of confidential material known about either party**, *and conflicts over "full" representation to each arise easily. For example, if a dual agent's keeping the confidence of a seller's motivation from the buyer hurts the buyer's ability to negotiate a lower price, the buyer may feel cheated,*

V. General: Laws of Agency (10 questions)
(5 Topic Areas; 15 Sub-Topics—each will be covered in its respective Topic Area)

perhaps enough to sue.

> *Some lawyers—and real estate instructors—doubt the basic validity of "dual agency": they argue it is a legal impossibility to act as a true fiduciary for opposing parties. They might even suggest it would be prudent for each party to engage separate lawyers and simply let the "dual agent" licensee play messenger and handle the transaction paperwork. All of this is way too advanced for testing, but illustrates how even "basic" dual agency is anything but simple.*
>
> *Those states that formally recognize dual agency have their own legal positions, definitions, guidelines, and regulations. All of these are tied closely to honest and fair dealing, and generally require getting written agreements before sharing sensitive, especially confidential, information.*
>
> *All questions on dual agency on this part of the exam will be based in the broadest application of common law; more detailed questions will be on the state-specific portion, if applicable.*

While misunderstandings arise all the time in the course of a transaction, when an agent, or another party, creates them through **making representations** involving **puffery**, **misrepresentation**, or **fraud**, whenever they are found out, before or after closing, litigation may not be far behind. The basic meaning of these terms includes

- **puffing**, or **puffery**, which refers to any general exaggeration found in promotional materials or agent comments intended to create a stronger impression of a property
- **misrepresentation** means any variety of misleading statements or undisclosed facts that an agent reasonably should have known and disclosed
    - **negligent misrepresentation**, which means making a careless statement where the exercise of due diligence and professional standards of care would have made the correct facts known
    - **material misrepresentation**, which means making a false statement – or failing to make a known, material disclosure – that is likely to induce a reasonable party to act against that party's own best interest
- **fraud** means intentional misrepresentation designed to persuade a party to make a decision the party would not have made had full and accurate disclosure been made

Where the line is drawn along the scale to distinguish one from the other among these terms, especially between misrepresentation and fraud, is often subjective and settled in court, where it generally rests on degree of knowledge and intent of the agent, and injury to the party suffering damages.

V-D. Responsibilities of Agent to Customers and Third Parties
(Expect 1-2 questions from this area)

As noted repeatedly for the sake of its importance: even though licensees have specific fiduciary duties to a client, they owe the obligations of **honesty and fair dealing** to all parties, **including customers.**

V. General: Laws of Agency (10 questions)
(5 Topic Areas; 15 Sub-Topics—each will be covered in its respective Topic Area)

*So, expect at least one question on this crucial point, and perhaps a second that presents a scenario in which a licensee's behavior toward unrepresented parties in a transaction applies this principle as **the best response**, though it will almost certainly either upset a client or be less lucrative.*

V-E. Termination of Agency (Expect 1-2 questions from this area)

An agency relationship is **terminated** for any of a number of reasons, all of which fall under the broad labels of **operation of law** or **acts of parties**.

Operation of law refers to legally "automatic" mechanisms, such as when a contract is terminated upon the discovery of the lack of one or more necessary elements, as when a party does not actually have legal authority to enter into a contract in the first place.

Such a contract termination is typically automatic due to existing laws requiring sufficient legal elements for it to remain in force.

Other commonplace occurrences that terminate contracts based on the operation of law include
- **completion** of the transaction through **performance**, or **fulfillment**, of contract elements
- **expiration** of the agency period
- **lack of legal elements** in the original contract, such as finding that the contract was made for an illegal purpose or that the "principal" lacked the legal capacity to create the contract

Acts of parties that can serve to terminate a contract generally include such circumstances as
- **mutual agreement** of the parties
- **revocation** of contract by the principal/client; as a unilateral act, it may incur liability for the client if it is successfully contested by the agent
- **renunciation** or **abandonment** of contract by the agent; like revocation, since it is a unilateral act, it may incur liability for the agent and/or brokerage if it is successfully contested by the principal/client
- **breach of contract** by one of the parties, which generally incurs liability for the party in breach

Listing agreements, like other agency agreements, may be terminated for reasons provided above. In addition to those factors, though, the following reasons may also provide grounds for terminating a listing
- **bankruptcy** of either party
- **loss of title by seller** through tax sale, foreclosure, or other legal action
- **condemnation** of the property under an eminent domain proceeding
- **destruction** of the listed property
- **death or incapacity** of one of the parties
- **revocation** of agreement by the principal, which may make the principal liable for breach of contract
- **renunciation** of agreement or **abandonment of agency services** by the agent, which may make the agent liable for breach of contract

V. General: Laws of Agency (10 questions)
(5 Topic Areas; 15 Sub-Topics—each will be covered in its respective Topic Area)

Most of the questions on agency relationships will be broad, such as listing several events and asking which one triggers the creation or termination of a particular type of agency, or which of several definitions best fits a particular type of agency.

<u>This ends the presentation of key terms and concepts likely to be either tested or used as distractors in this Content Outline Section.</u>

VI. General: Mandated Disclosures (7 questions)
(5 Topic Areas; 19 Sub-Topics—each will be covered in its respective Topic Area)

VI-A. Property Condition Disclosure Forms (Expect 1-3 questions from this area)

Though disclosure of property condition is a sound, ethical business practice that will limit a licensee's future liability in the event of post-sale discovery of defects, there are no federal requirements or standard forms for these disclosures.

However, the **Residential Lead-Based Paint Hazard Reduction Act of 1992** requires including a **lead-based paint disclosure notice either in or with sales contracts for residential properties built prior to 1978**, the year lead-based paint was banned.

*Questions in this area will most likely be based on this requirement or else present a scenario in which the licensee's **disclosure of material facts and/or known defects** will be the best answer.*

Despite there being no federal forms or requirements, an increasing number of states have developed a standardized form and specific regulations governing their use in residential real estate transactions.

These forms are commonly controlled by state requirements, and generally require the seller to complete them without the assistance of the licensee.

Further, in the event a seller misrepresents the property's condition, there may still be liabilities for the licensee in accepting the seller's self-reporting without performing a due diligence review and confirmation of the seller's statements.

Connecticut has property disclosure requirements and a special residential form, so expect questions on this topic in the state-specific portion of the exam.

VI-B. Warranties (Expect 0-1 question from this area)

Home warranties, or ***home protection plans***, are a ***type of insurance*** that generally have a one-year contract period and cover service and/or replacement costs for major systems, such as heating/cooling, ducts, hot water heater, electrical, and plumbing. They also cover major appliances, such as range, refrigerator, dishwasher, washer/dryer, ceiling fans, and garage door openers.

The details of coverage and cost vary depending on the number of insurers, if any, in a particular market, and the specific coverages offered.

A basic warranty policy may cost a few hundred dollars, and can be paid for by either party.

*Often a seller offers it as part of the contract in order to both demonstrate good faith and avoid after-closing problems with a buyer over the normal wear-and-tear failure of a covered system or appliance. **Most plans provide coverage even during the listing period**, so can be a seller's hedge against expensive surprises even while the property is on the market.*

If a listing does not offer a home protection plan, the buyer may either request one as a contract condition or purchase one as a new homeowner.

VI. General: Mandated Disclosures (7 questions)
(5 Topic Areas; 19 Sub-Topics—each will be covered in its respective Topic Area)

Regardless of which party pays, it is a useful service to the buyer to have information on these potentially major-expense saving policies available, if only because a warranty may also save the agent from angry calls from a buyer after closing regarding appliance or system failures.

Questions on these policies will be broad, since they are neither available nor uniform in coverages or prices in different markets.

*Questions on home warranties may also focus on **the important principle that licensees should provide information and choices, not conclusions or particular-company recommendations, on this and other professional services**.*

In the course of a real estate transaction, if a licensee steers a client to a particular company or professional for any service when there are a variety from which to choose, there are possible strong consequences for the licensee from both a dissatisfied client and competing service providers.

VI-C. Need for Inspection and Obtaining/Verifying Information
(Expect 1-3 questions from this area)

A licensee has an obligation to perform a ***due diligence property inspection and verification of information*** in order to ***discover material facts and/or defects*** that the ***licensee reasonably should have known about***.

This due diligence verification also applies to researching and ***confirming, or correcting, property data*** supplied by the owner or the owner's agent.

This generally involves reviewing information in ***the public record***, such as ***assessment data*** on ***annual taxes***, ***lot size and dimensions***, ***total square footage of any buildings***, ***zoning type and applicable restrictions***, as well as other general property expenses, such as utilities and heating/cooling costs.

In the course of verifying information, a licensee may see ***adverse consequences*** to property data that the seller will have to be prepared to address, either in price concessions or other remedies.

*For example, if the property is in a **flood zone** that requires special insurance, a seller will have to recognize that the cost of ownership for a new buyer may be higher than the buyer thought, and may use that expense and risk to justify a low-ball offer.*

In an actual instance, a seller had a combined residential and commercial operation that got sold to a buyer who continued the commercial operation only to have it shut down by a zoning enforcement officer's cease and desist order. As it happened, the property was not zoned for the previous owner's commercial activity, so continuing it represented an illegal activity. After suing the seller and the seller's broker for misrepresentation, the buyer went to the local zoning authority about this matter, and ultimately the property's commercial use was approved.

VI. General: Mandated Disclosures (7 questions)
(5 Topic Areas; 19 Sub-Topics—each will be covered in its respective Topic Area)

In this case, had the listing licensee confirmed the property's zoning classification, the seller could have either sought the zoning change or provided prospective buyers with accurate information and let them pursue a change.

Or a licensee may see unexploited property *opportunities* in zoning possibilities.

*For example, if the property is three acres with one house on it and its zoning classification requires one acre to build, an owner may want to consider **subdividing** the property and selling it in pieces. Or pricing and marketing the property for its subdivision potential, leaving the option to subdivide to the buyer.*

Also, for properties in **subdivisions** this means getting a copy of the **subdivision CCRs**, and for **common interest ownership properties**, this means getting the **homeowners' association rules** or comparable documents **and confirming all association fees**.

Incorrect or approximated property information needs to either be corrected or ***disclosed as unverified*** in order to provide notice to interested parties that the data is subject to change when verified by closer research, inspection, or measurement.

Even though an attorney or title company is likely to provide a ***title search*** in the course of the transaction, it is prudent to at least check the ownership/deed records under the name of the "owner." *(Title searches will be detailed in Section VIII-A, Title Insurance.)*

As noted in an earlier Section, a listing licensee in South Carolina was sued by a would-have-been buyer for not having discovered that the "seller" only had a life estate interest in the property. Regardless of what this interest means, this could have been avoided if the licensee had either checked the public records or requested, and then read, a title report.

Due diligence verification can also include matters related to requesting, interpreting, and explaining professional **appraisals**, **surveys**, **home inspections**, **property inspection reports**, or other tests, such as **tests of well water purity**, **soil contamination**, **septic tank condition** and **soil percolation**, or the age, location, and condition of **underground storage tanks** for home heating oil.

In the event of **nondisclosure of material facts and/or defects**, the seller and all of the seller's agents may incur **legal liability and various penalties**, depending on a court's finding of fault.

*While this standard of care may extend to **discovering stigmatizing conditions,** specific **disclosures** are either **governed by state-specific guidelines**, as in the case of a crime or death on a property**, or are sensitive enough to warrant a current, local legal opinion about how best to proceed.***

In addition, ***test questions about a seller being infected with HIV are most likely to make it a nondisclosable condition due to Fair Housing handicapping status***.

VI. General: Mandated Disclosures (7 questions)
(5 Topic Areas; 19 Sub-Topics—each will be covered in its respective Topic Area)

Liability refers to legal responsibility or accountability. ***Upon entering into an agency relationship, agents and principals become subject to a wide range of potential liabilities***, many of which outlive the agency relationship or closing of a particular property transaction.

Licensees and owners who demonstrate **negligence**, especially ***willful negligence***, in discovering and/or disclosing environmental and material problems that might reasonably be associated with a property may be subject to legal action.

There are ***liability considerations*** for various parties in the event of ***nondisclosure of material defects*** and other property condition issues.

Both the seller and all of the seller's agents, as well as even the buyer's agent, may incur ***legal liability and various penalties*** for nondisclosure and/or nondiscovery depending on a court's determination of fault.

Common ***types of legal liabilities*** include
- ***vicarious***, which refers to a ***supervisor*** or ***principal's responsibility*** for the acts of a ***subordinate*** or ***agent***, respectively; this is most commonly seen in the liability almost any employer has for the professional misdeeds of employees regardless of whether or not they were known to or authorized by the employer
    - ***some states***, *but far from all*, ***have specifically abolished vicarious liability*** *in real estate transactions, especially broker liability for actions of their agents, noting that there is* **"no imputation of knowledge"** *on the part of those parties not directly involved with the transaction*
- ***joint***, which means ***shared liability between two or more parties***
- ***several***, which means a ***liability of one party that can be legally pursued separately*** from other liable parties

An agent as well as a principal can incur legal liabilities for such actions as
- ***nondisclosure of property defects*** to a party interested in buying a property
- ***nondisclosure of environmental hazards*** to a party interested in buying a property
- ***nondisclosure of other material information*** to a party interested in buying a property, such as impending major changes to the neighborhood or immediate area

In addition, an agent can incur legal liabilities for such actions as
- ***nondisclosure of agency relationships*** to appropriate parties in a transaction
- ***lack of due diligence or breach of fiduciary duties***

A licensee's statement that "The seller told me the foundation was sound, and I figured, 'Who would know better than the owner?' So I never looked behind the empty packing boxes against the wall in the basement" is hardly a compelling legal defense should the seller actually be trying to conceal foundation problems.

*Depending on the claim brought by a party that feels wronged, the state may have a statutory time period, or **statute of limitations**, after which the party generally has lost the opportunity to get a legal hearing. Even when a statute of limitations does not apply, a court*

VI. General: Mandated Disclosures (7 questions)
(5 Topic Areas; 19 Sub-Topics—each will be covered in its respective Topic Area)

*may deny a claim based on the concept of **laches**, which means **an unreasonable delay or negligence in bringing a claim in a timely manner**.*

***Some questions in this Topic Area are likely to include the word <u>liability</u>**, and will be situational, meaning they will present a scenario **and ask which party or parties are most likely to incur liability** for not discovering, verifying, or disclosing a property condition, or if the property condition requires a disclosure.*

*But look for the word **liability**: it is a good tip that the question is following up on an important point about disclosures and is pointing out that there may be a legally painful consequence for not having made that disclosure at the earliest, or most appropriate, time.*

VI-D. Material Facts Related to Property Condition or Location
(Expect 1-2 questions from this area)

Property conditions that are ***material***, which means ***significant in a party's decision-making process*** of approving or disapproving a purchase, ***must, when known or reasonably should have been discovered*** by a seller, a seller's agent, or even a buyer's agent, ***be disclosed***.

Material facts have to do with discovery and disclosure of any of the elements discussed in the last Topic Area, as well as ***any other fact that is significant or essential to a buyer or seller's decision-making process***, even down to the types of available financing and date of closing or possession.

For example, if a buyer needs to move in July 1st but the seller cannot move out until Labor Day, that fact is material to the buyer's final decision and must be shared.

Generally, though, questions about material facts will deal with some of the following common types of ***physical or environmental material defects***.

Material defects can include
- **site or soil conditions**, such as being in an area where the water table is too deep for a steady water supply in a dry season, or the topsoil is easily washed away, or the soil is too sandy for grass or gardening
- **property location within a natural hazard zone**, or some other special study zone that may affect the property's insurability or insurance rates
- **undisclosed or undiscovered encroachments or easements**, such as a neighbor's fence that is actually placed within the subject property by three feet
- **structural property environmental problems (internal)**, such as the presence of
  - **wood infestation**, such as termites or other wood-boring insects
  - **lead-based paint**, which was banned in 1978, so sales contracts for residential properties built ***prior to 1978***, are, because of the Residential Lead-Based Paint Hazard Reduction Act of 1992, required to include a federal ***disclosure notice***; *this can be a separate document or a contract component*
  - **asbestos**, which was widely used for insulation and causes lung problems

VI. General: Mandated Disclosures (7 questions)
(5 Topic Areas; 19 Sub-Topics—each will be covered in its respective Topic Area)

- *radon gas*, which is a colorless, odorless gas that the Surgeon General has warned is the second leading cause of lung cancer, arises from the decay of radioactive minerals in the ground and can collect in a basement or other closed areas
- *urea formaldehyde foam insulation (UFFI)*, which was used extensively in the late 1970's for wall insulation, and may continue to exude formaldehyde gas, is an irritant and potential cancer-causing agent; its use was discontinued in 1980, but its presence in a property must be disclosed
- *toxic mold*, which is becoming an increasingly large problem nationwide
- *structural physical conditions*, such as a leaky roof, outdated wiring or plumbing, foundation cracks, a poorly working water heater or furnace, or some other condition that will become a surprise expense for a new owner

VI-E. Material Facts Related to Public Controls, Statutes, or Public Utilities
(Expect 1-2 questions from this area)

This Topic Area simply continues the lists from the previous Topic Area, but with a focus on material facts that are other-than site or structural in nature. These include facts related to

- *public controls*, such as discovering and disclosing information on
  - *local zoning and planning* that are currently in effect or may be subject to change
  - *municipal boundaries* that determine school and voting districts as well as availability of public utilities, such as sewer and water, and municipal services, such as waste and recycling pickup, and any special assessments associated with the subject property's specific location
- *property environmental problems (external)*, such as the on-site or nearby presence and effects of
  - *contaminated soil and/or groundwater*, from landfills, chemical discharges, spills, or toxic disposal
  - *underground storage tanks*, which may be deteriorating and/or leaking and contaminating groundwater supplies
  - *commercial, industrial, or utility concerns*, such as airport flight paths, railroad lines, interstate highways, steel or paper mills, nuclear power plants, high-voltage power lines, or cell-phone towers
  - *stigmatized, or psychologically impacted, properties*, such as one in which a crime or murder has been committed; *licensee discovery and disclosure requirements vary across state lines, and will be tested, if at all, on the state-specific portion of the test*
    - *Megan's law is a special area of concern for discovery and disclosure, since it deals with the federally mandated sex offender registry which is governed by state or local authorities; as with other psychologically impacted properties, how licensees conform with Megan's law requirements will be state-specific*

Property defects can be obvious, like sawdust piles that indicate wood boring insects, or they may be more concealed, or *latent*, which means that they are not readily discovered by a normal inspection, and often go undiscovered until after closing.

Latent defects abound, and include such examples as asbestos insulation in a chimney or around enclosed heat ducts, or a cracked foundation that is obscured by dry wall.

VI. General: Mandated Disclosures (7 questions)
(5 Topic Areas; 19 Sub-Topics—each will be covered in its respective Topic Area)

A listing *licensee's obligations* include discussing material property conditions with the owner and proceeding according to the legal requirements for the particular conditions.

Remember, *material defects must be disclosed*, and *if an owner instructs a licensee to either remain silent or lie about material defects, the licensee cannot legally obey those instructions*, despite the fiduciary duties of obedience and confidentiality.

If this comes up during a listing presentation, and *if the owner insists*, the licensee would be creating an *invalid contract since it would be based on an illegal purpose*, and so *must decline the listing*.

This ends the presentation of key terms and concepts likely to be either tested or used as distractors in this Content Outline Section.

VII. General: Contracts (10 questions)
(9 Topic Areas; 15 Sub-Topics—each will be covered in its respective Topic Area)

VII-A. General Knowledge of Contract Law (Expect 2-4 questions from this area)

This area of real estate relies directly on **basic contract law** for its technical understanding of commonly used **contract terminology**, including common contract **elements**, **provisions**, **contingencies**, and **termination** or **breach** issues.

The following list includes several **opposite pairings** that have specific legal interpretations in understanding the most basic nature of real estate sales contracts, which begins with **whether or not a contract exists**, and if so, **upon which parties it is binding**. For example

- a **valid** contract refers to one that includes **certain critical elements** (these will be itemized below) and so has full legal force and effect
    - an **invalid** contract **lacks at least one of those critical elements**, and is therefore either void or voidable
- a **void** contract is one that has no legal force due to its **lack of one or more elements** required for validity, and can be said to not be a contract at all
    - a **voidable** contract is seen as binding on one party but not on the other, who is free to pursue it or 'void' it
- a **unilateral**, or *'one-sided,'* contract is one in which only one party has made a promise to do something, such as offering a reward to the person who finds a lost pet
    - a **bilateral**, or *'two-sided,'* contract is one in which both parties have made a promise and are obligated to follow through on all of the contract's conditions or risk being in breach of contract
- an **enforceable** contract is one that meets the legal requirements for validity, and therefore is binding on all parties to observe their contractual obligations
    - an **unenforceable** contract may be **either a void contract or one that was valid when made but legally unenforceable** due to some technical fine point, such as the destruction of an unrecorded deed
- an **express** contract generally means that the understanding has been explicitly set out, **typically in writing, though it could be oral**
    - an **implied** contract generally refers to **the conduct of the parties** providing sufficient indication that they have a common understanding

Further, when parties enter into a contract and proceed to satisfy its conditions, the following terms apply

- the term **execute**, as a verb, as in, *"We expect them to execute the contract today,"* can mean <u>either</u>
    1. **to sign the contract** or
    2. **to fulfill and complete the contract's conditions**.
        Note: when used in the latter sense, an **executed contract** may also be termed **fully performed**, or **discharged**
- the term **executory** refers to a contract that is **in the process of being fulfilled**

The specific **basic elements of a valid contract** may vary slightly depending on what kind of contract it is. They may also appear, as is so common in legal language, under interchangeable terms.

VII. General: Contracts (10 questions)
(9 Topic Areas; 15 Sub-Topics—each will be covered in its respective Topic Area)

Some of the following terms will be further addressed in areas where they have more common applications. However, these elements are commonly identified as
- *legally competent parties*, which means they have *legal capacity* to enter into contracts. This usually *excludes* legal minors and those judged mentally incompetent.
- *offer and acceptance*, also known as a *meeting of the minds*, or *mutual assent*, which means that something is being offered by one party and accepted without qualification by the other
- *consideration*, which means the payment or promise of something of value, generally money, in exchange for what has been offered
- *legal purpose,* or *legality of object*, which means that *the contract is not for an illegal purpose*, such as disposing of toxic waste in an undeveloped residential subdivision, or a house rental in which illegal drugs will be produced
- *reality of consent*, which means that *both parties acted under their own free will*, without *duress*, and that all of the information they had at hand on which to base their decision was accurate and adequate

Other elements that may be required, depending on the contract, include that it
- *be in writing* if required by the *statute of frauds* or other applicable laws for commercial exchanges
  - the *statute of frauds* is a common law statute that has been specifically adopted by many states and requires contracts for the *sale or transfer of interest in real estate* or real estate *rentals for more than one year* to be *in writing in order to be enforceable in court*
- *include all signatures of parties* required to sign, for example, the grantor of a deed
- *give an adequate description of the property* as required for various real estate listing, sales, and mortgage contracts as well as deeds; street addresses may be acceptable for listings and rentals, whereas *an adequate legal description is required for deeds*

A relatively recent federal Act has made certain electronic transmissions legally valid substitutes for hand-written signatures and hard-copy transaction documents. **The Electronic Signatures in Global and National Commerce Act (ESIGN)** (2000) defines and covers the legal force of electronic signatures in **interstate and international commerce**.

ESIGN states that in interstate and foreign commerce, signatures, contracts, and other *transaction documents "may not be denied legal effect, validity, or enforceability solely because [they are] in an electronic form."* It also provides for electronic storage and retention of these records.

Most states have adopted some version of a related model Act, the **Uniform Electronic Transactions Act (UETA)***, in order to provide state-specific legal definition and validity to electronic records and signatures in business transactions.*

Increasingly, states are conforming with ESIGN standards by noting that the required records may be retained in any format, electronic or otherwise, capable of producing an accurate copy in paper format of the original document. *(Connecticut did this in 2002; see the State Exam, Section IV-G)*

VII. General: Contracts (10 questions)
(9 Topic Areas; 15 Sub-Topics—each will be covered in its respective Topic Area)

Breach of contract means a legally unsupportable violation of any of the contract terms by either party and generally gives rise to legal disputes over how to either pursue or abandon the contract. In the event that ***contract disputes*** arise during the executory period, legal action may follow.

Remedies for a breach include seeking
- ***contract rescission***, which basically means cancellation and return of deposits
- ***specific performance***, which is ***a judicial remedy*** that requires getting a court order for the party who breached the contract to honor it
- ***monetary damages***, which is another ***judicial remedy*** that means getting a court-ordered payment of financial restitution
- ***liquidated damages***, which is ***a nonjudicial remedy*** that means getting whatever any ***liquidated damages provision, default provision, or forfeiture clause*** in the contract stipulates, ***such as the forfeiture of earnest money*** in the case of buyer default

However, a ***liquidated damages*** provision in the contract may be written to entitle the seller to keep some or all of the earnest money deposit in the event of a simple ***contract cancellation***.

An all-purpose, quick introduction to the "Who's Who" in the legalese of real estate.

Entities, or ***parties***, involved in a real estate transaction may be businesses as well as individuals. They take on special names depending on their relationship in a transaction.

Since these terms appear on various transaction-related documents in the normal course of business, ***some of them may show up on a test as simple definition questions***.

These and similar terms will be categorized in whatever Content Outline Section is most appropriate for the term and/or the related topic being tested.

The *–er (-or)/-ee* distinction, as in employer/employee, is applied to a variety of pairings in real estate transactions. For here, though, the following are worth noting
- an ***offeror*** is the party that offers something, an ***offeree*** is the one to whom it is offered
- a ***vendor*** is the party that offers something for sale or trade, or actually sells something; a ***vendee*** is the one that purchases it
- a ***mortgagor*** is the owner of property that is being put up as collateral for a loan; the ***mortgagee*** is the one that finances the loan

Most unfamiliar terms that identify parties to a transaction should be pretty easy to figure out on sight if you look at the main word and think through what the –er(-or)/-ee endings mean.

PSI's expanded sub-topic listing includes a few contract-related terms and clauses in this Topic Area that are clustered elsewhere for more logical placement, but will get quick mention here, since it is quite likely that questions based on them will be tallied here
- ***assignment***, which means that a person is legally able to transfer their rights in a property; *this will be covered in upcoming Topic Area VIII-E*
- ***novation***, which means substituting one party to a contract for another, thus releasing the first party from further obligation while shifting that obligation to the new party alone; *this was covered as a financing/lender clause in Topic Area IV-E*

VII. General: Contracts (10 questions)
(9 Topic Areas; 15 Sub-Topics—each will be covered in its respective Topic Area)

- *acceleration* is another clause linked by PSI to this Topic Area; it was covered with other loan-related clauses some pages back in Topic Area IV-E

VII-B. Listing Agreements (Expect 1-3 questions from this area)

A *listing contract*, or *listing agreement*, is a contract that engages a real estate licensee's firm to market a property in exchange for receiving compensation, usually in the form of a commission, upon the sale and transfer of the property.

A licensee's disclosure and explanation of agency relationships to a principal includes explaining that since a licensee acts as a general agent for a broker, **when a licensee takes a listing, the licensee is actually creating an agency relationship between the principal and the broker/brokerage firm; the licensee's relationship is as subagent of the broker.**

This is the most logical place to note this important point about the creation of agency relationships; however, questions about a licensee's disclosure and explanation may be tallied in Section V-B, Creation and Disclosure of Agency.

Also, in a close, legal interpretation of agency relationships, it can be argued that because the agency relationship created by listing contracts is between the principal and the licensee's broker/brokerage firm, **the listing licensee** *is not a fiduciary for the principal—that's the position of the broker/brokerage firm—but* **does owe fiduciary duties to the principal on behalf of the broker/brokerage firm.**

These distinctions are legally too refined for testing, but are mentioned here to help address the finer distinctions that are commonly left unexplained in textbooks. They may also help you understand **the basic legal right brokerages have for retaining listings when listing licensees leave the firm**, *or even the authority to transfer listings to another agent, such as if the principal becomes dissatisfied with the listing licensee.*

Listing agreement contracts, like all contracts, *require some very specific elements* for their legal validity. In addition, though, they may contain a host of other components that address common practice, terms, and conventions in a particular market area or state.

The following elements need to be added to the basic elements necessary for a valid contract as detailed in Section VII-A, General Knowledge of Contract Law, to create a valid listing agreement
- *required signatures*, which include *all* of the owners *and* the listing licensee
- *property description* sufficient to identify the property; it need not be the legal description required on a deed and is often just the street address
- *list price* of the property
- *definite termination date*, which ensures that a property owner does not get locked into an arrangement that the owner has to actively terminate
- *broker compensation*, which describes when it is earned and how it is computed

The above elements are often reinforced by state regulations and tested in state-specific detail, where applicable, on the state portion of the exam. In most states, there are also ***property***

VII. General: Contracts (10 questions)
(9 Topic Areas; 15 Sub-Topics—each will be covered in its respective Topic Area)

disclosures as required by state law along with other elements, such as a definite starting date, prohibitions on automatic renewal clauses, and others.

Also, this area *may* contain questions similar to those in V-C, Responsibilities of Agent, on such *points about listing agreements* as the following
- *the seller* is *the final authority with responsibility for establishing a list price*, not the licensee preparing a CMA or an appraiser who has performed an appraisal
- *a listing agreement is an employment contract* that grants a licensee the authority for seller representation

The most common types of listing agreements are
- *exclusive right to sell*, which engages a single licensee to market the property and entitles that licensee to a commission regardless of who finds the buyer, even if it is the property owner; *this provides the greatest protection for the licensee to collect compensation*
- *exclusive agency*, which engages a single licensee to market the property and entitles that licensee to a commission if anyone **other than** the property owner finds the buyer; if the owner finds the buyer, the licensee gets no commission
- *open*, or *nonexclusive*, which allows the property owner to engage any number of licensees to market the property, and only entitles the licensee who procures the buyer to a commission; if the property owner finds the buyer, none of the licensees are entitled to any compensation
- *net*, which engages a licensee to market a property and receive as compensation all sale proceeds in excess of the owner's stated "net" for the property

   Note: net listings are illegal in many states and are widely viewed as unethical due to their potential for creating a licensee **conflict of interest**, or even direct exploitation of an unsophisticated seller. But they are defined here, and tested, because they represent a way of structuring a listing agreement and compensation, regardless of local rulings on their legality.

VII-C. Management Agreements [Broker Only]   (Brokers: Expect 0-2 questions from this area)

A *management agreement* refers to a contract between a licensee acting as a property manager and the property owner or principal. It defines the scope of authority as well as specific responsibilities, schedules, compensation arrangements, and other details of the relationship between the licensee and the property owner.

   This topic will be treated adequately in Section XI-A, Property Management; "extra" questions from that Topic Area may be tallied here for broker candidates.

VII-D. Buyer Broker Agreements/Tenant Representation Agreements
   (Expect 1-2 questions from this area)

A *buyer-broker agreement*, *buyer agency agreement*, or *agency employment contact*, is a contract that engages a real estate licensee to search for suitable property on behalf of a potential buyer in exchange for receiving compensation, usually in the form of a commission, upon the purchase and

VII. General: Contracts   (10 questions)
(9 Topic Areas; 15 Sub-Topics—each will be covered in its respective Topic Area)

transfer of the property. ***Tenant*** *may be substituted for* ***buyer*** *whenever appropriate for the situation under consideration, since agency relationship between a licensee and either type of consumer observes the same set of fiduciary duties and disclosures.*

In these arrangements the licensee is often referred to as a ***buyer's broker*** when representing only the buyer.

The most common types of ***buyer agency agreements*** are
- ***exclusive buyer agency***, which engages a single licensee to search for a suitable property and entitles that licensee to compensation regardless of who finds the property, even if it is the buyer – its listing agreement counterpart is the exclusive right-to-sell listing
- ***exclusive-agency buyer agency***, which engages a single licensee to search for a suitable property and entitles that licensee to a compensation if anyone other than the buyer finds a suitable property – its listing agreement counterpart is the exclusive agency listing
- ***open buyer agency***, or ***nonexclusive***, which allows the buyer to engage any number of licensees to search for a suitable property, and only entitles the licensee who introduces the buyer to the purchased property to compensation; if the buyer finds the property, none of the licensees are entitled to any compensation – its listing agreement counterpart is the open listing

*Note: **The above distinctions are gaining widespread recognition and even some state-specific acceptance, statutory definition, and use; they are presented here more for informational purposes than for testing.***

*However, read **all** questions regarding types of buyer brokerage very carefully – **the concepts and some terms are gaining sufficient national use to warrant appearing on the test as scored questions** instead of simple distractors.*

Questions on buyer agency will be very similar to those on listings, but the emphasis will be on an agent's ***duties as a buyer's agent*** rather than a seller's agent, which are the same, just on the opposite side of the transaction.

These questions may also present examples of licensee and agent conduct, identifying their obligations to disclose agency relationships to other parties in real estate transactions as well as explain different types of agency relationship, such as single or dual agency. If so, they will probably be tallied in Section V-B, Creation and Disclosure of Agency.

VII-E. Offers/Purchase Agreements   (Expect 2-4 questions from this area)

The paperwork and documentation trail in a real estate sales transaction proceeds from listing a property to ***offers***, ***counteroffers***, and ***sales contracts***.

Offers, like so many other real estate terms, may have a locally 'correct' label, such as ***offer to purchase***, ***offer to purchase and contract***, and similar terms. The purpose of an offer is ***to set forth the conditions the prospective buyer proposes to the seller.***

VII. General: Contracts (10 questions)
(9 Topic Areas; 15 Sub-Topics—each will be covered in its respective Topic Area)

But *an offer is not a contract*, since the offeree has not accepted it; *it may, though, become a contract upon acceptance of all of its conditions by the offeree*.

A *counteroffer* is the common term for the offer *if the offeree* makes *a change of any kind to it and returns it to the original offeror* (see the next Topic Area for more)

Earnest money is the term for the deposit, or down payment, that *accompanies an offer* to purchase real estate; it serves to demonstrate the buyer's good-faith, "earnest" intention to complete the transaction and supply the full purchase price, or consideration, at closing.

If the contract includes a *liquidated damages provision*, earnest money may also provide a source of funds *for damages to the seller in the event of buyer default*.

Both the use and the amount of earnest money are governed more by convention than law; *earnest money does not constitute "consideration" and is not a legal requirement for creating a binding sales contract*. However, most offers are accompanied by *some* earnest money, and *a buyer's seriousness of purpose* is commonly seen in direct proportion to the size of the earnest money check.

These and other critical earnest money considerations, such as *how much a buyer provides*, *conditions of its use and/or return* in the event of offer rejection or sales contract termination, and *liquidated damages provisions* are *all subject to negotiation between the parties*.

Once an offer or counteroffer has become a mutually accepted and binding contract, it is variously known as a *purchase agreement*, a *purchase contract*, a *sales contract*, a *purchase and sale contract*, an *agreement for sale*, or another similar term.

A properly executed purchase agreement identifies the specific property, sets out all of the contractual requirements for its transfer from one party to another, and generally serves as the complete agreement between parties.

As previously noted, *offer and acceptance* is a requirement of a valid contract, and is generally the final element needed for creating a valid real estate purchase agreement.

Once all of the contract details have been negotiated and there is a binding contract, each party acquires certain *contractual rights and responsibilities*. Some of these include
- *equitable title*, which means that the buyer, during the executory period of contract fulfillment, has a property interest, specifically *the right to acquire formal legal title*, which in turn *may allow the buyer to transfer or assign that right*
- *assignment*, which means that the buyer may transfer their rights in a property

Contract *provisions* refer to the particular information, conditions, and instructions provided in the contract that govern the many details that have to be addressed in *the 'performance' of the contract*.

Provisions are too numerous to list, or test, in detail, but include commonplace elements like
- *personal property included*, which specifies what stays, like firewood or appliances

VII. General: Contracts (10 questions)
(9 Topic Areas; 15 Sub-Topics—each will be covered in its respective Topic Area)

> (*Ownership of personal property* is legally transferred at closing through a *bill of sale*, which will trump all other options in a test question on this point.)

- *time is of the essence clause*, which serves to underline and *reinforce the importance of meeting contract dates*, and that *failure to do so will be considered a contract breach and grounds for cancellation of the contract*
- *rescission clause*, which allows one of the parties, generally through a contract-specific contingency or regulated-sale review period, to *rescind*, or *cancel* the contract without penalty. Rescind refers *to "unmaking" a contract* and *restoring the parties to their precontractual position, including the return of all monies* (more in VII-I)
- *option*, which is most often in *commercial property purchase offers* and serves to hold an offer open for a specified period *in exchange for some monetary consideration*, which is *generally (1) applied toward the purchase price* if all of the conditions are met and the sale goes through, *or (2) kept by the owner if there is no sale*
    - an *option is a unilateral contract*, which is *binding on the seller to sell, but not on the buyer to buy*
- *"as is"* refers to the property being sold in its existing condition without guarantees for its physical condition or title; *this provision generally does not protect a seller from liability for known material defects*
- *"subject to" a mortgage*, which refers to a seller retaining the mortgage and the liability for payments, but the new owner would pay the mortgage payments
- *liquidated damages*, which refers to a clause specifying particular amounts due to an aggrieved party in the event of breach or default, such as a seller keeping earnest money
    - *default provisions* in some states may include a *forfeiture clause*, which specifies how much (generally all) of an earnest money deposit may be kept by a seller in the event of buyer default on a binding contract
- *settlement or closing instructions*, which detail who pays for what, such as tax prorations, property repairs, title insurance, and other transaction expenses

A contract *contingency* is a *special condition* or provision inserted by either party that must be met in order for an approved offer to become a fully binding contract. *In the event the contingency is not satisfied, the contract is considered void.* (In practice, disputes may arise.)

Common contingencies include
- *financing*, which typically asserts that the contract is contingent on the buyer's being approved for a certain type of loan by a particular date
- *property sale*, which typically asserts that a buyer's current property must be sold prior to the target closing date for the new property
- *property inspection*, which typically asserts that a professional home inspection report must show that the true condition of the property is acceptable to the buyer

VII-F. Counteroffers/Multiple Counteroffers (Expect 1-2 questions from this area)

As previously noted, a *counteroffer* is the common term for the offer *if the offeree* makes *a change of any kind to it and returns it to the original offeror*. The following principles apply to offers and counteroffers

VII. General: Contracts (10 questions)
(9 Topic Areas; 15 Sub-Topics—each will be covered in its respective Topic Area)

- ***any change*** to the original offer legally ***terminates that offer*** and indicates the original has been ***rejected and replaced*** by the updated offer; the same is true of a counteroffer
- ***changes to offers and counteroffers should be initialed by all principals***
- an ***offer***, or ***counteroffer***, can be ***revoked by the offeror*** at any time prior to its acceptance
- the ***offeree may cancel*** the offer simply ***by letting the response period expire without responding***

Submission of offers and counteroffers is commonly understood to mean that an agent is responsible for ***submitting all offers***, regardless of the terms offered or whether the property is already under contract.

Further, even when the principal has instructed the agent not to present offers of a certain type or from certain parties, the agent is commonly expected to inform the principal of all offers.

*Some of the questions in this area will be scenario-type that serve to illustrate the above point of **submitting all offers**, not just the best, or those over a particular amount, or with certain conditions, but **all offers**.*

Other aspects of submitting offers, such as requirements to make e-mail correspondence, fax transmissions, or oral binders legally binding, are subject to local interpretations, so are unlikely to be tested on the general exam. Where there are state regulations on these matters, there may be questions on the state-specific portion of the exam.

A variety of other events can ***terminate offers and counteroffers***, many of which are examples of conditions that arise ***by operation of law***, which means that existing laws make them happen automatically, without any direct action or intent of a party. A few events that may terminate an offer or counteroffer include the

- ***death*** of a party to the contract, which automatically voids an offer or counteroffer, since there has been no completed ***offer and acceptance***
- ***bankruptcy*** of a one of the parties

VII-G. Leases and Lease-Purchase Agreements   (Expect 0-2 questions from this area)

As noted in Section I-D, Types of Ownership, ***estates in real property*** are divided into ***freehold estates*** and ***nonfreehold estates***, or ***less-than-freehold estates; nonfreehold estates*** are commonly referred to as ***leasehold estates***.

Leasehold estates are contracts, and ***are classified as personal property, not real property***. Therefore, whereas they typically entitle the lessee to all of the possession-and-use rights of ownership, ***they do not entitle the lessee to transfer title, encumber it with liens, or make alterations to the property*** without the knowledge and consent of the owner.

Since leases are contracts, the ***sale or other transfer of rental property*** ownership during a lease period ***typically has no effect on existing leases*** – new owners must honor the terms of all leases.

VII. General: Contracts (10 questions)
(9 Topic Areas; 15 Sub-Topics—each will be covered in its respective Topic Area)

Exceptions to this include *some foreclosure sales* and *most eminent domain condemnations*, which may cancel existing leases and other property use agreements.

Common *elements of a valid lease* include many of the same elements for other real estate contracts, such as a *description of the property*, that the lease must be for a *legal use of the property*, *mutual agreement*, *legal capacity of parties*, and *required signatures*.

In addition, the *statute of frauds* requires leases for *over a year to be in writing*; this means that *oral leases for one year or less are legally valid and binding*.

However, *an unwritten lease is subject to dispute* about who really promised what, so does not protect either party as well as a written agreement.

A *lease purchase* is *typically a rent-to-own arrangement* where an agreed-upon portion of the rent is applied toward the purchase price and either when the tenant can arrange other financing or when the full price is paid, ownership transfers

Types of leases, leasehold estates, and *lease clauses and provisions* provide over 20 definitions that are presented in XI-A, Property Management and Landlord/Tenant. You would do well to read through that Topic Area to become familiar with the most common of them, since a few definitions there may get tested and tallied in this area.

VII-H. Options and Right of First Refusal (Expect 0-2 questions from this area)

The term *option* commonly refers to either an *option, most commonly seen in commercial property purchase offers*, or a *lease-option*; options are similar to, yet quite different from, a *right of first refusal* arrangement.

An *option* in a *commercial property purchase offer* serves to hold an offer open for a specified period *in exchange for some monetary consideration*, which is *generally*
(1) applied toward the purchase price if all of the conditions are met and the sale goes through, *or*
(2) simply kept by the owner if there is no sale.
- an *option is a unilateral contract*, which is *binding on the seller to sell, but not on the buyer to buy*

A *lease-option*, or *lease with an option to buy*, is a mixture of a lease and a purchase contract, but begins as a lease with *a clause allowing the tenant to exercise an option to purchase the property*.

A *right of first refusal* clause may be included in a lease when the tenant wants the opportunity to purchase the property in the event the owner decides to sell; *it gives the tenant the right to review any sales offer the owner receives and either match it or else let the owner proceed with a sale to a different party*

The information on lease-options is presented here for comparison with option contracts for purchases; lease-options will most likely be tallied for testing in the previous Topic Area.

VII. General: Contracts (10 questions)
(9 Topic Areas; 15 Sub-Topics—each will be covered in its respective Topic Area)

VII-I. Rescission and Cancellation Agreements (Expect 0-2 questions from this area)

Rescission means that one of the parties, generally through a contract-specific contingency or regulated-sale review period, may *rescind*, or *cancel* the contract without penalty.

As noted previously, this term refers *to "unmaking" a contract* and *restoring the parties to their precontractual position, including the return of all monies.*

Several events may *terminate a sales contract*, most obviously the *completion* of the sale and transfer of title at closing/settlement. As noted previously, this means that all contractual commitments have been *fully performed*, or *discharged.*

Similarly, *sales contracts may be terminated* by such occurrences as
- *failure to satisfy a contract contingency*
- *eminent domain* proceedings

However, in the case of any contract termination, *one or both parties may incur liabilities* that may be remedied by either existing contractual agreements or litigation.

As noted previously, an agency relationship is *terminated, or cancelled* for any of a number of reasons, including
- *completion* of the transaction through *performance*, or *fulfillment*, of contract elements
- *expiration* of the agency period
- *mutual agreement* of the parties
- *breach of contract* by one of the parties, which generally incurs liability for the party in breach
- *lack of legal elements* in the original contract, such as finding that the contract was made for an illegal purpose

Listing agreements, like other agency agreements, may be terminated or cancelled for reasons provided above, including *bankruptcies, destruction* of the property, *death or incapacity* of a party, *abandonment of agency services* by the agent, or *condemnation* of the property under an eminent domain proceeding.

This ends the presentation of key terms and concepts likely to be either tested or used as distractors in this Content Outline Section.

VIII. General: Transfer of Title (4 questions)
(7 Topic Areas; 13 Sub-Topics—each will be covered in its respective Topic Area)

VIII-A. Title Insurance (Expect 1-2 questions from this area)

Regardless of which type of deed is used to convey and warrant title, there may be a **defect in the title**, or something that might put a **cloud on the title**, meaning that there are conflicting claims that prevent the absolute legal conveyance of **clear title**.

Title insurance is a common way to address the risk of buying a property with ***existing, undiscovered title defects***, since title insurance ***insures the policyholder against the <u>future discovery</u> of <u>certain past problems</u>***.

> ***Common defects*** include ***forged documents*** or ***undisclosed third-party interests***, such as a ***lis pendens***, which is Latin for "a pending lawsuit," ***liens***, ***undiscovered ownership interests*** of spouses or family members, and ***unrecorded prior transfers or assignments***.

> A professional ***title search*** generally discovers all of the recorded information about the property's ***liens***, ***lis pendens***, and ***chain of title***.

>> *This chain may extend from the present back to the original owner, who may have received title through a **grant** from the King of England, ruler of France or Spain, or a **warrant** or **patent** from the state or federal government, depending on the state.*

>> *However, local convention as well as statutory provisions in many states only requires searching the past 40-60 years or so to provide a due-diligence confirmation of marketable title.* **In Connecticut, the statutory requirement is 40 years**, *though most searches will go back an additional 20 years (see Connecticut General Statutes, Chapter 821, Land Titles, Section 47-33c).*

>> *In some states, attorneys handle title searches and prepare an **attorney's opinion of title**, whereas in others the name for the most thorough type of search, which summarizes all documents in all official sources, is an **abstract of title**, and is performed by an **abstractor**.*

> If the search identifies a ***cloud on the title***, it may be resolved through a ***quiet title action*** or ***quiet title suit***, or ***suit to quiet title***, which is a court pleading that leads to a judge's decision on the matter. Or the cloud may also be lifted, and the need for a quiet title action removed, by ***getting a quitclaim deed*** from the newly discovered party with a real, or potential, interest in the property.

Title insurance policies are commonly classified as ***standard coverage policies*** and ***extended coverage policies***, and though the extended coverage insures against more risks, such as unrecorded mechanics liens or undisclosed survey and zoning problems, standard coverage policies typically include common basic coverages such as problems arising from

- ***forged documents***
- ***unknown or undisclosed heirs***
- ***hidden incompetency of grantors***
- ***public record errors***, such as misfiled documents
- ***incorrect marital statements***

VIII. General: Transfer of Title   (4 questions)
(7 Topic Areas; 13 Sub-Topics—each will be covered in its respective Topic Area)

When a ***title insurance company*** performs a title search, it generally prepares what is commonly known as a ***title report***, or ***preliminary title report***, or ***certificate of title***, that shows whether the title is clear and insurable.

If it is, the company will provide a ***commitment for title insurance***, or ***title commitment***, or ***binder***, which is ***the policy offer, explanation of coverages, and commitment to insure***.

The two most common types of policies are
- ***owner's policy***, which covers the new property owner for the purchase price of the property; it remains in effect even beyond the new owner's selling the property later on *and may be paid for by either party, depending on the sales contract and/or local convention*
- ***lender's policy***, or ***mortgagee's policy***, or ***loan policy***, which covers the lender for the remaining loan balance at the time of a claim; these policies expire as soon as the loan is fully repaid *and are typically paid for by the borrower*

*In the event a claim has to be paid to buy out a legitimate, undisclosed interest, the title insurance company exercises its right of **subrogation**. This means, roughly, that since they have made the payment to, or on behalf of, the insured, the company is entitled to recover its costs by suing for and keeping damages from any wrongdoers or other liable parties.*

*Note: the term above, **subrogation**, is not appropriate for real estate testing since it is specific to insurance processes; it is mentioned here both for informational purposes* and *because it may be used as a distractor, especially in questions about **subordination provisions** in loans.*

Title insurance ***premiums*** are typically made in a ***single payment, due at closing***.

VIII-B. Conveyances After Death   (Expect 0-2 questions from this area)

The ***transfer of property by inheritance*** involves some terms that are worth noting here. Some of these are
- ***testate*** refers to ***having a will***; a ***testator*** is someone who has made a will
- ***intestate*** refers to a situation where ***a person dies without a valid will***
- ***probate*** is the public, legal process of executing the terms outlined in a will, or determining how to settle the estate if there is no will
  - ***personal representative*** is, in more and more states, the person designated to see that the terms of a will are carried out; or the following names may apply
    - an ***executor*** is/was the term for a personal representative ***appointed by the testator in the will*** to execute the terms of the will; the term ***executrix*** refers to a female representative, *though **executor** is increasingly used in a gender-neutral way to identify this position*
    - an ***administrator*** is/was the term for a personal representative ***appointed by probate when someone died intestate, or when there is a will and the court sees a reason to appoint an administrator***; the term ***administratrix*** refers to a female

VIII. General: Transfer of Title (4 questions)
(7 Topic Areas; 13 Sub-Topics—each will be covered in its respective Topic Area)

representative, *though **administrator** is increasingly used in a gender-neutral way to identify this position*
- ***intestate succession*** refers to the distribution of an estate that is not governed by a will, and follows state ***laws of descent and distribution*** (or ***devise and descent***) for ***intestacy***
  - ***escheat***, as noted above, is the process of property reverting to the state in the event someone dies intestate and with no heirs
- ***types of wills*** include
  - ***formal***, *or witnessed, which are typically prepared with the help of an attorney*
  - ***holographic***, *or handwritten and unwitnessed*
  - ***oral***, *or **nuncupative**, which is a will spoken by the person who is near death and written down by a witness*
- <u>real</u> ***property disposed of in a will*** is known as a ***devise***; the recipient is a ***devisee***
- <u>personal</u> ***property disposed of in a will*** is known as a ***legacy*** or ***bequest***; the recipient is a ***legatee***
- ***real property transfers*** to a devisee or a buyer in order to pay estate obligations may be ***conveyed by*** an ***executor's deed*** or an ***administrator's deed***, depending on whether or not there is a will
  - *State-specific terms for conveyance instruments that transfer title of certain properties, especially family-retained property, of a deceased owner vary.* **In Connecticut**, *probate courts issue a* **Certificate of devise, descent, or distribution** *to convey willed and family-retained properties – these generally function legally as quitclaim deeds granted either directly by or on behalf of the deceased. Check with a real estate attorney for other available transfer instruments and applicable terms.*

VIII-C. Deeds (Expect 1-2 questions from this area)

A ***deed*** is ***a written instrument by which land is conveyed***. There are several areas of note about deeds: terminology, elements of validity, common types of deeds, covenants and warranties, and title issues.

The ***terminology*** for parties to a deed includes knowing that the one who is ***granting***, or giving away, ownership is referred to as the ***grantor***, and the new owner is known as the ***grantee***.

There are some ***legal elements of validity*** that are required in order for a deed to be legally ***valid*** and ***enforceable***. While some states require a few more than others, most require, at a minimum, the following elements or conditions
- it must be ***in writing***
- the grantor must have ***legal capacity***, that is, be of legal age and mental competence
- ***identification of the parties***, that is, the grantor and the grantee must be named
- ***statement of consideration***, or what is being paid/exchanged for the property. While this is often expressed as a nominal sum, as in "for $10 and other good and valuable consideration," increasingly it is the actual sales price
- ***words of conveyance***, or a ***granting clause***, such as, "I do hereby grant and convey"
- ***a legal description of the property***
- ***signature of the grantor***

VIII. General: Transfer of Title (4 questions)
(7 Topic Areas; 13 Sub-Topics—each will be covered in its respective Topic Area)

- ***delivery*** and ***acceptance*** (or ***registration*** when using the ***Torrens system*** in those 10 states that recognize it)

In some states, there are additional requirements, such as
- an ***habendum clause***, which defines the extent and limitations of the interest conveyed; it generally begins with the words "to have and to hold," and so is often referred to as the ***"to-have-and-to-hold" clause***. Sometimes it is considered part of the granting clause.
- a ***seal***, or mark of authentication. It is often just the printed, or written, word "Seal" or the initials "L.S." (for the Latin term meaning "the place of the seal") by the line for the grantor's signature.

Other common parts and processes of deed creation may include
- the ***date***
- ***relevant exceptions and restrictions***
- ***acknowledgement***, or formal statement that the grantor is the one signing the deed and is doing so voluntarily
- ***recording*** the deed in the public records to provide notice of its existence
    - *public records may be housed and maintained by the municipality itself or centralized in either a county or state location, depending on the type of document (birth, marriage, and death certificates; divorce decrees; probate records; etc.) as well as the state: the county system is used widely, but not exclusively, nationwide for land records.*
    - ***NOTE: though Connecticut does NOT use a county recording system, the exam MAY use that term, so be ready to overlook this particular imprecision in your search for the answer that will give you credit!***

Recording a document provides what is referred to as ***constructive notice***, or ***legal notice***, which means that a ***due diligence*** review of the public record would make the existence of the document known to the reviewer. This differs from ***actual notice***, which means that a party ***has personally received the notice***, as when a process server delivers a subpoena to appear in court.

Recording the deed provides ***constructive notice that title has been transferred*** to the new owner.

This is critically important in protecting an owner's title interest, since ***proper, legal recording establishes a new owner's position and rights within the chain of title***.

The specific process for recording deeds and other documents ***may*** involve formal ***acknowledgments*** of signatures by witnesses and/or ***notarization*** in order to create a legally valid recordation; ***the process details for recording documents are state-specific and therefore not testable on this section of the test***.

Types of deeds are as varied as the purposes they serve and the covenants and warranties they include. Some of the more common ones are

VIII. General: Transfer of Title (4 questions)
(7 Topic Areas; 13 Sub-Topics—each will be covered in its respective Topic Area)

- *general warranty deeds*, or *warranty deeds*, which **include all of the five covenants listed below**, and **offer the greatest protection for the grantee of all deeds**
- *special warranty deeds*, which warrant the **title against title defects that arose only during the grantor's ownership**
- *bargain and sale deeds*, which contain **no guaranty from the grantor about the validity of title, but implies that the grantor has an interest** that is being sold to the grantee
- *quitclaim deeds*, which have **no covenants or warranties**. They simply relinquish any and all interest the grantor may have in a property. They are commonly used to ensure that a particular party will not decide to interfere later; **they provide the least protection for the grantee** against other potential problems with the title.

The following **additional types of deeds** are less common than those above but do appear in various national textbooks. ***Some are state-specific or go by different names in different jurisdictions, so are not fair game for testing, except as distractors, on this part of the test***. They include

- *grant deeds*, which are used in a few states, notably in the West, in place of a general warranty deed, which contains additional warranties
- *tax deeds*, which transfer ownership after a tax sale
- *sheriff's deeds*, which transfer property for certain forced or judicial sales
- *correction deeds*, which simply correct errors or omissions in a previous deed
- *confirmatory deeds*, which is often the same as a correction deed, but in some states is used to affirm title based on a final order in a suit to quiet title
- *gift deeds*, which are deeds given for either a nominal sum or "love and affection"
- *mortgage deeds*, which are deeds used in some states, **including Connecticut**, whereby a property owner borrowing money secured by the property gives a lender, who is sometimes the seller using this deed for seller-financing, **legal title and specific contractual rights** to claim and/or sell the property if the borrower is in breach of loan provisions
- *executor's deeds*, or *administrator's deeds*, which are used in some states to convey property of those who died with or without a will, respectively
    - *certificate of devise, descent, or distribution* or some other state-specific form may be used by a probate judge to convey willed and family-retained properties

Special note: Since **trust deeds**, or **deeds of trust**, are mortgage financing instruments, the term(s) would only appear in this Topic Area as a distractor.

Deeds may include a variety of **covenants and warranties**. Covenants are **formal agreements or promises**; warranties are **guarantees**. The **five most common** are the

- *covenant of seisin*, which means the grantor claims to be the owner of the property and is therefore legally entitled to convey it; *seisin is a Middle English/Old French word for* **"possession,"** *and is related to—and pronounced like—the word* **"seize"**
- *covenant of quiet enjoyment*, which means the grantor promises that no one will disturb the new owner with claims against the property, such as an undisclosed co-owner or a long-lost heir

VIII. General: Transfer of Title (4 questions)
(7 Topic Areas; 13 Sub-Topics—each will be covered in its respective Topic Area)

- ***covenant of further assurance***, which means the grantor assumes responsibility for any additional documentation necessary to ensure the grantee's title, such as releases from family members who should have signed the original transfer deed
- ***covenant against encumbrances***, which means the grantor promises that any and all easements or liens have been properly disclosed and is liable for damages if others are discovered after the transfer
- ***covenant of warranty forever***, or ***warranty of title***, which means the grantor promises to bear the cost of defending the title against undiscovered or undisclosed flaws existing at the time of transfer – sometimes seen as synonymous with the covenant of quiet enjoyment

*As stated in the preceding Section on Title Insurance, regardless of which type of deed is used to convey and/or warrant title, there may be a **defect in the title** that prevents the absolute legal conveyance of clear title.*

VIII-D. Escrow or Closing (Expect 1-2 questions from this area)

Escrow is a generic legal term used to refer to both (1) ***an account***, as in, "We put the rent deposit money in escrow." In this sense, escrow is interchangeable with ***escrow account***, ***impound account***, and, in some states, ***trust account***, and (2) ***the 'signed-contract to delivered-deed' period*** of a real estate transaction, as in, "The property is in escrow."

Real Estate Settlement Procedures Act (RESPA) literature states that the terms "*'settlement' and 'closing' can be and are used interchangeably.*"

However, **since the PSI outline uses the term "escrow"** for this Topic Area, wherever its meaning could be interpreted as referring to the 2nd meaning above, **simply accept it as a synonymous term for the settlement/closing process**.

Also, despite local preferences and conventions that use one over the other, in most cases here, and perhaps on the PSI exam, **"settlement" will be used instead of "closing,"** *if for no other reason than because it is the term printed prominently on every* **"Settlement Statement (HUD-1)"** *form nationwide.*

The ***purpose of settlement*** is to ***consummate the transaction*** by ***fulfilling the contract conditions, disbursing required funds, and transferring title***.

Some settlement conventions and processes vary from state to state. For example, in some states lawyers are an integral part of closings whereas they are rarely involved in any part of a routine transaction in others.

Due to such differences in practice, details that are not uniform nationwide will not be tested on the general exam, but may appear on the state-specific exam if they are tested at all. Nevertheless, certain terms or processes may appear in distractors.

VIII. General: Transfer of Title (4 questions)
(7 Topic Areas; 13 Sub-Topics—each will be covered in its respective Topic Area)

So, take note of the following terms
- *settlement agent* is the term for to the party authorized to process the closing/settlement details, regardless of whether it would be a lawyer, a title company representative, an 'escrow agent,' or another official by any name
- *escrow/trust account* is the term you might see rather than escrow or trust account to refer to a *property sales transaction account* – this term **clarifies, for testing purposes, the interchangeable nature of these terms** and allows all candidates to readily understand, within the context of question, that the question is about a sales transaction situation rather than an office trust account question.

The settlement agent acts in a fiduciary capacity regarding all transaction funds and details.

Further, the settlement agent oversees the checklist of details and contingencies created by the *sales contract* and *loan-related specifics*. These may include such elements as
- securing the *satisfaction and release of contingencies*
- verifying the documentation necessary for the *satisfaction and release of liens*
- gathering and reviewing documents regarding *encumbrances*, *restrictions*, *title and property insurance*, and other contract-specific requirements
- *disbursing transaction funds* according to *priority of liens*, which generally get paid, first to last, in the following order
  - *property taxes*
  - *special assessments*
  - *first mortgage*
  - *other liens*, generally by date of recordation
  - *other closing/settlement fees*
  - *balance*, if any, *to the seller*, or *foreclosed owner in a forced sale*
- *recordation* of pertinent documents, e.g., releases for any extinguished lien(s) and/or encumbrance(s); new deed and lien(s)
- *filing IRS form 1099-S*, *Proceeds from Real Estate Transaction*, with the IRS and getting a copy to the seller for reporting on the seller's tax returns

A settlement statement is the document that provides *the transaction's final, detailed accounting summary*. The particular form of the settlement statement may *vary from state to state as well as from transaction to transaction*.

However, a "default" for references to settlement statements will be the uniform *Settlement Statement (HUD-1)*, or just *HUD-1*, since they are used nationwide for residential loans governed by the Real Estate Settlement Procedures Act (RESPA), which is implemented through the Department of Housing and Urban Development (HUD).

A list of *critical documents* that are commonly included in the closing process for the sale of a residential property secured by a loan would, at a minimum, be likely to include
- *RESPA loan documents*
  - The *Settlement Statement (HUD-1)*, with a final, summary accounting of all settlement costs for both the buyer and the seller

VIII. General: Transfer of Title (4 questions)
(7 Topic Areas; 13 Sub-Topics—each will be covered in its respective Topic Area)

- the **Initial Escrow Statement**, which itemizes the estimated taxes, insurance premiums and other charges anticipated to be paid from the impound/escrow account during the first twelve months of the loan. (Although the statement is usually given at settlement, the lender has 45 days from then to deliver it.)
- **deed** for the real property included in the transaction
- **bill(s) of sale** for all **personal (unattached) property** included in the transaction
  *It is worth repeating here that **real property ownership is transferred by a deed**, while the **transfer of personal property ownership** is formally accomplished through a **bill of sale**. Both provide evidence that **title** has also been passed.*
- **title insurance policy(ies)** as required
- **property insurance** as required
- **reduction certificate**, which is a loan document that shows the remaining principal balance, interest rate, and date of maturity; it is used by a seller who needs to know the exact payoff amount on the day of closing as well as to verify the terms and amount of an existing loan that a buyer may be assuming
- **satisfaction piece**, or **satisfaction of mortgage**, which is the certificate a mortgagee provides to a mortgagor that states the debt has been paid; typically it is recorded to confirm the title is free of the seller's mortgage lien's encumbrance
- **estoppel certificate**, or **offset statement**, or **certificate of no defense**, which is a statement from a tenant or a mortgagee attesting to relevant conditions, such as the tenant's security deposit or a mortgage's balance, that is used to stop the party from claiming different facts later
- **IRS form 1099-S** for reporting the proceeds of the sale

Many of the costs involved in a real estate transfer **are negotiable**, even when convention has one party or the other as typically responsible.

Closing costs as presented on the closing/settlement statement are commonly referred to as **credits** and **debits**, which means, respectively, that funds are **due and payable to a particular party** or that funds are **to be provided by a particular a party.**

Common costs and responsible parties include
- **buyer's closing costs**, where applicable
  - **refunds to seller** of prorated portion of remaining fuel oil and other prepaid utility and property expenses
  - **deed and new mortgage recording fees**
  - **appraisal fees for loan funding**
  - **home inspection fees**
  - **new loan or assumption fees**
- **seller's closing costs**, where applicable
  - **cost of clearing title**
  - **loan payoff**
  - **termite inspection**
  - **broker's commission**

VIII. General: Transfer of Title (4 questions)
(7 Topic Areas; 13 Sub-Topics—each will be covered in its respective Topic Area)

While some questions in this area will focus on which party is responsible for certain charges, who pays how much will be addressed in the appropriate Topic Area of Section X, Real Estate Calculations.

VIII-E. Foreclosure, Short Sales (Expect 0-1 question from this area)

Foreclosure is an area of special note since it is the most common recourse for lenders, and refers to the legal proceeding initiated by certain property creditors to **force the sale of a property in default on a loan or in arrears for taxes in order to repay the debt**.

A foreclosure sale is an example of **involuntary alienation, or involuntary transfer, of property ownership.**

Foreclosure types and processes are too varied and state-specific to address here, though it is worth noting that the two-party mortgage and the three-party deed of trust have different basic sets of processes

- *generally, the processes are known, respectively, as (1)* **judicial**, *which means by a legal action in court that results in* **a sale by court order**, *or* **writ of execution**, *and (2)* **nonjudicial**, *which means things proceed according to contract terms alone*
- *at a settlement for a foreclosure sale, the* **priority of liens**, *or the order of repayment to creditors with the sale proceeds, is important; if the proceeds do not cover all property liens, the creditors may be entitled to seek a* **deficiency judgment** *against the foreclosed property owner*

*Special **nontestable, information-only** Connecticut note: In Connecticut,* **the judicial foreclosure process** *is carried out by either* **strict foreclosure** *or a* **decree of sale**.

- **Strict foreclosure** *permits the lender to get a court order showing the borrower has defaulted on the mortgage terms and thereby* **acquire an immediate transfer of title**, *though there is* **a court-determined redemption period for the borrower**. *If the borrower is unable to redeem the property, the process continues and* **the lender soon receives absolute title rights to the property's full market value, not just the remaining loan balance**.
- *A* **decree of sale** *is a court-directed process by which the court appoints* **a committee to sell the property, the time and place of the sale,** *and* **three appraisers to help determine the price**; *typically the lender only recovers the loan balance and costs from the sale.*

Depending on the particular case as well as the state in which the foreclosure occurs, some form of the following types of **protections** and/or **remedies** for **the owner** may come into play.

Since many of the following terms, concepts, and processes are not uniformly available or applied nationwide, **they are provided for informational purposes and may be used on exams as distractors.** *Their specific applicability in your own state, however, may make them a part of your state-specific exam.*

Some common terms associated with **alternatives to foreclosure, homeowner protections,** and **other remedies** include

VIII. General: Transfer of Title (4 questions)
(7 Topic Areas; 13 Sub-Topics—each will be covered in its respective Topic Area)

- *forbearance*, which refers to an alternative by which the creditor refrains from taking legal action against a borrower in default after being satisfied that the borrower is taking acceptable measures to satisfy the debt; commonly referred to as **workout**, forbearance may involve adjustments to the payment schedule or amounts due, as well as some other negotiated **mortgage modification**
- a *deed in lieu of foreclosure*, or *deed in lieu*, and also known as a **"friendly foreclosure,"** is, as the name suggests, a situation in which the owner gives a lender the deed rather than going through a foreclosure proceeding
- *redemption*, which refers to the right to pay off a debt, even after mortgage default, and reclaim the property; this remedy varies widely in its particulars
    - **redemption rights** vary from state to state, but may include a before-foreclosure-sale right known as the **equitable right of redemption**, or even a statutory period after a sale, known as a **statutory right of redemption**
- *homestead laws*, in states where they exist, such as Florida, may provide a **homestead protection** that shields part or all of a residence against creditors. This protection is often referred to as a **homestead exemption**, because the protection may 'exempt' property from creditor attachment
    - however, 'exemption' more widely refers to any homestead <u>tax exemption</u> **program(s)** available from an owner's state or local taxation authorities that reduces the annual property tax for qualifying owners, **generally based on income, age, veteran status, or handicap**
- *tenant rights* regarding *leased occupancy of a foreclosed property* were introduced both federally and in many state laws, including Connecticut, in the wake of the subprime mortgage crisis. **For properties with federally-related mortgages**, **federal law** requires lenders to honor existing leases and/or provide at least **ninety (90) days' notice of intention to terminate**, depending on the specific circumstances; under Connecticut law, there is a sixty (60) day protection period that begins upon transfer of title.
    - The federal law is currently only effective through the end of 2012. Both laws have requirements that should be reviewed by a tenant's legal counsel to ensure the tenant's particular situation is interpreted correctly, and subsequent rights and protections are made effective.

A **short sale** is another alternative to foreclosure on certain distressed properties that have a ready, qualified buyer; it involves the sale of the property with a lender-approved reduction, often about 20%, of the outstanding mortgage balance, and can also involve new-owner assumption of the reduced mortgage

- short sales typically involve a lawyer negotiating with the lender on the actual reduction amount; short sales can benefit the lender financially by avoiding the cost of full foreclosure and subsequent property maintenance, marketing, and sales commission expenses, as well as possible lender accounting benefits

With the well-publicized rise in home foreclosures stemming from both subprime loans and prime loans on properties that have lost significant value, you are likely to see the terms **"upside down"** *or* **"underwater"** *for properties with* **property values that have dropped below their mortgage balance**.

VIII. General: Transfer of Title (4 questions)
(7 Topic Areas; 13 Sub-Topics—each will be covered in its respective Topic Area)

These terms, now much more mainstream than ever before, may appear in test questions that describe particular distressed property scenarios and then ask you to identify resolution options for either the lender or the borrower.

VIII-F. Tax Aspects of Transferring Title to Real Property
(Expect 0-1 question from this area)

Most tax aspects of property transfers are locally controlled revenue generators, so cannot be tested in this Topic Area; such state or municipality specific questions may appear in the State-specific portion of the exam, or as a math question with all of the variables provided.

Internal Revenue Service (IRS) capital gains allowances generally top the list of test questions about the ***tax aspects of property transfer***.

Broadly speaking, IRS capital gains on a property are computed by subtracting the actual sales price a seller gets from the amount the seller bought the property for earlier.

*In practice, it would typically take an accountant to compute the reportable capital gain—or loss—after subtracting the original purchase price, cost of improvements, and other deductible expenses, from the gross proceeds as reported on **IRS Form 1099-S, Proceeds from Real Estate Transaction**.*

Questions on capital gains for residential properties will be based on the ***Taxpayer Relief Act of 1997***, which says that on the sale of a ***primary residence*** that has been ***owner-occupied for two of the past five years***, the owner(s) are allowed to exempt capital gains of
- ***$250,000 for a single seller***, or
- ***$500,000 for a married couple filing jointly***

The Act also specifies that these ***exempt sales can be repeated***, and so creates incentives for certain kinds of real estate speculation; previously, capital gains in the same range had to be reinvested within a specified post-sale period to remain exempt.

The provisions of the 1997 Act are in stark contrast to ***the law it replaced***, which ***allowed homeowners over 55*** years of age a ***once-in-a-lifetime exclusion of $125,000 worth of capital gains*** on the sale of a primary residence.

The particulars of the outdated law are noted here in case they appear as distractors.

As noted in Section IV-A, General Concepts (of Financing), ***IRS tax issues*** regarding the costs, benefits, and tax implications of property financing include the following borrower-related items that are worth remembering during a property transfer
- ***interest payments*** on mortgage loans are deductible if the owner itemizes deductions, though for homeowners with low-balance loans and few other deductions, the standard deduction may be better than itemizing
- ***real estate taxes*** are deductible
- ***certain costs*** of financing and refinancing may be deductible, such as ***origination fees***, ***discount points***, and loan ***prepayment penalties***

VIII. General: Transfer of Title (4 questions)
(7 Topic Areas; 13 Sub-Topics—each will be covered in its respective Topic Area)

Another common property-related tax matter is the ***1031 exchange***. Named for the Internal Revenue Code Section 1031, it refers to situations where an investor takes the ***proceeds from a property sale and defers paying capital gains taxes by reinvesting the funds in different, but like-kind properties***.

*Not surprisingly, 1031 exchanges have a whole set of rules, such as a **time limit for qualifying reinvestment purchases** and numerous accounting details, that are too complex for entry-level licensure testing; some regulators would argue that even simple definition questions on this topic should only be used on broker exams.*

However, since 1031 exchanges are not uncommon in practice, you should be familiar with the basic concept. Besides, the term may appear as a distractor!

Boot *is another term commonly associated with 1031 exchanges for **additional cash** required over the reinvestment amount from sold properties. However, it typically refers to any cash or other goods added to any transaction to make up for differences between a new property's value and funds available from a sold/exchanged property.*

Special reminder: to limit your liability as well as ensure greater accuracy, refer clients to an accountant or tax attorney for answers to tax-related questions.

VIII-G. Special Processes [Broker Only]   (Brokers: Expect 0-2 questions from this area)

The terms and processes given below, especially voluntary and involuntary transfers, are basic real estate material, some of which PSI may test and tally in other Topic Areas.

*So **you would be well-advised to read what follows**. Even if there are no questions on the Salesperson exam regarding these processes, you should be familiar with the information below, since some of the associated terms are likely to appear as distractors, and more importantly, in your upcoming professional life.*

The ***transfer***, or ***alienation***, or ***conveyance*** of title to property ownership from one party to another can be categorized as being either ***voluntary*** or ***involuntary***.

*The terms **transfer** and **alienation** are interchangeable, so either one may appear in test questions; **alienation** is used almost exclusively when property transfers are **involuntary**.*

Voluntary transfer refers to the free-will transfer of property by its owner using methods such as
- ***deeding*** it after selling it or making it a gift
- ***assigning*** it to another
- ***dedicating*** it for public use
- ***willing*** it to an heir

Property ***dedication*** refers to the donation of private property for public use. For example, a developer may ***dedicate*** roads and some common-use areas in a subdivision as part of its plan, so the municipality will own and maintain them.

VIII. General: Transfer of Title (4 questions)
(7 Topic Areas; 13 Sub-Topics—each will be covered in its respective Topic Area)

Also, if the public uses **nondedicated** private land as if it were public, the property may become subject to a municipal easement, much like a prescriptive easement for individual users, and legally turn into **dedicated property**.

> *Note: All over the country, there are privately owned roads, public places, and sections of sidewalks that the owners may mark somehow as "nondedicated property" and/or actually close off to the public one day a year to interrupt public use and thereby demonstrate such use has been allowed under a revocable license. By doing this, the owner helps avoid loss of control through a claim of dedication.*

Involuntary transfer, or **involuntary alienation**, refers to any situation where **title transfers** in a manner that the owner may not have any control over or would generally prefer not to have happen. Examples of these would include

- **foreclosure** due to financial default, including tax sales
  - **distress sale** is a term applied to most forced or below-market property sales; distress sales have become a strong niche market in the real estate industry
- **condemnation** through the process of **eminent domain**
  - **inverse condemnation**, which is when the owner forces a governmental agency to either step-up the payment on a condemned property or actually condemn it due to a court-determined decline in use or value based on some governmental action, like building a military airport right next to the owner's residence
- **escheat** due to an owner's dying intestate with no heirs
- **adverse possession** as a result of a court's approval that a claimant deserves to acquire title to a property due to legally adequate and compelling **open, notorious, and hostile** use of a particular property for a statutory period
- **partition** by a court-ordered sale of a property with multiple owners, one or more of which cannot get the other(s) to buy their interest, and so petition the court to force a sale in order to receive their share of the proceeds
- **reversion** due to a breach in the terms of the deed or contract

---

This ends the presentation of key terms and concepts likely to be either tested or used as distractors in this Content Outline Section.

IX. General: Practice of Real Estate (12 questions)
(8 Topic Areas; 24 Sub-Topics—each will be covered in its respective Topic Area)

IX-A. Trust Accounts (General) *[Regulatory Details in State Portion]*
(Expect 1-2 questions from this area)

This area presents, in a general way, the **common law basics of trust accounts** and their use in **ensuring that licensees faithfully observe their fiduciary duty of accounting for transaction funds.** As noted in the heading, regulatory details will be found in the state portion of the exam.

> However, in general, **the purpose of trust, or escrow, accounts** is to provide an account that is **separate from operational or personal accounts** in which **to maintain and account for transaction-related funds.**

Typically the are required to be opened in a bank doing business in the licensee's state, and are the responsibility of the firm's primary broker to establish and oversee. Generally, even if the primary broker is allowed to delegate account management, the ultimate responsibility—and liability—for proper handling of monies remains at the top.

Questions in this area will be necessarily broad, and probably develop scenarios demonstrating expected standards of accounting.

> *Though licensees are often expected to submit all transaction-related funds to their broker and the funds are expected to be deposited within a statutory period, such as "three banking days" or "forty-eight-hours, excluding weekends and holidays," any questions about such details will be written using phrases like "within the required period" rather than a specific number of days*

Though mentioned in the last Section in outlining fiduciary duties, it is worth repeating that as a fiduciary, any licensee who accepts transaction-related funds has an obligation of *accounting*, which means the licensee is obligated to avoid either of the following situations with those funds

- *commingling*, which means mingling, or combining, transaction funds with other funds that are required to be maintained separately; this could result from putting the funds in the wrong account, either business or personal
- *conversion*, which refers to **converting funds to another use than the one intended by the principal**, or **misappropriating them**, as in using earnest money to pay office expenses *or for any personal use*; conversion is generally preceded by commingling

*Additional particulars regarding the **handling of monies**, such as **to whom it is given**, **into which account it gets deposited**, the **time period within which it must be deposited**, and **method(s) of disbursal, especially when there is a dispute**, are all state-specific and may be tested on the state portion of the exam.*

Remember that even though licensees have specific fiduciary duties to a client, they owe the obligations of **honesty and fair dealing** to all parties, including customers, and this extends to handling any customer funds entrusted to the licensee.

> *Further, review your own state statutes governing accounts and recordkeeping to determine the regulatory requirements for holding and maintaining transaction funds as well as tenant deposits; for example, some states that have Landlord/Tenant Acts often require deposits be held in an account that bears nominal interest for the tenant.*

IX. General: Practice of Real Estate (12 questions)
(8 Topic Areas; 24 Sub-Topics—each will be covered in its respective Topic Area)

And each state has its own requirements for which records to maintain, acceptable methods to store them, such as electronic or original hard copy, and how long they must be retained in the event the regulatory agency wants to examine them.

IX-B. Fair Housing Laws (Expect 3-4 questions from this area)

In a nutshell, the ***Civil Rights Act*** and the federal ***Fair Housing Act*** are terms that encompass and refer to all Fair Housing legislation, beginning with the ***Civil Rights Act of 1866*** through the federal ***Fair Housing Act of 1968***, also known as ***Title VIII of the Civil Rights Act of 1968***, and the federal ***Fair Housing Amendments Act of 1988***. The ***Americans with Disabilities Act (ADA)*** is separate, though related, and deals with access to public buildings.

Note: You should NOT be tested on what specifically became protected at which time along the way.** Despite any appearance to the contrary by the use of slightly different terms, test vendors have historically been aware that **the real estate license exam is not the place for a mini-test on "The History and Evolution of the Fair Housing Law."

*Ultimately, a real estate licensee's obligation regarding Fair Housing is simple: **do not discriminate**. And just to be sure you know how to spot it when you see it, you should know the following basic protections, provisions, and violations.*

The ***Civil Rights Act of 1866*** asserted ***one basic protection***: there was to be ***no race-based discrimination in the housing market***. The U. S. Supreme Court decision of ***Jones v. Mayer (1968)*** reaffirmed this position as the law of the land.

The accumulated provisions of the federal ***Fair Housing Amendments Act of 1988*** include prohibiting discrimination in the sale, rental, or advertising of residential property for ***protected classes*** based on the following personal characteristics
- ***race or color***
- ***national origin***
- ***religious preference***
- ***sex***
- ***handicapping conditions***, which means having a physical or mental disability, including infection with the HIV virus or recovery status for drug and alcohol dependence, that substantially limits one or more major life activity
- ***familial status***, which means ***one or more individuals under 18 years of age being domiciled*** with a parent or custodian, or the legal designee of the parents, and also ***applies to any person who is pregnant*** or in the process of securing legal custody of any individual under 18 years old
    - ***older persons exemption*** to familial status protection for multi-unit properties ***may apply*** to housing that is
        - intended for and ***solely occupied by*** persons ***62 years of age or older***
        - intended for older persons and ***80 percent or more of the units*** are occupied by ***at least one occupant 55 years of age or older***

IX. General: Practice of Real Estate (12 questions)
(8 Topic Areas; 24 Sub-Topics—each will be covered in its respective Topic Area)

Practices that would be *violations* of Fair Housing laws include
- *steering*, which means showing prospective buyers of a particular protected class properties only in areas that have a high representation of the same class
- *blockbusting*, which means 'spreading the word' that property values may decline due to an increased presence in the area of a particular protected class, so owners should consider selling before the 'price drop'
    - *this may also be called **panic-peddling**, or **panic selling**, under which there may be no discrimination involved in a licensee's marketing based on a fear of falling prices; examples include real or trumped-up anticipation of change, such as a zoning change allowing a low-income housing project in an affluent neighborhood*
- *redlining*, which applies to a *lender's* designation of a particular area as a 'loan-free zone' due to the presence in that area of a protected class

Federal Fair Housing laws are **administered and enforced by the Department of Housing and Urban Development (HUD),** which also provides an **Equal Housing Opportunity poster** for real estate offices.

*This **HUD poster** is expected to be **displayed prominently** in the office as a statement that the office supports non-discriminatory practices in housing sales and rentals. **Its absence** can be used against the office broker and/or other licensees being investigated for discrimination by HUD as **evidence of discriminatory practices**.*

The HUD symbol and an anti-discrimination notice are often included in company listing forms, marketing materials, and advertising as a further demonstration that the company and its licensees adhere to Fair Housing guidelines.

Be sure that in preparing all materials and advertising that no language is used that singles out any protected class, regardless of whether it is offering discounts or discouragement – and watch on the test for questions that ask you to identify an example of acceptable, discrimination-free advertising!

Some property transactions are exempt from federal Fair Housing laws. These include
- *sale or rental of a single-family dwelling by owner* without a real estate licensee's involvement
- *rental of rooms or units in one- to four-family dwellings if one is owner-occupied*
- *preferences shown by a religious organization for its own members* in the sale, rental, or occupancy of real estate, as long as the organization does not restrict membership based on any of the protected classes
- *preferences shown by a private club for its own members* in a rental or occupancy of residential real estate, as long as the club is not open to the public and the lodging is not operated commercially

The sale or rental of a single-family dwelling unit is *NOT exempt from Fair Housing laws whenever there is a real estate licensee involved*, and
- under the Civil Rights Act, even properties exempt from Fair Housing laws are *protected against discrimination whenever it is based on race*

IX. General: Practice of Real Estate (12 questions)
(8 Topic Areas; 24 Sub-Topics—each will be covered in its respective Topic Area)

Important Fair Housing note for property rentals: In residential property rentals covered by Fair Housing requirements, a *landlord must allow a handicapped tenant to make reasonable modifications to a unit at the tenant's own expense*, typically *with the obligation to return the unit to its previous condition when moving out.*

Special clarification: This requirement is based on Fair Housing laws, NOT the Americans With Disabilities Act (ADA) requirements, which apply to public accessibility. (Questions on this may be categorized and tallied in Section XI-A.)

The **Americans with Disabilities Act (ADA)** includes provisions for **handicapped access and accommodations in public buildings**. This includes ramps, wheelchair-accessible rest room facilities, and elevators. It also has a host of details that are more appropriately the responsibility of developers, builders, and architects rather than real estate licensees. However, a few key definitions, concepts, and requirements include

- **disability** means a **physical or mental impairment that substantially limits one or more major life activities**
- **places of public accommodation include real estate offices**
- **employers with 15 or more employees** must comply with ADA requirements for both nondiscriminatory employment practices and employee workplace accommodations

IX-C. Advertising (Expect 1-3 questions from this area)

As noted in the previous Topic Area, a licensee needs to observe Fair Housing guidelines when advertising properties for sale or rent, so Fair Housing questions on advertising may be tallied in this area. And there are other federal requirements for certain types of advertising, especially loan terms (see below) as well as additional requirements in the state-specific portion of most state outlines, commonly that a licensee must include the agency's name in ads.

But the most likely area where a licensee could go afoul of acceptable guidelines is in simple property descriptions. Advertisements typically engage in some form of highly subjective "property enhancement," sometimes referred to as **puffing** or **puffery**, by describing run-down properties as "handyman specials," small homes as having a "modest floor plan," or a site as offering "the best view of the mountain" compared to others with arguably similar views.

*So, questions in this area may also focus on examples or definitions of **puffing** or **puffery**. They may also ask you to determine whether a misleading description is based on poor information, and possibly just **negligent misrepresentation**, or **willful misrepresentation**.*

*For example, advertising a property as having a 1,520 square foot floor plan is a verifiable fact. If a licensee's advertisement presents this as "nearly 2,000 square feet!" the licensee may be guilty of **misrepresentation** rather than just engaging in puffery.*

*However, if a buyer then relies on that statement as a fact and the licensee **deliberately avoids correcting the "fact"** before the buyer is damaged by relying on that information, it is quite likely that a judge would rule the licensee had gone beyond **deliberate misrepresentation** and had ultimately committed **fraud**.*

IX. General: Practice of Real Estate (12 questions)
(8 Topic Areas; 24 Sub-Topics—each will be covered in its respective Topic Area)

Under the provisions of the *Federal Trade Commission Act*, there are specific *truth-in-advertising* rules and guidelines. These include requiring advertisers to ensure that
- *advertising must be truthful and non-deceptive,* which means that the ad includes no statement, and omits no information, that is either likely to mislead or material to misleading consumers
- *advertisers must have evidence to back up their claims*, and
- *advertisements cannot be unfair*, which means it causes or is likely to cause unavoidable consumer injury

The federal *Truth in Lending Act (TILA)*, a part of the *Consumer Credit Protection Act*, has a detailed set of loan *disclosure* and *advertising* requirements for lenders who originate residential loans. *Regulation Z* is the regulation that implements the Act and explains how lenders are to comply with those parts of TILA that bear on consumer credit.

> *Style Note*: Testing convention combines these terms, making them the **Truth-in-Lending Act (Regulation Z)** *for most test questions, especially those regarding Regulation Z. This ensures they are properly linked on the test as they are in practice, while avoiding both the possibility and the appearance of testing on which one does what, which are distinctions better left to lenders and lawyers.*
>
> *For clarity in presenting a general overview here, though, they will separated briefly; the test questions will typically bring them back together.*

TILA is intended to enable the customer to examine loan offers to determine
- the *cost of a cash-versus-credit transaction*
- the *difference in the cost of credit among different lenders*

Regulation Z is intended to spell out how to ensure that customers get meaningful, accurate, and complete information to make informed credit comparisons and decisions.

> *It is important for licensees to understand key elements of TILA and Regulation Z as they relate to mortgage loans in order to explain them to customers and clients.*
>
> *However, since they govern the professional activities of <u>lenders</u>, their intricacies **are not appropriate** for real estate examinations. (For example, they apply to certain other consumer credit transactions, but for our immediate purpose here, so what?)*

Key elements of TILA are that it
- is a *federal* law, though states may have their own adaptations
- *seeks to ensure the informed use of consumer credit* by borrowers
- requires lenders to provide *meaningful disclosures of credit terms and costs*
- *applies to loans secured by a personal residence* (among others)

Key elements of Regulation Z include that it
- *provides the specific requirements of TILA*

IX. General: Practice of Real Estate (12 questions)
(8 Topic Areas; 24 Sub-Topics—each will be covered in its respective Topic Area)

- requires *disclosure standards for advertisements* when the ad includes details for certain credit terms, known as *trigger terms*. These include
    - *amount or percentage of down payment*
    - *amount of any payment*
    - *number of payments*
    - *period of repayment*
    - *dollar amount of finance charges, or that there is no charge for credit*

    > An advertisement containing details for any of the above trigger terms, such as "only $500 down!" must *disclose all* of the following information
    > - *down payment information*
    > - *the cash price or loan amount*
    > - *terms of repayment (number, amount, and schedule)*
    > - *the annual percentage rate (APR) and possibility of any increases*
    > - *some* sales also require the *total of all payments*

- requires lenders to make certain *disclosures on loans* within three business days after their receipt of a written application and again at the time of loan closing, if the loans are subject to the *Real Estate Settlement Procedures Act (RESPA)* – (see IV-F, Financing/Credit Laws for more on RESPA). There are 18 required disclosures, which include *the amount financed, the finance charge, the annual percentage rate (APR),* and *the total of all payments*

- allows a borrower a *limited three-day right to rescind* a loan contract, or revoke it without penalty, after signing *for certain home improvement loans*, but *NOT* for a primary residential mortgage *(though some refinancing arrangements may invoke the rescission right)*

*Remember the earlier note: **real estate licensees are NOT lenders**, who are the ones who need to know the fine-line, ever-changing details, such as the other 14 RESPA disclosures. So do not panic over memorizing all 18 disclosures -- review them if they are in your main textbook, then move on.*

A final note on advertising: the laws above and any others require that *disclaimers and disclosures must be clear and conspicuous*, regardless of the medium, including the Internet.

IX-D. Agent Supervision (Expect 1-3 questions from this area)

This Topic Area is most likely to contain scenario and/or application questions about the liability a broker has for the actions of affiliated licensees. As noted previously, common *types of legal liabilities* include

- *vicarious*, which refers to a *supervisor* or *principal's responsibility* for the acts of a *subordinate* or *agent*, respectively; this is most commonly seen in the liability almost any employer has for the professional misdeeds of employees regardless of whether or not they were known to or authorized by the employer
    - *some states*, but far from all, *have specifically abolished vicarious liability* in real estate transactions, especially broker liability for actions of their agents, noting that there is *"no imputation of knowledge" on the part of those parties not directly involved with the transaction*

IX. General: Practice of Real Estate (12 questions)
(8 Topic Areas; 24 Sub-Topics—each will be covered in its respective Topic Area)

- *joint*, which means **shared liability between two or more parties**
- *several*, which means a **liability of one party that can be legally pursued separately** from other liable parties

Most details about a broker's responsibility to supervise affiliated licensees, including providing them with office policies and training opportunities, are either state-specific or company-generated, so there is not much material available for general testing.

However, it is common for licensees to enter into an ***independent contractor arrangement*** with a ***principal broker***, or ***broker-in-charge***, or ***designated broker***, or ***broker-of-record***, or some other jurisdiction-specific term for the "boss" authorized to "employ" other licensees.

As independent contractors, licensees are responsible for sending in quarterly estimated taxes, paying self-employment taxes, and providing their own health insurance.

Federal requirements governing the relationship between a firm and its licensees are primarily seen in the IRS distinction of ***employee*** versus ***self-employed***, or ***independent contractor***, status for tax purposes. According to the government, a licensed real estate agent may be treated as self-employed if
- ***substantially all pay*** for services as a real estate agent ***is directly related to sales or other output rather than to hours worked***
- the services are performed under a written contract that provides ***the real estate agent will not be treated as an employee for federal tax purposes***

There are more extensive guidelines that clarify the distinction between an employee and an independent contractor. However, they generally point out that when acting as an independent contractor, a licensee does not receive health, vacation, sick-day, or other benefits from the agency.

Further, the licensee is allowed to work according to the licensee's own schedule and pay all self-employment, federal, and other taxes rather than having them withheld and processed by the agency.

Contractual agreements between a broker and a licensee are quite likely to require state-specific elements, such as making sure that a copy of the company's policy manual or other critical documents are included as part of the agreement. So, general questions on contract agreements are most likely to focus on the IRS distinctions given above.

It is important to note that in some states, ***brokers who establish independent contractor rather than employee relationships with affiliated licensees do NOT distance themselves against legal liability*** *for claims that may arise regarding licensee misdeeds.*

This distinction MAY be addressed as part of another question, such as the following:

<u>Question:</u> *Which of the following statements about the difference between a licensee who is an independent contractor rather than an employee is CORRECT?*

IX. General: Practice of Real Estate (12 questions)
(8 Topic Areas; 24 Sub-Topics—each will be covered in its respective Topic Area)

<u>*WRONG*</u>
Answer: A broker is not legally liable for the professional actions of a licensee who is an independent contractor but is for licensees who are employees.

This option would be wrong because it is not a uniformly correct statement nationwide.

*Neither is a requirement for a brokerage to carry **errors and omissions (E&O) insurance**, or require affiliated licensees to do so, though in some states it is a legislated requirement as a means of recovery if an important—and costly—transaction detail is overlooked.*

IX-E. Commission and Fees (Expect 1-2 questions from this area)

Commission and fees are common components of ***compensation agreements***, which are increasingly reflecting a host of creative compensation arrangements nationwide, even though the traditional commission percentage arrangement is still quite common.

Compensation agreements detail elements like a ***commission percentage*** rate, who is entitled to collect, ***commission-splitting*** arrangements for ***cooperating brokers***, as well as other compensation arrangements, such as a ***flat-fee for services*** rather than a commission, or ***reimbursements*** for certain marketing expenses.

However, ***compensation arrangements in a buyer agency agreement*** can be complicated by whether or not the buyer pays the agent directly for specific assistance in locating and securing a property or allows the agent to collect a listed property's commission split.

Plus there has been a recent rise in ***companies offering to help market property*** under some form of ***flat-fee for limited services***, often just signs, property information flyers, and a posting in a multiple listing service (MLS), rather than charging a conventional commission for conventional full-service marketing. Some such companies set charges based on a list of ***fees-for-services*** plus ***reimbursements*** for specified costs.

An ***important consideration*** in setting commissions and compensation arrangements has to do with ***maintaining open market competition*** rather than ***agreeing with competitors to standardize rates and fees***, so as noted elsewhere, they are ***established by negotiation*** between the ***principal and the agent***.

Standardized compensation arrangements invite scrutiny—and potential penalties—as violations of antitrust laws; this will receive elaboration in an upcoming Topic Area.

The following compensation arrangements also invite scrutiny for their basic ethical nature and legality under antitrust laws, especially when they are undisclosed
- ***referral fees***, which are fees earned by referring business to someone
- ***kickbacks***, which means the return of a portion of a payment received by a vendor to another individual involved in the vendor's getting some business, especially when it is part of a secret agreement.

IX. General: Practice of Real Estate   (12 questions)
(8 Topic Areas; 24 Sub-Topics—each will be covered in its respective Topic Area)

The best way to handle these situations is to avoid them. The next-best way to handle *any compensation payments to or from anyone*, be it a commission, referral fee, gift, bonus, *"finder's fee"* to unlicensed parties, or anything else of value, is to *get the written, informed consent of all parties* to the transaction, even if it is not a specific requirement in your state.

*This practice **may be a specific requirement in your state**, but if not, is a good safeguard against basic misunderstandings and financial disputes anywhere.*

Compensation disputes often arise in cases where a licensee introduces a party to a property and then that party either buys through another licensee or finds a way to deal directly with the owner.

These disputes are often legally resolved based on the application of the concept of **procuring cause**, which refers to determining if a licensee's efforts were instrumental in leading to the sale of real estate and is therefore generally entitled to a commission.

The traditional test for procuring cause, and arguable entitlement for an earned commission, is finding a buyer who is **ready, willing, and able to meet the seller's terms**.

In some states this is determined by who introduced the buyer to a property, regardless of who actually writes the offers and counteroffers for the buyer.

Also, in many states, finding a ready, willing, and able buyer who meets the seller's terms is all that is required for a licensee to be entitled to a commission.

*In those states, commonly referred to as **"procuring cause states,"** if the seller backs out of a contract, or refuses to accept an offer that meets the listing specifications, the licensee may be able to successfully sue for compensation.*

Further, many jurisdictions allow various forms of protection for licensees in the event a principal acts unethically by telling an interested buyer to wait until after the agency agreement period expires and then return as a "free" party to pursue the transaction without having to incur a sales commission.

*Commonly known as **broker protection clauses**, they may be written into agency employment contracts using language that reinforces the agent's right to collect a commission for particular sales that occur even after contract termination.*

They are generally market-area specific, and may include a definite post-contract time period during which a sale still entitles the original agent to compensation. Such protection clauses may also involve a "protected persons" list of those who were introduced to the property by the agent, so could entitle the agent to compensation if one of them purchases the property.

*Over twenty states also have **broker lien laws** that generally cover a commercial agent's right to put a lien on a property when the owner fails to pay rental commissions. **In some states, though, like Connecticut, the applicability of the law extends to all types of property transactions**.*

IX. General: Practice of Real Estate (12 questions)
(8 Topic Areas; 24 Sub-Topics—each will be covered in its respective Topic Area)

IX-F. General Ethics (Expect 1-3 questions from this area)

This Topic Area is most likely to contain scenario and/or application questions that refer to ethical choices based on material covered in other Topic Areas, most notably Section V, Laws of Agency as well as the other Topic Areas in this Section.

For example, the question posed in the Agency area regarding a couple asking for advice about how to take title could be written to fit in this Topic Area by having the licensee provide a definitive answer without recommending they confirm it with an attorney.

*The licensee's definitive response **exceeds the licensee's authority**, and represents both **unethical behavior** and the **illegal practice of law**. Further, the licensee may be subject to legal action later on if the buyers relied on the information and were damaged by it.*

Additional topic treatments that raise ethical issues could include situations illustrating self-dealing, conflicts of interest, net listings, nondisclosure of agency relationships, misrepresentation of material facts, antitrust arrangements, and kickbacks, among others.

Agency duties include recognizing circumstances under which licensees should ***refer parties to other professionals*** for advice that exceeds the ***limits of their professional competence or expertise*** and ***license authority***.

There are numerous examples in this area, such as referring parties to
- ***real estate lawyers*** for legal opinions on types of deeds or property restrictions
- ***accountants or tax attorneys*** for detailed financial and tax advice
- ***surveyors*** for property boundary and encroachment questions
- ***home inspectors*** for detailed property reports
- ***appraisers*** for property valuation
- ***other professionals*** as appropriate

For example, in most states, real estate sales contracts and many other transaction documents must be prepared by attorneys, and then simply used by licensees. In such states, preparing these documents may constitute grounds for ***practicing law without a license***.

*At least one state, Arizona, specifically authorizes licensees to draft sales contracts from scratch, so test questions on this are likely to specify that **it might be** beyond a licensee's authority or expertise to draft an especially complicated document.*

Remember, failure to recommend the appropriate professional could mislead and harm a party, who in turn could take legal action against the licensee.

In addition, the exam may ask identification and recognition questions on such matters as ***how to take title,*** or ***the use of preprinted forms,*** or ***the need to get the principals to initial any changes to contracts.***

Exam, and professional practice, note: *the exam may ask identification and recognition questions on the above matters, such as*

IX. General: Practice of Real Estate (12 questions)
(8 Topic Areas; 24 Sub-Topics—each will be covered in its respective Topic Area)

Question: M and K took title in such a way that (plug in some description of ownership here). Which of the following terms identifies this type of ownership?

Answer: The answer would simply be a matter of fact, not opinion, and be based on a term and its definition that would be supported by textbooks and legal dictionaries alike.

However, as a professional, it is important to protect yourself against giving advice that might present legal trouble, such as explaining different ways to hold title in a way that also sounds like a <u>recommendation</u> of how to take title.

Or sounding like the last word on a property's physical condition, or real estate tax matters, or anything else that, in short, exceeds the limits of your professional authority or expertise.

So, on the test, watch out for application-type questions, such as

Question: M and K are interested in taking title in such a way that (plug in some description of ownership here) and ask the licensee who is working as their agent which form of ownership they should use. Which of the following statements indicates the licensee's BEST response?

Answer: **For this question, the answer will probably identify the form that they have described, <u>but should include</u> a recommendation to seek an attorney's advice.**

If it does not, it leaves you, as a test-taker, with the incorrect impression that giving legal advice is just part of the real estate licensee's job. Such a question would itself be questionable, and quite remiss in its duties to both test and instruct.

In practice, be careful even if you have other professional credentials -- there's a difference between "speaking as an agent" and "speaking as an attorney."

Some *federal marketing controls* that serve as guidelines for ethical and legal behavior in the course of real estate transactions include such regulations as the following, most of which are of greater importance to experienced licensees and brokers than to entry-level licensees. These controls and regulations include
- ***Truth in Lending Act (TILA), Regulation Z***, which has to do with lending practices and advertising *(discussed above)*
- ***Equal Employment Opportunity Commission (EEOC)***, which is responsible for enforcing federal laws that make it illegal to discriminate against a job applicant or an employee because of the person's race, color, religion, sex (including pregnancy), national origin, age (40 or older), disability or genetic information
  - *it is also illegal to discriminate against a person because the person complained about discrimination, filed a charge of discrimination, or participated in an employment discrimination investigation or lawsuit*
  - *most employers with at least 15 employees are subject to EEOC requirements, for age discrimination cases it is 20 or more employees*

IX. General: Practice of Real Estate (12 questions)
(8 Topic Areas; 24 Sub-Topics—each will be covered in its respective Topic Area)

- *Uniform Commercial Code (UCC)*, which is a "uniform act," or proposed set of laws, that most states have adopted to govern commercial transactions of moveable, personal property, *including secured transactions*, such as ones in which a fixture, like a new heat pump, is purchased under a financing agreement and may be considered personal, 'detachable' property under a *security agreement* and/or *financing statement* until it is paid off
    - the *Bulk Sales Act* is Article VI of the Code, and covers *the transfer of inventory in order to avoid fraudulent conveyances designed to defraud creditors*;
        - the UCC is most applicable for licensees that go into commercial real estate and need to know more about their clients' business environment; any test questions on the Code or its Bulk Sales Act are most likely to be marked for broker-exams only
- *Interstate Land Sales Full Disclosure Act*, which *requires land developers to register certain large subdivisions with HUD and provide each purchaser with a disclosure document called a Property Report* before the signing of the contract or agreement; some states have their own adaptation of the federal Act
- the *Securities and Exchange Commission (SEC)* establishes *federal securities regulations*, some of which *apply to real estate investments that can be categorized as a security*, such as some limited partnerships in real estate; *selling such securities requires a securities license*
    - state legislation governing securities transactions are known as *"Blue Sky Laws"*
- the *Telephone Consumer Protection Act of 1991 (TCPA)* and subsequent laws regulate telemarketing activities. Provisions include, among other measures, *restricting the hours for calling (between 8 a.m. and 9 p.m. local time), maintaining a free "do-not-call list"* for those who ask to be on it (*it takes 31 days after registering* before complaints can be brought), and *prohibiting recorded messages*, *fax solicitations*, and *automated dialing*, or *"robocalls."*
    - The *Do Not Call Registry* is *managed by the Federal Trade Commission (FTC) and enforced by the Federal Communications Commission (FCC) and state-level agencies*; for more information and how to ensure your own real estate telemarketing conforms with the law (violations begin at $500-1,500/illegal call), see www.donotcall.gov

IX-G. Issues in Use of Technology (Electronic Signatures, Document Delivery, Internet Advertising) (Expect 0-1 question from this area)

Although technology is clearly driving and changing the way many real-estate-related tasks get done, the prelicensing exam is not the place to test a candidate's knowledge, skills, or abilities with software, Web platforms, or productivity gizmos.

Yet as both clients and companies become more tech-dependent in the performance of basic real estate functions, the exam has to remain open to including future basics once they uniformly affect entry-level licensees nationwide, especially with Web-based applications. This already includes such functions as marketing, researching property information, correspondence and contracts, and electronic filing of deeds and other land records.

Right now, *technology is most visibly applicable* to daily entry-level activities in the federal law that asserts legal status for properly sent and received *electronic documents*.

As noted earlier, a relatively recent federal Act has made certain electronic transmissions legally valid substitutes for hand-written signatures and hard-copy transaction documents. *The Electronic*

IX. General: Practice of Real Estate (12 questions)
(8 Topic Areas; 24 Sub-Topics—each will be covered in its respective Topic Area)

Signatures in Global and National Commerce Act (ESIGN) (2000) defines and covers the legal force of electronic signatures in *interstate and international commerce*.

> *ESIGN states that* in interstate and foreign commerce, signatures, contracts, and other *transaction documents "may not be denied legal effect, validity, or enforceability solely because [they are] in an electronic form."* It also provides for electronic storage and retention of these records.
>
> *Increasingly, states are conforming with ESIGN standards by noting that the required records may be retained in any format, electronic or otherwise, capable of producing an accurate copy in paper format of the original document. (Connecticut did this in 2002; see the State Exam, Section IV-G.)*
>
> *According to ESIGN, "electronic record" means a contract or other record created, generated, sent, communicated, received or stored by electronic means.*
>
>> Some states have specifically identified these records to include *faxes*, *email*, *telexes*, and *Internet messages (IMs)*. Even though these are not specifically named in the federal law, they are each reasonably understood to be a type of "electronic record," so may appear in a question about the legality of relying on particular documents.

Further, there are numerous states that have enacted regulations governing advertising and marketing via Web postings for real estate listings and services, typically that the firm identify itself on every page as well as update information at specific intervals.

And, with the emergence of the many, many business and personal uses for social media on the Internet, there are additional concerns regarding both firm and individual liability for licensee blogs, postings, videos, and other Internet exchanges. You may see these addressed in Policy Manuals of real estate firms, and hear of new regulations and court cases for years!

IX-H. Antitrust Laws (Expect 1-2 questions from this area)

Compensation arrangements and marketing practices are governed by federal and state *antitrust laws*. Federal antitrust law is grounded in the Sherman Antitrust Act (1890) and the Clayton Antitrust Act (1914), commonly referred to as the *Sherman Antitrust Act*, or just *antitrust law*.

The primary purpose of antitrust law is to outlaw illegal monopolies, or monopolies that could be shown to be using their power to squelch competition; its primary lasting effect has been to stimulate open competition through regulating business practices that attempt to monopolize the market. The key terms that arise in antitrust considerations include

- *monopoly*, which means that one firm or person is the only player in a particular business
- *price-fixing*, which means that selected competitors agreeing to standardize prices as a way to reduce or remove additional competition by restricting the prices available for the consumer
- *market allocation*, which occurs when competitors agree to parcel up market areas and only do business in their designated area, leaving it free from competition in exchange for not encroaching on the competitor's 'protected' zone

IX. General: Practice of Real Estate (12 questions)
(8 Topic Areas; 24 Sub-Topics—each will be covered in its respective Topic Area)

- ***boycotting***, which occurs when a group of competitors band together to refuse to either do business with or recommend the services of a particular company
- ***tie-in agreement***, or ***tying arrangement***, which refers to the practice of requiring a party to use a particular service or vendor, such as a lender requiring a borrower to hire a particular home inspector or closing attorney

Antitrust laws regarding price-fixing make it ***illegal for competing real estate companies to standardize commission rates*** or brokerage compensation arrangements. Rather, as noted above, ***they are established by negotiation between the principal and the agent***.

It is worth noting here that there are significant court precedents nationally that have upheld verdicts against licensees for antitrust violations in their business conduct.

Some cases are based in situations where "the word was out" about the "local" commission rate, i.e., price-fixing, but no formal "agreement" among the competing agencies which uniformly adopted the same rate was found.

Penalties have included felony convictions and significant damage awards.

The following compensation arrangements also invite scrutiny for their basic ethical nature and legality under antitrust laws, especially when they are undisclosed
- ***referral fees***, which are fees earned by referring business to someone, and may be seen as a violation of antitrust laws if they are related to a tie-in agreement
- ***kickbacks***, which means the return of a portion of a payment received by a vendor to another individual involved in the vendor's getting some business, especially when it is part of a secret agreement. Like a referral fee, it may be a violation of antitrust laws if it is part of a tie-in agreement.

This ends the presentation of key terms and concepts likely to be either tested or used as distractors in this Content Outline Section.

X. General: Real Estate Calculations (7 questions)
(6 Topic Areas; 22 Sub-Topics—each will be covered in its respective Topic Area)

General comments about this Section, and about real estate Math

There are six Topic Areas specifically labeled in the PSI Content Outline Real Estate Calculations Section; there are seven test questions from the entire Section.

Hmmm ... simple math tells us that asking seven questions from six Topic Areas means that only about nine percent (8.75% to be precise) of your total test score rides on doing math.

Further, if every Topic Area gets one question, only one Topic Area is likely to get even two questions on the test.

So, relax, and do NOT let the list of math topics make you think there is too much math to master – though you should know everything, you do not need to in order to pass!

Most of the seven math questions on the test will not be particularly complicated. Those that are simply require you to take a deep breath and think a little harder.

Also, in most cases the questions will include all the numbers, conditions, and other information necessary to perform the math, as well as all conditions of who pays for what and whether prorations are based on 30-day versus 31-day months and 360-day versus 365-day years.

As for individual questions, the chances are good that you will be able to at least rule out a few of the answer choices and then be able to make a better-odds guess at whatever's left.

Special Note: PSI's math questions typically use "none of the above" as the fourth option.

*This means **you MUST be confident** in the answer you arrive at through your computations, since **the correct answer MAY NOT be among those given** and your answer may be based on a commonly made math error.*

So be careful and double-check your work for the greatest confidence in your conclusions.

For those of you with math anxiety, one strategy for tackling them is to mark them on the testing device with the colored "Mark" key as soon as they appear, then move on immediately to the next non-math question.

After answering all of the <u>non-math</u> questions, you can then return to <u>JUST</u> the "marked" questions and work them as a group, doing the ones that look easiest first.

The six topics presented in this outline section are bulleted below with a brief, "textbook-reminder" definition. If you need a more detailed explanation to perform a particular type of math computation, refer to the applicable pages in the math chapter of a full-blown textbook.

All of the math questions will be about items a licensee *might reasonably need to compute in order to <u>provide, confirm, correct, or explain</u>* figures in the course of a real estate transaction.

X. General: Real Estate Calculations (7 questions)
(6 Topic Areas; 22 Sub-Topics—each will be covered in its respective Topic Area)

The questions cover issues commonly applied to determining property valuation, buyer financing options, seller proceeds, typical settlement expenses, rental properties, and real estate investment concerns, including depreciation.

These include, at a minimum, the following elements related to property value
- *making adjustments* to a comparable property's sales price
- *determining the price of a subject property* from data on comparables
- *computing replacement or reproduction cost* given the necessary basic price information
- *determining property value* from data related to one of the three approaches to value

Plus, regarding buyer financing, common settlement expenses, and seller proceeds, questions may reasonably address issues such as
- *principal, interest, tax, and insurance (PITI)* totals and sub-parts for impound accounts
- *property taxes*, prorations and determination from assessed value and mill rate
- *property insurance premiums* and prorated portions
- *mortgage insurance premiums (MIP)*
- *title insurance premiums*
- *prorations of prepaid expenses*
- *mortgage interest payments* and *principal balance* at a specified time
- *proration of rents* at closing
- *special assessment charges*
- *brokerage fees*
- *property sales price determinations* from a variable, such as taxes due, commission paid, or a LTV percentage and loan amount
- *buyer's total cost of purchase*
- *seller's net after sale*

Topic Areas A through F will each have 0-2 questions on the exam.

A. General Math Concepts
Grade-School Math and Percentages
Percentage computations are commonly used in determining proportions of ownership interest, land or building lot useable area, commission splits, taxes, prorations, points, interest rates, and other relatively straightforward addition, subtraction, multiplication, and division problems.

Areas, including Acreage
Area computations are most likely to concentrate on determining property square footage *(remember, use the outside dimensions)*, lot sizes, and acreage (43,560 square feet/acre).

B. Property Tax Calculations (not Prorations)
Taxes
Property taxes are common in every town, city, and county nationwide, though the method of computing and collecting them are not.

X. General: Real Estate Calculations (7 questions)
(6 Topic Areas; 22 Sub-Topics—each will be covered in its respective Topic Area)

Of all of the Topic Areas in this section, taxation is the most likely to have at least one, if not two, questions, so here's a quick look at basic tax terminology and amounts.

You may find that the question(s) present conditions that do not apply in your state, such as referring to an annual bill while yours is billed semi-annually.

Remember, while taking the test you are in "the testing state," not your home state, and all the clues you need should be clearly presented in the question.

Tax rates are commonly expressed as a **mill rate**, or **millage rate**, or **mills**, which translates into **one mill = 1/1,000 of a dollar**, or **1/10 of one cent (.1¢)**.

The tax bill will multiply the mill rate by the assessed value to arrive at the annual taxes due, regardless of whether or not they are paid in installments.

For example, a property assessed at $85,500 in a town with a mill rate of 34.5 will have an annual tax liability of: $85,500 multiplied by 34.5 divided by 1,000, which equals an annual tax of $2,949.75.

A quick way to translate the "one mill = 1,000th of a dollar" is to just change the comma at the thousand-dollar point in the property's assessed value to a decimal point and multiply that number by the mill rate. So, in the example above, it could be computed as $85.50 times 34.5 equals $2,949.75.

Practical AND testing note: *some state taxation systems vary in their use of terms and applications of the basic, common process illustrated above.*

For example, at least one state begins with a property's "fair market value" for taxes, or "tax appraised value," which corresponds to most jurisdictions' "assessed value." This amount is then multiplied by a "tax assessment ratio" of 4% for an owner-occupied primary residence (there are other rates and rules, but they are of no importance here) to arrive at the property's "assessed value." This value, which is MUCH lower than in other states, is multiplied by a mill rate that is MUCH higher.

So, an owner-occupied property with a "tax appraised value" of $200,000 will have an "assessed" value of $8,000, and may have a mill rate for that year of 375. Its tax bill would be $3,000.

For testing purposes, do NOT make any such state-specific adjustments to the basics of assessed value and millage rates provided in a question! If you do, you will NOT find the answer that will get you credit among the choices given, including "none of the above"!

C. Lending Calculations
Loan-to-Value Ratios
As noted in Section IV-A, loan-to-value (LTV, or L/V) ratios are simply that: the loan amount divided by the value of the property.

X. General: Real Estate Calculations (7 questions)
(6 Topic Areas; 22 Sub-Topics—each will be covered in its respective Topic Area)

LTV ratios divide loan amounts by *the lesser of the appraised value or sales price*, so be careful to avoid using list prices, high sales prices, or other large amounts that might be included in the question's details as an alternative property values.

For example, a property listed for $327,000, appraised at $315,000 and sold for $310,000. If the LTV is 80, the loan amount would of $248,000.

Discount Points
As noted in Section IV-A, a "point" is one percent of the face value of a loan amount.

Questions about points are most likely to present transaction information and ask either the amount that will be charged for a certain number of points, or what the loan amount is based on a total dollar amount charged for a certain number of points.

Equity
As noted in Section IV-A, equity is the amount of principal a property owner has in a property after deducting liens and claims against it.

Questions about equity are most likely to include elements such as loan amounts, other property indebtedness, appraised value, and list and/or sales prices, and then ask for the owner's equity.

Pre-sale equity is determined using appraised value. Equity calculations based on sales price may vary somewhat if the sales price is close to the appraised value, though a sales price that is much lower than appraised value due to a foreclosure, family member, or estate sale does not present an accurate valuation of the equity.

Also, the proceeds to the seller are not the same as equity, since proceeds are what is left after transaction expenses, such as brokerage fees and prorations, are deducted from the equity a seller manages to get out of a property.

Qualifying Buyers
These questions will provide variables such as buyer income, savings, and other resources and then ask how much a buyer can afford to either borrow or pay per month for a mortgage.

The critical elements needed to compute these amounts will be provided, so read any question on qualifying buyers carefully to make sure you *use only* the applicable factors when computing the *maximum loan amount or monthly payment* a buyer can afford.

D. Calculations for Transactions
Prorations
Prorations are *proportionate amounts*, or *apportionments*, of any shared expense, and can either be a credit or a debit to either party. Common shared expenses include taxes, sewer, special assessments, and unused fuel, such as heating oil or bottled gas.

For example, if a sale includes the buyer reimbursing the seller for 350 gallons of heating oil remaining from the seller's recent purchase of 500 gallons, the proration would involve

X. General: Real Estate Calculations   (7 questions)
(6 Topic Areas; 22 Sub-Topics—each will be covered in its respective Topic Area)

determining the price per gallon based on the seller's bill for the 500 gallons then multiplying that amount by 350.

In most cases, the questions will include all the numbers and information necessary to the math, as well as ***all*** conditions of who pays for what and whether prorations are based on 30-day versus 31-day months and 360-day versus 365-day years.

Commissions and Commission Splits

These questions will be among the easiest, and are good candidates for a "none of the above" answer.

But the compensation arrangements will be carefully spelled out. Just remember that commission percentages are based on sales price, not on appraised value, loan amount, or seller's net proceeds, and that these three values are commonly used to compute attractive distractors.

One twist on commissions may be to determine sales price based on what the licensee received for a commission. Should you see one of these, simply work backwards, dividing the licensee's compensation amount by the prorated commission percentage the licensee receives.

For example, if a licensee earns $18,000 on a 30% share in a 6% brokerage commission, the licensee's $18,000 is 1.8% of the sales price, or $18,000/.018 = $1,000,000.

Seller's Proceeds of Sale

Sale proceeds are the heart and soul of a real estate transaction, so expect to see at least one question that includes a variety of transaction details, then asks "How much did the seller make on this sale?"

These questions may require you to make several calculations from other areas and combine them to get the "bottom line" for the seller, or a prorated amount for a party with a specified interest in the sale.

For example, three heirs to a property may have a 50 percent, 25 percent, and 25 percent interest, respectively, and the question may ask how much the first heir will receive from the sale proceeds

Total Money Needed by Buyer at Closing

How much money the buyer pays for the property as well as all buyer-paid financing and closing costs is crucial to a successful closing. So expect to see at least one question that lists a lot of expenses and prorations, then asks "How much did the buyer need to close?"

Transfer Tax/Conveyance Tax/Revenue Stamps

Taxes paid on property sales vary from place to place, as do what the taxes are called.

Questions on these taxes will include all necessary variables. As noted in the Topic Area on taxes above, you are in the "testing state," not your home state, so answer the question based solely on the information, and names, provided.

X. General: Real Estate Calculations (7 questions)
(6 Topic Areas; 22 Sub-Topics—each will be covered in its respective Topic Area)

E. Calculations for Valuation

Comparative Market Analysis (CMA)

As noted in Topic Area III-C, CMAs are similar to appraisals, but with a lot of shortcuts.

Questions on this topic will use a licensee's preparation of a CMA as a way of applying the principles of the appraisal process either to specific elements of a property's value or to determining a recommended listing price.

A common source of questions in this area is adjusting the value of comparable properties to arrive at the value of a subject property – remember to add and/or subtract the value of a comparable property's differences to the comparable's sales price, not to the subject property.

Other appraisal principles tested here may include determining (1) the cost of an improvement, such as replacement carpeting or paint, (2) an outbuilding's value based on per-square-foot replacement cost, and (3) a recommended listing price after reviewing details of several comparable property sales.

Net Operating Income

This topic will most likely include questions on rents, expenses, and investment returns associated with both residential and commercial properties; these questions will provide all of the details you need to answer them.

The question you may see will probably focus on a common income property issue like (1) *gross rental revenue*, (2) property manager or licensee's *compensation*, (3) owner or investor's *return on investment*, or (4) *rental rates based on factors such as square footage and type of lease*.

Other questions that might appear in this Topic Area could present information related to determining such matters as *occupancy rates, gross income determinations, property manager's income, property capitalization rate, owner's taxable income, general budget review, or net operating income (NOI).*

The following *three categories of income* are important to remember for rentals and other investment properties. *The last of these is the one to use for computing cap rates.*
- *potential gross income*, or *projected gross income*, or *scheduled gross income*, which means the *maximum rental income* at 100 percent occupancy
- *effective gross income*, which means the *actual income* after subtracting vacancies and rent collection losses
- *net operating income (NOI)*, which is *what's left of the effective gross income after subtracting all of the property's operating expenses*, such as maintenance, taxes, insurance, reserves for replacements, and other recurring expenses (but not debt service, such as mortgage interest)

Depreciation

This topic will most likely include questions based on a set of property depreciation variables given in the question.

X. General: Real Estate Calculations   (7 questions)
(6 Topic Areas; 22 Sub-Topics—each will be covered in its respective Topic Area)

Any depreciation computation will most likely be a component of a CMA/appraisal question, asking you something like, "If property values in a particular subdivision have been declining by an average of 4.9 percent annually, how much should a licensee preparing a CMA depreciate a comparable property sale that is eight months' old?"

Capitalization Rate

As noted earlier, to **compute the capitalization rate** for a particular property, simply **divide the property's net operating income by its price**.
- For example, a $200,000 property that has a $20,000/year net operating income has a capitalization rate of 10 percent.

To **estimate a property value from a cap rate**, analyze several recent comparable sales to determine their cap rates, develop an appropriate composite cap rate for the subject property, then **divide the subject property's NOI by the cap rate**.
- For example, if an area's market currently supports a cap rate of 5 percent and the NOI for a property is $10,000, the estimated property value would be $200,000.

Gross Rent and Gross Income Multipliers (GIM, GRM)

Another income approach method of estimating value is the *gross rent multiplier (GRM)*, or *gross income multiplier (GIM)* method.

Using recent sales, **divide each comparable property's sales price by its gross income, either monthly or annual**, using the same time-period standard (monthly/annual) for all, to determine their respective GRMs.

Then, after developing a representative GRM from a reconciliation of the collective GRMs, **multiply the subject property's income by the GRM** to arrive at a general estimate of value.
- For example, if there is a GRM of 135 for monthly rents in an area, and a property has a monthly rent of $1,200, the property's value would be expected to be around $162,000.

F. Mortgage Calculations
Down Payment/Amount to be Financed – Amortization – Interest Rates – Interest Amounts – Monthly Installment Payments

This area commonly focuses on total payment amounts as well as individual components. Questions will provide the necessary variables for calculating such amounts as
- *principal portion* of a monthly payment
- *interest portion* of a monthly payment
- *total monthly payment* given a particular interest rate and annual charges for taxes and property insurance *(PITI – principal, interest, taxes, and insurance)*
- *reserve, or impound, or escrow amounts* held by a lender based on the variables presented, such as a particular percentage of annual taxes and property insurance
- *mortgage insurance premiums (MIP)* charged for loans with an LTV over 80%
- *remaining principal* given the interest rate, term period, and number of payments already made

X. General: Real Estate Calculations (7 questions)
(6 Topic Areas; 22 Sub-Topics—each will be covered in its respective Topic Area)

Refer to your primary text for explanations of how to perform these mortgage calculations, and remember that you may not even get a single question from this area.

Finally, remember these points as you go into the test

- *If you miss <u>all and only</u> the math questions, you would score 91% on the test*
- *If you miss <u>all and only</u> the math questions, you would still be at least 15 points above the pass/fail line*
- *It is highly unlikely that you will get more than two questions from any Topic Area*
- *It is highly likely that you will get NO questions from one or more Topic Areas*
- *Most of the seven math questions on the test are not particularly complicated*
- *Those that are simply require you to take a deep breath and think a little harder*
- *Expect the questions themselves to provide all the numbers and information necessary to do the math*
- *You should be able to at least rule out a few of the answer choices and then be able to make a better-odds guess at whatever's left*
- *"Mark" any question you need to spend time on, then come back to it*
- *Leave no question unanswered: pure guessing gives you 1 out of 4 odds*

This ends the presentation of key terms and concepts likely to be either tested or used as distractors in this Content Outline Section.

XI. General: Specialty Areas (4 questions)
(4 Topic Areas; 0 Sub-Topics)

XI-A. Property Management and Landlord/Tenant (Expect 0-2 questions from this area)

General note on this entire Section, XI-Specialty Areas

For test preparation purposes, you can probably stop reading this book right here and still know more than enough to pass the test handily. After all, the Topic Areas presented here from Section XI only get four questions on the test.

But as a real estate professional, you would be well advised to read on, since the topics presented here are "part of the territory."

Besides, if you do read on, it will bring together a host of issues and topics from your main textbook in a concise way, which will certainly give you a few more correct answers on the test, as well as in your first real estate job!

Plus, for those who rent, or want to own rental properties, the following four pages could be of great personal value. For the rest of you, the types of leasehold estates, leases, lease provisions, and trade fixtures could actually be tallied for testing in Section I-Property Ownership.

And despite the low test emphasis on the following topics, they are nevertheless important in their own right. So here goes . . .

Property management topics begin here with a look at types of leasehold estates.

*Note for the following description of **types of leasehold estates**: these names appear in textbooks using the terms "estate" and "tenancy" interchangeably, as in "estate for years" and "tenancy for years," the convention here, as in both common practice and test questions, will be to use "tenancy."*

Common types of leasehold estates include
- *tenancy for years*, which means that there is **a definite termination date. Vacation rentals** as well as **commercial leases** are often written this way, and may run for whatever time period suits both parties, such as Memorial Day through Labor Day for the former, or a few days for storage to many years for an industrial site for the latter. An important characteristic of these leases is that **no notice is required for termination**, at which time the old tenant simply has to be out to make way for whatever new use or tenants the landlord has for the property. However, some contracts may have **an option to renew with a deadline for exercising that option**.
- *tenancy from period to period*, or *periodic tenancy*, which means there is **no definite termination date, just recurring time periods (e.g., year-to-year or month-to-month)** during which one party or the other may exercise an option to terminate it. This is a **common tenancy arrangement in residential leases,** which may include an automatic renewal, or 'evergreen' clause, that allows the lease to automatically renew for the same period and general terms unless one of the parties cancels the renewal by providing proper notice to terminate.
- *tenancy at will*, which is **similar to a tenancy from period to period except that there is no specified periodic nature** to it – it is simply at the will and discretion of the landlord and

XI. General: Specialty Areas (4 questions)
(4 Topic Areas; 0 Sub-Topics)

may be terminated at almost any time by either party. These situations may include an owner letting a tenant remain in a property being taken by eminent domain right up to the last minute, or tenants being given the option to move out whenever a job transfer or alternate housing situation arises.
- *tenancy at sufferance*, which means that a tenant has *refused to vacate* at the end of a tenancy for years or periodic tenancy and *remains in possession of the property against the will of the landlord*. Generally, a landlord will not accept or cash rent checks to avoid appearing to approve the tenant's continuation.
    - *holdover tenant* is the term used to describe a tenant who remains against the landlord's will in a tenancy at sufferance.

The names of various *common lease types* suggest the financial structure of the revenues, or *method of payment*. Some of these include
- *gross lease*, or *straight lease*, which means the *tenant pays a flat fee out of which the owner pays all standard property expenses*, such as taxes, association fees, and, in some cases, utilities. *Most residential leases are gross leases*.
- *net lease*, under which the *tenant pays a base rent and some or all of the property expenses*, beginning with utilities, taxes, and special assessments; *some appraisal authorities consider this term synonymous with net-net and net-net-net leases*
    - *net-net leases* are negotiated to require additional tenant obligations, typically insurance – these are not very common in current practice
    - *net-net-net leases*, or *triple-net leases*, are generally negotiated to make the *tenant responsible for paying all expenses*, including maintenance, repairs, and in some cases, the owner's mortgage interest
    - *absolute net lease*, cover extensive expenses according to contract negotiations, as well as typically making the tenant responsible for structural maintenance
- *full-service lease* is a lease in which *the landlord agrees to pay all maintenance, property taxes, and insurance*
- *percentage leases* have a *fixed base rental fee plus a percentage of the gross or net income in excess of a predetermined minimum sales volume*; these are *common in retail properties*
- *graduated leases*, which establish a *schedule for rent increases, generally based on a business tenant's anticipated growth* of gross or net income
- *index leases* are *similar to graduated leases, but the rental amounts may go up or down, generally in reference to the consumer price index* or the *cost-of-living index*
- *lease purchase*, which is *typically a rent-to-own arrangement* where an agreed-upon portion of the rent is applied toward the purchase price and either when the tenant can arrange other financing or when the full price is paid, ownership transfers
- *lease-option*, or *lease with an option to buy*, is a mixture of a lease and a purchase contract, but begins as *a lease with a clause allowing the tenant to exercise an option to purchase the property*

Some other types of leases refer to the *property type* rather than payment type. Examples of these include
- *ground lease*, or *land lease*, generally is *a long-term commercial or industrial lease of land only, with the tenant typically erecting a building* that reverts to the landowner at the end of

XI. General: Specialty Areas (4 questions)
(4 Topic Areas; 0 Sub-Topics)

the rental period, which may be as long as 99 years. ***Ground leases are commonly structured and paid as some form of net lease***.

- *oil-and-gas lease*, which grants the right to extract oil and gas from a specified property, usually in exchange for ***an up-front fee and royalties*** from any oil or gas produced

Common *lease provisions and clauses* include

- *covenant of quiet enjoyment*, which entitles the tenant to ***undisturbed possession and use of the property***. Most leases qualify this right to allow the landlord to enter the premises periodically during business hours for maintenance and inspections, as well as for emergencies.
- *term of lease provision*, which generally ***gives the start and end dates, may also, in the case of a periodic residential lease, include an automatic renewal provision***, or *evergreen clause*, which extends the lease unless one of the parties specifically terminates it according to the process indicated in the provision
- *escalator clause*, or *escalation clause*, or *step-up clause*, which ***specifies the terms and conditions of rent increases***; they are central to graduated leases, though they can be found in any lease
- *right of first refusal* clause may be included in a lease when the tenant wants the opportunity to purchase the property in the event the owner decides to sell; ***it gives the tenant the right to review any sales offer the owner receives and either match it or else let the owner proceed with a sale to a different party***
- *subletting*, or *subleasing*, which refers to a ***tenant leasing the property to someone else***. When not prohibited, ***the original tenant remains primarily liable to the landlord for rents and property condition***.
- *assignment* refers to a tenant ***transferring the lease and some or all of its liability to another person***. In some cases, the landlord or the lease will allow the complete substitution of the original tenant by the new tenant regarding lease responsibilities and let the new tenant assume sole, primary responsibility for the rest of the lease period.

Owned and leased inclusions represent an especially important provision in commercial leases to ensure clear mutual understandings about whether ***tenant improvements*** are owner or tenant owned and/or reimbursable.

Fixtures, mentioned in Section I, are of special importance in leased property. Generally, anything a residential tenant ***attaches*** to a rental unit in a permanent manner can be argued as becoming real property and thus must be left in the unit at the end of the lease period.

Separation and removal, regardless of whether it is approved by both parties, is known as ***severance*** and ***turns whatever was severed from the real property into personal property***.

Trade fixtures are more commonly understood to remain the tenant's property, though all tenant-provided ***improvements***, both residential and commercial, should be spelled out as ***owned or leased inclusions*** to avoid confusion.

Reversionary rights in property management generally refer to ***the reinstatement of the owner's full ownership and possession rights at the end of the lease period***

XI. General: Specialty Areas (4 questions)
(4 Topic Areas; 0 Sub-Topics)

The term for the *transfer of ownership of improvements* is *accession*, and is often part of an owner's *reversionary right*.

This is of particular importance in many long-term commercial and industrial leases, since lease terms often make tenant improvements, including buildings and facilities, the landowner's property at the end of the term.

Abandonment refers to a tenant's *vacating a rental property prior to the end of the lease term and defaulting on the rent*. A few terms related to the property of a tenant in default is
- *distrain*, *distraint*, or *distress*, which refer to the right of a landlord, generally after a court order, to seize a tenant's personal property for rent in arrears

*Some states have specific time periods and legal language to clarify what constitutes **legal abandonment** and a landlord's rights to enter and regain possession of the property, as well as the tenant's continued financial liability. Where applicable, these may be part of the state-specific portion of the test.*

Evictions may be *initiated by either the landlord or the tenant*. Although they are handled according to state-specific procedures, they are commonly referred to by the same terms
- *actual eviction* is the *landlord's recourse* when a tenant has breached the lease, such as nonpayment of rent or exceeding the occupancy limit. This is typically effected by the landlord's bringing a *suit for possession* in court; *the legal details and timing vary from place to place.*
- *constructive eviction* is the *tenant's recourse* when the landlord has breached the lease by *letting the property become uninhabitable through conscious neglect*. This kind of neglect on the part of the landlord *relieves the tenant from the obligation to pay rent*. Again, though, the *details of the process may vary from place to place*.

A *property management contract* defines the relationship between a property manager and an owner. Through the contract, the owner typically authorizes the *property manager to act as a general agent*, able to make a wide range of binding decisions in the course of managing the property. These activities include, but are not limited to, the authority to
- *select tenants*
- *prepare and sign leases*
- *collect and deposit rents*
- *hire and pay employees*
- *contract* with maintenance and repair contractors
- *make risk management decisions*, such as selecting insurance coverages
- *prepare operating budgets*
- *determine gross effective income*
- *maintain office accounts*
- *monitor and pay fixed operating expenses* such as salaries and taxes
- *establish a reserve account* for variable expenses, such as repairs and supplies

The property management agreement itself generally includes the following *key elements*
- *property description*

XI. General: Specialty Areas (4 questions)
(4 Topic Areas; 0 Sub-Topics)

- *contract period and termination provisions*
- *property management's duties, scope of authority, and limitations*
- *statement of the owner's purpose or objective*, such as maximizing income or increasing property value: *trying to achieve the owner's objective is generally considered to be the primary duty of a property manager*
- *statement of the owner's obligations and duties*
- *frequency and types of reporting to the owner*
- *management compensation arrangements*, which are generally based on a percentage of gross income. However, rates for property management services *are established by negotiation between the principal and the property manager*

Rental related discriminatory laws include many federal laws presented above for property sales, but with direct application to property management processes and particulars.

Special Note: much of the following, especially the federal laws, is adapted from previous material to reinforce their direct application to property management processes and particulars.

In the course of renting properties, the landlord or owner has to pay attention to many of the same *federal Fair Housing, lending, and credit laws* that govern property sales, plus some *handicapped access requirements* and *property condition disclosures*.

Federal Fair Housing laws provide *protection against discrimination in the <u>rental</u>, or <u>advertising</u> of residential property* for *protected classes* based on the same personal characteristics identified in Topic Area V-A regarding property sales.

Protected classes under Fair Housing laws include *race or color, national origin, religious preference, sex, handicapping conditions,* and/or *familial status*.

As a reminder here, the particulars of handicapping conditions and familial status will be repeated to both reinforce their details and save you from having to flip back to IX-B.

- *handicapping condition*, which means having a physical or mental disability, including infection with the HIV virus or recovery status for drug and alcohol dependence, that substantially limits one or more major life activity
- *familial status*, which means *one or more individuals under 18 years of age being domiciled* with a parent or custodian, or the legal designee of the parents, and also *applies to any person who is pregnant* or in the process of securing legal custody of any individual under 18 years old
  - *an age exemption* to familial status protection for multi-unit properties *may apply* to housing that is
    - intended for and *solely occupied by* persons *62 years of age or older*
    - intended primarily for *"55 and over,"* meaning *80 percent or more of the units* are occupied by *at least one occupant 55 years of age or older*

Important Fair Housing reminder for property management: In residential property rentals covered by Fair Housing requirements, a *landlord must allow a handicapped tenant to make*

XI. General: Specialty Areas (4 questions)
(4 Topic Areas; 0 Sub-Topics)

reasonable modifications to a unit *at the tenant's own expense*, typically **with the obligation to return the unit to its previous condition when moving out.**

Special clarification/reminder: This requirement is **based on Fair Housing laws, NOT the Americans With Disabilities Act (ADA)** requirements, which apply to **public accessibility**.

Also, just as in property sales, licensees and unlicensed property managers alike must avoid the following ***discriminatory practices in marketing and tenant selection*** that are ***violations of Fair Housing laws***

- *steering*, which means showing prospective renters of a particular protected class properties only in areas that have a high representation of the same protected class
- *blockbusting*, which means 'spreading the word' that the neighborhood may be about to decline in safety and quality of life factors due to an increased presence in the area of a particular protected class, so ***tenants should consider relocating***

Equal Credit Opportunities Act (ECOA), which applies when a property manager is reviewing an applicant's credit and employment history – *the property manager is required to ignore the following factors about an applicant when reviewing a credit application*
- *race or color*
- *religion or national origin*
- *sex or marital status*
- *age (over the age of majority)*
- *receipt of income from public assistance programs, such as food stamps*

Lead-Based Paint Hazard Reduction Act, which applies to both the sale and rental of ***residential properties built before 1978***, and requires landlords to provide tenants of units covered by the Act as well as all rental applicants with a ***standard disclosure pamphlet*** and also ***to attach a disclosure form to new leases, unless the disclosure information is included in the text of the lease***

NOTE: Connecticut adapted a model 1972 federal law known as the ***Uniform Residential Landlord and Tenant Act*** and now we have ***Title 47a, Landlord and Tenant***, which covers many of the matters in this Roman Numeral Content Outline Area. It is the subject of the State Outline Topic Area IV-B, so expect to see questions about it on the state-specific exam.

XI-B. Common Interest Ownership Properties (Expect 0-2 questions from this area)

Common interest ownership is a type of ownership that refers to multiple owners having an overlapping, inseparable interest in a property complex; ***condominiums***, ***townhouses***, ***coops***, and ***timeshares*** are the most common examples, and were discussed in Section I-B.

However, one type of common interest ownership was not presented there, yet is important to municipal plans and may earn a test question: Planned Unit Developments (PUDs).

A ***Planned Unit Development (PUD)*** is a specialized category of subdivision that is both a regulatory process and a type of building development. A ***PUD encourages mixed land use***, and

XI. General: Specialty Areas (4 questions)
(4 Topic Areas; 0 Sub-Topics)

may include clustered residential properties with open space, recreational, commercial, and even industrial areas.

PUDs often allow developers to integrate ***multiple land uses with a more flexible application of zoning restrictions***, such as smaller residential lots and reduced setbacks, to meet overall community zoning goals. Not unlike condominium ownership, ***units are individually owned in fee*** while ***common areas are either owned and managed jointly or deeded to the local government and reserved for PUD-resident common use***.

XI-C. Subdivisions (Expect 0-2 questions from this area)

Property subdivisions require the subdivider to comply with all applicable regulations regarding lot size, utility and water lines, street construction, and many other details, which are often simply called ***mapping requirements***, in order to be able to get the plan approved, recorded, and underway.

As noted above in Section II-C, Private Controls, ***subdivisions are typically created with a list of private restrictions*** often known as ***subdivision covenants, conditions, and restrictions (CC&Rs)*** or ***owners' association rules***, that encumber the use and/or transfer of property.

Private restrictions generally seek to accomplish similar ends, such as allow or disallow pets in a subdivision, or clarify where to put trash and recyclables, regardless of which of the following names they may use. Depending on the property type and local conventions for terminology, they may be referred to as

- ***deed restrictions***
- ***restrictive covenants***
- ***covenants, conditions (or codes), and restrictions (CC&Rs)***
- ***condominium owners' association rules*** for condominium-specific restrictions
- ***homeowners' association rules*** for subdivision-specific restrictions

Private restrictions are often more restrictive than local zoning ordinances, which means they may either ***enhance or detract from property values***.

Private restrictions on land use are ***contractual rather than statutory*** and are prepared by ***subdivision developers*** as well as ***individual property owners*** to limit the use of a property by future owners. For example, a ***developer*** may sell lots with restrictions on building styles or property uses.

CC&Rs, as well as most other enforceable deed restrictions, ***are generally available in the public record***; a ***court injunction may be required to stop violators***.

Note, however, that ***illegal restrictions, such as those that violate federal Fair Housing laws, are not enforceable***.

XI-D. Commercial, Industrial, and Income Property (Expect 0-2 questions from this area)

Commercial property generally involves a variety of ***corporate and business ownership structures*** that are typically more intricate than others presented in this book.

XI. General: Specialty Areas (4 questions)
(4 Topic Areas; 0 Sub-Topics)

For office buildings, professional complexes, and other commercial ventures, there are a variety of ***partnerships***, such as a ***syndicate, joint venture, limited liability corporation (LLC)***, and more, that are simply too sophisticated for entry level agents to either encounter or be expected to know in detail.

However, the following ***three categories of income*** are important to understand for commercial rentals and other industrial, income or investment properties, especially since they have direct application to math Topic Area X-E, Calculations for Valuation

- ***potential gross income***, or ***projected gross income***, or ***scheduled gross income***, which means the ***maximum rental income*** at 100 percent occupancy
- ***effective gross income***, which means the ***actual income*** after subtracting vacancies and rent collection losses
- ***net operating income (NOI)***, which is ***what's left of the effective gross income after subtracting all of the property's operating expenses***, such as maintenance, taxes, insurance, reserves for replacements, and other recurring expenses (but not debt service, such as mortgage interest)

The ***Americans with Disabilities Act (ADA)*** apply to ***public building and workplace access and other accommodations*** for those with disabilities.

Since commercial and income properties involve a wide variety of public ***retail and business properties***, the provisions of ADA especially affect owners and landlords by making them responsible for such access concerns as designated parking, curb and building-entry ramps, elevators, automatic doors, larger rest room stalls with grab bars, and lower public telephones.

And as another matter that is of much more common concern to investors in all types of properties, there is the previously mentioned ***1031 exchange***, which affords investors the opportunity to ***reinvest funds from a property sale in like-kind properties*** and thereby ***defer*** their accumulated ***capital gains tax liability.***

For example, a person may have bought a house as a primary residence twenty years ago for $200,000 and moved out-of-state ten years ago, turning the property into a rental. If the property is sold today for $500,000, the owner's tax liability for capital gains of $300,000 may be deferred indefinitely by purchasing another residential rental property for $500,000.

*Not surprisingly, 1031 exchanges have a whole set of rules, such as a **time limit for qualifying reinvestment purchases** and numerous accounting details, and all must be met for the above scenario's new property to qualify as a reinvestment. The rules are too complex for entry-level licensure testing; some regulators would argue that even simple definition questions on this topic should only be used on broker exams.*

However, since 1031 exchanges are not uncommon in practice, you should be familiar with the basic concept. Besides, the term may appear as a distractor!

XI. General: Specialty Areas (4 questions)
(4 Topic Areas; 0 Sub-Topics)

Boot is another term commonly associated with 1031 exchanges for **additional cash** required over the reinvestment amount from sold properties. However, it typically refers to any cash or other goods added to any transaction to make up for differences between a new property's value and funds available from a sold/exchanged property.

This ends the presentation of key terms and concepts likely to be either tested or used as distractors in this Content Outline Section.

The Connecticut State-Specific Statutory Summary Begins after the Orientation Notes on the Next Page.

You have completed the exam-prep review for the General Exam; the State-Specific review material begins on the next page.

You may take the General Sample Exam now by skipping to the back of the book, or wait until you feel ready to take the General and the State together, just like on Test Day.

The choice is yours; there is probably no harm in taking them separately.

Whether you take them separately or at the same time, you should retake/review them both a few days before your scheduled exam so you can do a final, close review of key areas based on the questions that still trip you up.

Now, on to the Connecticut State-Specific portion!

Preface and Orientation to the Following State Law Sections

The Connecticut General Assembly meets periodically to propose, debate, amend or reject, and pass legislation in the form of Bills and Public Acts. These are used to revise the Connecticut General Statutes, which are organized according to Title, Chapter, and Section; each Chapter is a named collection of specific sections. (These can be found on the web at www.cga.ct.gov by clicking on "statutes" and then "browse statutes.")

The bulk of the statutory basis for Connecticut Real Estate License Law can be found under
- **Title 20: Professional and Occupational Licensing, Certification, Title Protection and Registration. Examining Boards.**
  - **Chapter 392: Real Estate Brokers and Salespersons**
    Note: Chapter 392 is comprised of Sections 20-311 to 20-329gg where "Section 20" refers to the number of the Title and the following numbers identify the particular section. In references noted in this book, periodically there will be some that do not begin with "Section 20." This means the reference is from another Title, such as "Section 21a-4," which is from Title 21a: Consumer Protection, part 4, which is simply one of the sections in Chapter 416: Department of Consumer Protection.

The references herein are drawn almost exclusively from Chapter 392, which also is incorporated in a 58-page document available on the Department of Consumer Protection's Website (www.ct.gov/dcp) under "Connecticut Real Estate Laws and Regulations." The latter document refers to a few other Statutory Sections and Commission Regulations that have a bearing on real estate practices or administrative policies; this text also refers to applicable sources that supplement the intent or application of Chapter 392's Statutes governing licensees.

If you are already familiar with that document, you will appreciate the larger-font, straightforward Exam-Outline organization of the central, testable material here, as well as the summaries and commentary on the regulatory sections excerpted for presentation.

Note on exam questions: *In preparing and reviewing questions for use on a licensing exam, committees of Subject Matter Experts (SMEs) are generally asked to confirm that each one is **relevant** to a topic in the Topic Area being tested, **appropriate** for the **knowledge expected of entry-level candidates**, and that its scored answer is **accurate**, especially if it is complex.*

*Further, the SMEs also consider whether each question stands up to the challenges of **"Should they know this?"** and **"Do they need to know this?"** and **"Does knowing this in any way protect the public?"** and **"If a candidate fails by one point, and this question is it, should it still be asked?"** and the biggest question-killer of all, **"Who cares?"***

On the License Law portion of the test, some questions are going to be administrative, such as who is responsible for reporting a change in a licensee's broker/firm affiliation. Most, though, should concentrate on knowledge of regulations that clearly protect the public, such as required disclosures versus details of nonresident/reciprocal licensing. Disclosures? They're important for public protection. Details for nonresident licensing? For testing, who cares?

Disclaimer: Though the author believes the presentation of and occasional interpretations in the following material to be legally supportable based on the law presented, there may be additional statutes or legislation that bear on final determinations that have not been recognized or considered here. <u>*Nothing herein is to be construed as legal advice*</u>, and should not be substituted for a differing legal opinion by your own legal counsel. This material is intended for exam purposes only; <u>*in practice always seek legal verification*</u>.

Connecticut General Statutes & Regulations (State Portion) Real Estate Exam Content Outline

30 questions for Salesperson exams
(Your exam may include an extra five unscored "pretest" questions for a total of 35.)

I. Connecticut Real Estate Commission and Licensing Requirements (5 questions)
    A. Real Estate Commission purpose, powers, and duties
    B. Activities requiring a license
    C. Exemptions from licensure
    D. License types and qualifications
    E. License renewal, continuing education, and transfer
    F. Real Estate Guaranty Fund
    G. License suspension and revocation

II. Connecticut Laws Governing the Activities of Licensee (10 questions)
    A. Broker/salesperson relationship
    B. Duties to parties
    C. Handling of deposits and other monies
    D. Misrepresentation
    E. Disclosure of nonmaterial facts
    F. Advertising
    G. Commissions and compensation
    H. Unlicensed personal assistants

III. Connecticut Real Estate Agency (8 questions)
    A. Agency: the representing of a client vs. working with a customer
    B. Agency agreements
    C. Agency disclosure
    D. Subagency limitations
    E. Dual agency
    F. Designated agency
    G. Confidential information
    H. Interference with agency relationship

IV. Connecticut-Specific Real Estate Principles and Practices (7 questions)
    A. Connecticut-specific property ownership and transfer issues
        1. Co-ownership forms and shares
        2. Adverse possession/prescriptive easement time
        3. Land records and recording
        4. Real property taxes and assessments
        5. Conveyance tax
        6. Residential property condition disclosure
    B. Connecticut Landlord-Tenant Act
    C. Connecticut Common Interest Ownership Act
    D. Connecticut fair housing law
    E. Connecticut lead paint laws
    F. Connecticut disclosure of off-site conditions law
    G. Connecticut Uniform Electronic Transactions Act

V. For Broker Exam Only: *These topics are omitted since this book is primarily for Sales candidates; Broker candidates will be prepared for Sections I-IV by reading this book.*

I. Connecticut Real Estate Commission and Licensing Requirements
(Expect 5 questions from this Outline Section)

> ### SPECIAL EXAM NOTE
>
> *There are seven Topic Areas in this Roman Numeral Content Area, but only five test questions. This means there will be <u>at least</u> two areas from which you will receive no <u>scored</u> questions.*
>
> *In reality, though, the Commission identifies some Topic Areas as being worth more emphasis than others for testing, so your version of the test may present more than one question from a particular Topic and none from certain others. Other test takers, however, will get questions from Topics your test version may have omitted.*
>
> *And that is why each Topic Area in this book has a range of questions—to indicate its relative importance within its Roman Numeral Content Area.*
>
> *However, the testing company "pretests" five questions on each exam that do not get counted toward your score, but are on the test to gather <u>statistical data on their performance</u>. So, <u>you may actually see one or more questions</u> from each Topic Area.*
>
> *Since you will not be able to tell the difference between scored and pretest questions, <u>answer every question as if it counts – it just might!</u>*

I-A: Real Estate Commission Purpose, Powers, and Duties
(Expect 1-2 questions from this area)

Most Real Estate Commissions are created with the express, primary purpose of protecting the public by promulgating regulations regarding licensing and professional conduct for real estate licensees. In those states, the **primary purpose of the Real Estate Commission** is a basic test question.

> Connecticut statutes, however, simply create a Real Estate Commission with various administrative powers and duties, the foremost being licensure. **The Commission's duty to protect the public has to be inferred** from the fact that it falls under the Department of Consumer Protection and is charged with direct responsibility for **granting licenses "only to persons . . . competent to transact the business of real estate . . . in such manner as to safeguard the interests of the public. . . .[and] with due regard to the paramount interests of the public . . ."**
>
> (References: Sections 20-311a and 20-314(a),(b))

As noted above, **the Connecticut Real Estate Commission operates under the Department of Consumer Protection**, to which the Commission delegates numerous administrative duties, such as preparing forms, processing licensing applications, and overseeing the development, administration, and passing standards for real estate licensing exams. (References: Sections 20-314(b),(c))

> Though **there are <u>eight</u> Commission members** and **they are appointed by the Governor**, a licensee's **knowledge of such administrative details <u>does nothing</u> to protect the public**.

I. Connecticut Real Estate Commission and Licensing Requirements
(Expect 5 questions from this Outline Section)

*Nor does it protect anyone for a licensee to memorize for exam purposes that Commissioners represent a mix of **three brokers**, **two salespersons**, and **three public members** drawn **from each congressional district**, or that the Commission **composition cannot have more than a bare majority from the same political party**, or that the Commission keeps records and submits reports to the Governor.*

So, these "facts," however important they may be in the smooth operation of the Commission, are irrelevant to gauging an entry-level licensee's preparation to protect the public, and are unlikely to be asked on the exam. **To be safe, though, you should note these details (eight Commissioners appointed by the Governor, etc.), just in case . . .**

The Commission administers legislative provisions regarding real estate licensure and the issuance, renewal, suspension, or revocation of licenses; further, the Department of Consumer Protection is authorized by the Commission to process and issue the physical licenses to real estate salespersons and brokers. (Reference: Section 20-311b)

The Commission delegates many other enforcement and administrative responsibilities to the Department.

- ***The Commission may request the Department of Consumer Protection to investigate the actions of any real estate broker or real estate salesperson or any person who assumes to act in any of such capacities within this state***, generally in response to a complaint. (Reference: Section 20-320)

In addition, the following regulation applies to Commission powers as well as licensee conduct related to *investigations*:

- A *licensee shall cooperate* with Department staff if the licensee is contacted in connection with an investigation performed by the Department of Consumer Protection *concerning possible violations* of real estate statutes or regulations. *A licensee shall not make any untruthful or misleading statements in connection with any* Department of Consumer Protection or Real Estate Commission *investigation or hearing*.
(Reference: Section 20-328-3a)

Other related regulations are mostly administrative and follow the principle that *licensee cooperation is expected*; reluctance to respond willingly, honestly, and fully can have serious consequences for the licensee.

For example, when licensees are either in violation of license law or uncooperative during investigations, the Commission has the authority to issue cease and desist orders for particular activities, issue letters of reprimand, place a practitioner on probationary status, limit the licensee's practice, require periodic reports to the Commission, stipulate additional professional education, and impose fines. (Reference: Section 21a-7)

Among the powers and duties of the Commission is determining ***whether or not provisions of the license law have been violated***, and ***determining appropriate penalties and/or fines***.

I. Connecticut Real Estate Commission and Licensing Requirements
(Expect 5 questions from this Outline Section)

In many other states, real estate exam questions about license law violations are grouped into a separate category labeled something like, **"violations, investigations, and penalties."**

Since there is no similar Topic Area grouping in Connecticut's Content Outline, questions regarding violations may be tallied in this area if the thrust of the question focuses on the power or duty of the Commission to assess particular penalties for certain violations listed below.

Or, the violations and penalties below may be categorized and tallied in other Topic Areas if the question focuses on penalties for, say, particular types of misrepresentation, violations of advertising requirements, or other specific license law infraction.

Nevertheless, **specific fines for particular violations of license law** *are brought together below to provide the most comprehensive, inclusive presentation of statutory guidelines and limits; the violations in Section A are also grounds for license suspension and revocation, so will be mentioned again in that Topic Area, I-G.*

According to Connecticut Real Estate License Law,

A. *No more than $2,000* may be imposed as a fine for a licensee *found guilty of obtaining a license by false or fraudulent misrepresentation*; or any of these other offenses:
   (1) making any *material misrepresentation*;
   (2) making any *false promise of a character likely to influence, persuade or induce*;
   (3) *acting as an agent for more than one party in a transaction without the knowledge of all parties for whom the licensee acts*;
   (4) *representing or attempting to represent a real estate broker* other than the licensee's employer or the broker with whom the licensee is affiliated, *without the express knowledge and consent of the licensee's employer or affiliated broker*;
   (5) *failing, within a reasonable time, to account for or remit any moneys coming into the licensee's possession that belong to others*;
   (6) *entering into an exclusive listing contract or buyer agency contract that contains* a fixed termination date if such contract also provides for *an automatic continuation of the period of such contract beyond such* date
   (7) *failing to deliver immediately a copy of any instrument to any party or parties executing the instrument*, where such instrument has been prepared by the licensee or under the licensee's supervision and where such instrument relates to . . any matters pertaining to the consummation of a lease, or the purchase, sale or exchange of real property or any other type of real estate transaction in which the licensee may participate as a broker or a salesperson;
   (8) *conviction in a court of competent jurisdiction of forgery, embezzlement, obtaining money under false pretenses, larceny, extortion, conspiracy to defraud, or other like offense or offenses . . .* ;
   (9) *collecting compensation in advance of services* to be performed *and failing, upon demand of the person paying the compensation or the commission, to render an accounting of the use of such money*;
   (10) *commingling funds of others with the licensee's own, or failing to keep funds of others in an escrow or trustee account*;

I. Connecticut Real Estate Commission and Licensing Requirements
(Expect 5 questions from this Outline Section)

    (11) *any act or conduct that constitutes dishonest, fraudulent or improper dealings*;

    (12) *failing to provide the disclosures required by section 20-325c*; or

    (13) *a violation of any provision of this chapter or any regulation* adopted under this chapter. (Reference: Section 20-320)

*On July 1, 2008, the list above was expanded to include a **prohibition against influencing real estate appraisals**. By that the statute means **to either refuse or intentionally fail to refer a homebuyer to a lender or mortgage broker who uses an appraiser whose appraisal is less than the sale contract price**. This action also applies to any licensee who encourages any other licensee to do the same.* (Reference: Section 20-320b)

B. *No more than $1,000* may be imposed as a fine for a licensee found guilty of *receiving a fee, commission, or other form of referral fee for referring any buyer to (1) an attorney at law* or the attorney's affiliates or *(2) a mortgage broker or lender* or their affiliates

(Reference: Section 20-320a)

Similarly, attorneys as well as mortgage brokers and lenders are prohibited from receiving referral fees from real estate licensees under sections 51-87b and 49-7f, respectively, **and can be disciplined and fined by their own regulatory authorities** (not the Real Estate Commission) for doing so.

*These penalties for attorneys, mortgage brokers, and lenders who accept referral fees should make it clear to real estate licensees that such arrangements are prohibited; **if asked to provide such a fee, the licensee may point out it is for the other party's own good not to do so***.

*Finally, **anyone found guilty of engaging in the real estate business without a license may be fined not more than $1,000 and/or be imprisoned not more than six months**, and prohibited from getting a license for up to a year.*

The last violation should serve as a warning NOT to jump into licensee-level real estate activities between the day you pass the exam and the day your affiliated broker receives your license certificate.

Also, beware of asking unlicensed assistants to do too much, and be sure to renew on time! Brokers, especially, can lose track of renewals, and all affiliated licensees are technically operating illegally when their primary broker is in a lapsed/expired/late-renewal situation!

*Further, **this provision may apply later in your career if you fail to renew your license on time yet continue to collect commissions or perform activities requiring a license**. The meeting minutes of the Commission contain numerous examples of actions against individuals who continued real estate activities without renewing their license.*

(Reference: Section 20-325)

I.	**Connecticut Real Estate Commission and Licensing Requirements**
	(Expect 5 questions from this Outline Section)

    C. *No more than $500* may be imposed as a fine *for any person* found guilty of:
- *willfully misrepresenting any fact* required to be disclosed in any application or in any other form, paper, or document *required to be filed with the Commission in connection with an application for a license*

    It is worth noting that ***this infraction also subjects a violator to the prospect of imprisonment for up to six months.*** *(Prison sentences may be recommended, but not imposed, by the Real Estate Commission; a court of competent jurisdiction must take the next step of imposing the sentence.)* (Reference: Section 20-324)

The following two points are noteworthy as a summary of the above laundry lists of violations and fines; there will be more on each one in later Topic Areas:
- ***Before refusing, suspending, or revoking any license, or imposing any fine under this chapter, the Commission shall give notice and afford an opportunity for hearing*** as provided in the regulations adopted by the Commissioner of Consumer Protection.
(Reference: Section 20-321)

- Most of the money collected from fines is deposited in the Real Estate Guaranty Fund; most of the money from general licensing fees goes to the State's General Fund by way of the State Treasurer, who also pays some to the University of Connecticut for its Center for Real Estate and Urban Economic Studies.

    The details of which monies and how much go where, or how the funds are processed, while of some general interest to a few, are too administrative to have any place on exams for any position other than internal DCP accounting.
(References: Sections 20-311e; 20-320; and 10a-125)

Finally, whereas the vast majority of States specifically insulate their respective Real Estate Commissions from becoming embroiled in disputes between licensees over compensation, Connecticut Real Estate License Law says, "Jump right in!"

- ***The Commission shall have the power to act as a board of arbitration to consider and decide any dispute over commissions arising between brokers or salespersons*** that is voluntarily submitted to the Commission by the parties to such dispute.
(Reference: Section 20-311f)

I-B. Activities Requiring a License	**(Expect 0-1 question from this area)**

According to Connecticut Real Estate License Law, ***activities requiring a real estate license*** are defined broadly under the definition of ***"engaging in the real estate business,"*** which means
- ***acting for another and for a fee, commission, or other valuable consideration*** in the listing for sale, selling, exchanging, buying or renting, or offering or attempting to negotiate a sale, exchange, purchase or rental of, an estate or interest in real estate or a resale of a mobile manufactured home, as defined in subdivision (1) of section 21-64, or collecting upon a loan secured or to be secured by a mortgage or other encumbrance upon or transfer of real estate
(Reference: Section 20-311(3))

I. Connecticut Real Estate Commission and Licensing Requirements
(Expect 5 questions from this Outline Section)

These activities above are clarified by the Commission as including, but *not necessarily limited* to:
- *hosting open houses*, kiosks, home show booths or fairs, *or handing out materials at such functions*
- *showing property*
- *answering any questions from consumers on listing, title, financing, closing, etc.*
- *contacting cooperative brokers*, whether in person or otherwise, *regarding any negotiations* or open transactions
- *discussing or explaining a contract*, offer to purchase, agreement, listing, or other real estate document with anyone outside the firm
- *being paid on the basis of commission*, or any amount based on listings, sales, etc.
- *negotiating or agreeing to* any commission, commission split, or referral fee on behalf of a licensee
- *placing calls that would require a license* such as cold calls, soliciting listings, contacting expired listings or for sale by owners, or extending invitations to open houses
- *attending inspections or pre-closing walk-throughs* unless accompanied by licensee

(Reference: Connecticut Real Estate Commission Policy on Use of Unlicensed Persons by Licensees, 12/5/1996)

In order to engage in the above activities, *an individual or business entity*, as defined in the License Law, *must be licensed as either a salesperson or broker*, unless exempt from licensure as provided in the next Topic Area. (References: Sections 20-311(1),(2),(4); 20-312)

I-C. Exemptions from Licensure (Expect 0-1 question from this area)

Questions in this Topic Area will concentrate on most of the activities, circumstances, or individuals that are exempt from licensure requirements.

However, exceptions to licensure requirements include the special *subcategory of unlicensed personal assistants*, which has its own Topic Area, II-G, for exam question categorization and tallying, so they will only be discussed here as necessary *to clarify basic distinctions between activities that require a license and activities that do not*.

The statutory definition of *"salesperson," specifically excludes "employees of any real estate broker whose principal occupation is clerical work in an office, or janitors or custodians engaged principally in that occupation."* These exclusions help distinguish office staff and maintenance workers from those who need to be licensed to perform broker-delegated sales, rental, or property management duties. (Reference: Section 20-311(2))

Additional statutory exceptions include ten categories, plus a stray reference to Commission-approved student interns acting temporarily under broker supervision (Section 20-316), but the most important for entry-level testing are
- *any person who as owner or lessor* performs any of the acts enumerated in section 20-311, with reference to property owned, leased or sought to be acquired or leased by the person, *or to the person's regular employees who are employed as on-site residential*

I. Connecticut Real Estate Commission and Licensing Requirements
(Expect 5 questions from this Outline Section)

superintendents or custodians, with respect to the property so owned or leased or sought to be acquired or leased when such acts are performed in the regular course of, or incident to, the management of such property and the investment therein

- The Commission has interpreted this law as requiring all of the following conditions for the exemption to apply: The individual must (1) be a regular employee, (2) be employed as a superintendent or custodian, (3) work on a residential site where he engages in licensed activities, and (4) reside at the location where he works and engages in those licensed activities.

    (Declaratory Ruling, Connecticut Real Estate Commission, April 1, 1999)

- *any person acting as attorney-in-fact* under a duly executed power of attorney from the owner authorizing the final consummation by performance of any contract for the sale, leasing or exchange of real estate, *or to service rendered by any attorney-at-law in the performance of the attorney-at-law's duties as such attorney-at-law*;

- *a receiver, trustee in bankruptcy, administrator, executor or other fiduciary, while acting as such*, or any person selling real estate under order of any court, or to a trustee acting under a trust agreement, deed of trust or will, or the regular salaried employees thereof

    (Reference: Section 20-329)

I-D. License Types and Qualifications   (Expect 0-1 question from this area)

Connecticut recognizes *three types of licenses: salesperson, broker,* and *nonresident/reciprocal.*

A *salesperson* is a person *affiliated with any real estate broker as an independent contractor or employed by a real estate broker*, and performs any of the activities listed in Topic Area I-B (above) as those requiring a license.   (Reference: Section 20-311(2))

A *broker* is a person authorized to perform all of the actions of a licensee *as well as the additional authority to act as a principal, even sole proprietor, in a real estate firm* and contract with other licensees to conduct real estate activities under their authority. "Broker" may also mean partnerships, corporations, or other business entities that meet Commission licensure requirements.

(Reference: Section 20-311(1),(4))

*Technically, licensed brokers who work under another broker's supervision fall under the broad definition of salesperson. For that reason, most test questions will use the term **licensee** to refer generically to both sales and brokers, and **broker only when it refers to the specific individual principal** of a firm or company, generally to stress or test additional authorities, responsibilities, or liabilities that individual has assumed.*

A *nonresident/reciprocal* licensee is a licensee with either a salesperson or broker license in another jurisdiction that has received recognition and approval from the Real Estate Commission to conduct real estate activities in Connecticut.

Provided that the jurisdiction licensing the nonresident has substantially similar, or higher, requirements to those of Connecticut, out-of-state licensees who are currently practicing competently and are not involved in disciplinary proceedings may be granted a nonresident license to practice in Connecticut. The licensee must also

- conform to all provisions of Connecticut Real Estate License Law

I. Connecticut Real Estate Commission and Licensing Requirements
(Expect 5 questions from this Outline Section)

- file an irrevocable consent that service for suits and actions arising against the licensee be made on the chair of the Connecticut Real Estate Commission and bind the licensee to action in the state judicial district where the action arose

(Reference: Section 20-317)

Also, Connecticut has *reciprocity understandings* with numerous states, and *"non-resident holders of license-by-reciprocity who become Connecticut residents have a valid Connecticut license and are not required to qualify with course, experience, and examination requirements in order to maintain the validity of their license."*

(Reference: Legal Opinion, Connecticut Attorney General's Office, 6/11/99)

In order *to qualify for a real estate license*, salesperson or broker, in the State of Connecticut, *an applicant must* meet the following requirements
- be *at least eighteen years old*
    - *Curious note*: this applies to both salesperson and brokers, though *broker applicants are required to have been "actively engaged for at least two years as a licensed real estate salesperson under the supervision of a licensed real estate broker in this state"* Perhaps being eighteen instead of twenty only applies to reciprocal brokers?
- bear a good *reputation for honesty, truthfulness, and fair dealing*
- be *competent* to transact the business of real estate in such manner as to *safeguard the interests of the public*
- *not have been rejected for licensure or have had a license revoked* in any state (or DC) *within a year of applying* for licensure in Connecticut
- submit an original *certificate of completion for sixty hours* of Commission-approved coursework in principles and practices of Real Estate
    - pre-licensing education-hour requirements for both salesperson and broker applicants may be waived by the Commission if it determines an applicant has equivalent experience or education
    - *broker candidates have to also successfully complete thirty hours of Appraisal I, thirty hours of an elective real estate related course, and have at least two years of active engagement as a salesperson for a Connecticut broker*
- pass a written examination
    (Duh and double-duh! Do not expect a question on the exam about whether or not passing the exam is a requirement for licensure. However, I have seen them used in several states, and, fortunately, got them tossed from those exam pools.)
- complete the application and pay the license fee *within two years* of the date of passing the examination (References: Sections 20-314; 20-316; and Commission forms)

I-E. License Renewal, Continuing Education, and Transfer
(Expect 1-2 questions from this area)

There are several testable elements in this area. They include some of the following points
- *all licenses expire annually*
    - the *salesperson* license *annual renewal fee is $285*
        - *license renewal in even-numbered years*, e.g., 2012, 2014, etc., requires

I. Connecticut Real Estate Commission and Licensing Requirements
(Expect 5 questions from this Outline Section)

- completing *12 hours of continuing education (CE)*, <u>OR</u>
- passing a *40-question Connecticut CE Exam** *(administered by PSI at its testing sites for $52; see www.psiexams.com--also* **look into the CE prep book at www.On-the-Test.com!)**
- equivalent educational experience or study as approved by the Commission
  Note: CE requirements for 2012 renewals do not apply to those who <u>pass the original licensing exam</u> between 6/1/10 and 5/31/12.

- the *broker* license *annual renewal fee is $375*
  - *license renewal in even-numbered years*, e.g., 2012, 2014, etc., requires
    - completing *12 hours of continuing education (CE)*, <u>OR</u>
    - passing a *40-question Connecticut CE Exam** *(administered by PSI at its testing sites for $52; see www.psiexams.com--also* **look into the CE prep book at www.On-the-Test.com!)**
    - equivalent educational experience or study as approved by the Commission
      Note: CE requirements for 2012 renewals do not apply to those who <u>pass the original licensing exam</u> between 4/1/10 and 3/31/12

Special Note: Those of you who are studying for the licensing exam now will not need to comply with CE requirements until the 2013/2014 renewal cycle. Clearly, CE requirements will not apply to you directly for some time yet.

---

*from <u>Sec. 20-319. Renewal. Continuing education requirements. Regulations.</u> *(emphases below added)*
Applicants for an annual renewal license . . shall . . . in any even-numbered year, [comply] with the continuing education requirements . . . *The continuing education requirement may be satisfied by successful completion of any of the following during the two-year period preceding such renewal*:
(1) A course or courses, approved by the Commission, of continuing education in current real estate practices and licensing laws consisting of not less than twelve hours of classroom study; or
(2) *a written examination . . . which demonstrates a knowledge of current real estate practices and licensing laws*; or
(3) equivalent continuing educational experience or study as determined by regulations adopted . .

However, the test may have questions about the current CE requirements out of concern that you will be better prepared for the profession by recognizing that the Real Estate Commission expects licensees to remain abreast of topics that are subject to periodic updates.

So, even though the requirements may have been adjusted by then, the course requirements for 2012 renewal are (1) *three hours of "Connecticut Real Estate Fiduciary Agent Duties Review and Law Update"* and (2) *nine hours of approved real estate elective courses*.

If a licensee does not renew the license at the correct time, *it expires and may be reinstated for two years* provided unpaid renewal fees are made.

The following license law details, though, should NOT be tested even though they are part of either the Statutory Sections most applicable to this area, Commission-updated requirements posted on the Department of Consumer Protection's Website, or CREC meeting minutes
- *in even-numbered years, the renewal fee goes up by $8.00 as a CE processing fee*

I. Connecticut Real Estate Commission and Licensing Requirements
(Expect 5 questions from this Outline Section)

- since the 2004 renewal year, licensees have been required to retain original CE certificates for three years in the event of an audit rather than submit them at renewal; though the Department is now requiring CE providers to upload attendee rosters to a database for use in electronic auditing, it would be wise to ask for, and hold onto, some proof of CE course attendance
    - *Note: minutes of Commission meetings reveal that if an audited licensee cannot prove compliance with CE requirements, the Commission may impose a $1,000 fine, license suspension of at least 30 days, and additional CE*
- if a licensee joins the military and lets the license expire, the licensee has two years from expiration to apply for reinstatement without payment of any fee
- three dollars of each annual renewal fee shall be payable to the Real Estate Guaranty Fund
    - 8.75% of each license fee, initial and renewal, shall be paid to the University of Connecticut for the Center for Real Estate and Urban Economic Studies

(References: Sections 20-314; 20-319; 21a-4; 10a-125; Commission forms and Commission Meeting Minutes of 8/04 & 9/04)

As previously noted, **anyone found guilty of engaging in the real estate business without a license may be fined not more than $1,000 and/or be imprisoned not more than six months**, and prohibited from getting a license for up to a year. **This provision may apply later in your career if you fail to renew your license on time yet continue to collect commissions or perform activities requiring a license.** (Reference: Section 20-325)

When any licensee **transfers affiliation from one broker or company to another**, regardless of whether the licensee acts as an employee or independent contractor, **the licensee (_not_ the broker) "shall register such transfer with, and pay a registration fee of twenty-five dollars to, the Commission."** After receiving the proper form and fee, the Commission will issue a new license certificate to the licensee through the new broker or firm. (Reference: Section 20-319a)

I-F. Real Estate Guaranty Fund (Expect 0-2 questions from this area)

The Real Estate Guaranty Fund provides a State-backed last resort for consumers who got shafted by a licensee, especially through embezzlement or fraud, and have won a court judgment against the licensee for damages the licensee subsequently proves unable to pay.

By law, **the Real Estate Guaranty Fund is structured to build to a maximum of $500,000**, after which **excess funds are passed over to the State's General Fund**.

There is a complex, extensive set of requirements and procedures for consumers who appeal to the Fund for monetary compensation, all of which are procedurally too involved for entry-level testing. Besides, it would undoubtedly be up to prosecuting attorneys to wade through ways to tap the Fund for their clients, so don't sweat the fine print.

A few key points, though, that might be pulled out for testing include
- **compensation levels max out at $25,000 per transaction**
    - **this total is _an aggregate per transaction_, _NOT per party_ involved**

I. Connecticut Real Estate Commission and Licensing Requirements
(Expect 5 questions from this Outline Section)

- *an application for compensation* made to the Connecticut Real Estate Commission **must meet the following requirements**
  - *the applicant must already have a valid judgment in a Superior Court against a licensee and/or firm*
  - *the judgment amount must remain unsatisfied* after all legal efforts to collect them from the responsible parties have been exhausted
- *a licensee against whom an application is made is subject to the following penalties*
  - *automatic license revocation* upon the entry of the judgment against the licensee
  - *no reinstatement of the license until the following condition is met*
    - *repayment to the Fund in full, plus applicable interest*, even if the licensee has been awarded a bankruptcy discharge of financial obligations
- *there is a two-year statute of limitations on filing an application for collection* from the Fund
  - this two-year period is triggered either by the date of the judgment's final determination or the expiration of time to appeal it, as applicable

Interestingly, an application for recovery of damages from the Fund cannot be brought by the spouse of an offending licensee, either directly or through a representative . . . there must be a story behind this restriction!

(References: Sections 20-324a; 20-324c; 20-324d; and 20-324e)

A licensee has a contributory obligation to the Fund as follows
- when paying for the *initial license, there is a separate $20 fee that is credited to the Fund*
- *three dollars of each annual renewal fee* shall be payable to the Fund

Also, most fines collected for licensee infractions are deposited into the Fund.

(References: Sections 20-314(f); 20-320; 20-324b; and 20-324e)

I-G. License Suspension and Revocation (Expect 0-1 question from this area)

The Commission may *temporarily suspend or permanently revoke* any license *if the Commission finds that the licensee is guilty of any of the offenses itemized in Topic Area I-A above* for which the Commission may impose a fine, *including receiving a fee for referring buyers to a particular attorney or mortgage broker*. (References: Sections 20-320; 20-320a)

In addition, a *court's conviction on any violation* of Section 20-320(8), i.e., forgery, embezzlement, obtaining money under false pretenses, larceny, extortion, conspiracy to defraud, or other like offense or offenses, warrants license *revocation* after due process.

The process begins with the clerk of the court that renders any such conviction forwarding a certified copy of the conviction to the Commission, which shall make written notification within ten days to the licensee of the license revocation. (Reference: Section 20-323)

Also of note in this Topic Area about suspension and revocation are the points made earlier regarding the Commission's powers and duties over license law violations and penalties:

I. Connecticut Real Estate Commission and Licensing Requirements
(Expect 5 questions from this Outline Section)

- *Before refusing, suspending, or revoking any license, or imposing any fine under this chapter, the Commission shall give notice and afford an opportunity for hearing.*
(Reference: Section 20-321)

- *The Commission may request the Department of Consumer Protection to investigate the actions of any real estate broker or real estate salesperson or any person who assumes to act in any of such capacities within this state*, generally in response to a complaint.
(Reference: Section 20-320)

- A *licensee shall cooperate* with Department staff if the licensee is contacted in connection with an investigation performed by the Department of Consumer Protection *concerning possible violations* of real estate statutes or regulations. *A licensee shall not make any untruthful or misleading statements in connection with any* Department of Consumer Protection or Real Estate Commission *investigation or hearing*. (Reference: Section 20-328-3a)

- If the Commission determines license suspension or revocation is not the most appropriate course, it may take other measures. These include such actions as imposing fines, issuing cease and desist orders for particular activities, issuing letters of reprimand, placing a practitioner on probationary status, limiting the licensee's practice, requiring periodic reports to the Commission, and stipulating additional professional education. (Reference: Section 21a-7)

This ends the presentation of key terms and concepts likely to be either tested or used as distractors in this Content Outline Section.

II. Connecticut Laws Governing the Activities of Licensees
(Expect 10 questions from this Outline Section)

II-A. Broker/Salesperson Relationship   (Expect 1-2 questions from this area)

This Topic Area will focus primarily on the following four points
(1) *whether the professional relationship* between a broker and an affiliated licensee *is as an employee or an independent contractor*
(2) the *responsibilities of employing brokers for all subordinates*, licensed, unlicensed, or anyone working for affiliated licensees
(3) the *liability of a broker for acts of affiliated licensees*
(4) *licensee termination/transfer* issues, especially the handling of records, client agreements, and final compensation

The first point includes the following basic definition and list of *points that distinguish an independent contractor from an employee*.

As noted in a previous Topic Area, technically, licensed brokers who work under another broker's supervision fall under the broad definition of salesperson.

*For that reason, and to avoid confusion, the term **licensee** will be used here to refer generically to both salespersons and brokers. **Broker will only refer to the specific individual principal** of a firm or company, generally to stress the additional authorities, responsibilities, or liabilities that individual has assumed.*

A licensee *shall not be considered an employee* if
- *substantially all of the remuneration* for the services performed by such licensee *is directly related to sales or other output rather than to the number of hours worked*, and
- such *services are performed by the licensee pursuant to a written contract* that contains the following provisions:
    (1) the licensee, for purposes of workers' compensation, is engaged as an independent contractor associated with the person for whom services are performed;
    (2) the licensee shall be paid a commission based on the licensee's gross sales, if any, without deduction for taxes, which commission shall be directly related to sales or other output;
    (3) the licensee shall not receive any remuneration related to the number of hours worked and shall not be treated as an employee for purposes of worker's compensation;
    (4) the licensee shall be permitted to work any hours the licensee chooses;
    (5) the licensee shall be permitted to work out of the licensee's own home or the office of the person for whom services are performed;
    (6) the licensee shall be free to engage in outside employment;
    (7) the person for whom the services are performed may provide office facilities and supplies for the use of the licensee, but the licensee shall otherwise pay the licensee's own expenses, including, but not limited to, automobile, travel and entertainment expenses; and
    (8) the contract may be terminated by either party at any time upon notice given to the other.   (Reference: Section 20-312b)

II. Connecticut Laws Governing the Activities of Licensees
(Expect 10 questions from this Outline Section)

The second point has to do with *the broker's responsibility for subordinates of all kinds*, and is discussed in the following language in Commission Policy Statements:

> Licensees, both brokers and salespersons, often use unlicensed persons, either employed or contracted, to perform various tasks related to a real estate transaction that do not require a license. Such persons, for example, are used as personal assistants, clerical support staff, closing secretaries, etc.
>
> Employing brokers, whether they are employing unlicensed persons or whether licensees under their supervision are using unlicensed persons as personal assistants or the like, are responsible for assuring that such unlicensed persons are not involved in activities that require a license and/or activities that violate this policy.
>
>> Brokers should establish guidelines for the use of unlicensed persons and procedures for monitoring their activities. *It is the responsibility of the designated broker to assure that unlicensed persons, either directly employed or contracted, or employed or contracted by licensees under his or her supervision, are not acting improperly*.
>> (Reference: Connecticut Real Estate Commission Policy on Use of Unlicensed Persons by Licensees, 12/5/1996)

Agency relationships between brokers and affiliated licensees are also considered automatic in some cases. The Connecticut Real Estate Commission Policy on Agency specifically states: *"Agency runs to the brokerage firm, not individual licensees."*

> The Policy clarifies the establishment of subagency and the exception of designated agents.
>
>> *In general, agency runs from a client to the broker in a brokerage firm and all licensees in that brokerage firm*. This means that if the brokerage firm has entered into a listing agreement with a seller, then all of the licensees in that firm are agents of that seller, represent that seller, and owe fiduciary duties to that seller.
>>
>> Likewise, if the brokerage firm enters into a buyer agency agreement with a buyer, then all of the licensees in that firm are the agents of the buyer, represent that buyer, and owe fiduciary duties to that buyer. Further, once a seller consents to letting a cooperating broker act as a subagent, all licensees affiliated with that broker are that seller's subagents for the listed property.
>>
>> *The only exception to this is in the case of the appointment of designated agents.*
>> (Reference: Connecticut Real Estate Commission Policy on Agency)

The third point, regarding *broker liability for subordinates*, is based in a common law agency principle that has been codified by Connecticut General Statutes.

> In Connecticut, *brokers who establish independent contractor rather than employee relationships with affiliated licensees do NOT distance themselves against legal liability* for licensee misdeeds, according to the following

II. Connecticut Laws Governing the Activities of Licensees
(Expect 10 questions from this Outline Section)

- In any action brought by a third party against a real estate salesperson affiliated with a real estate broker as an independent contractor, such broker shall be liable to the same extent as if such affiliate had been employed as a real estate salesperson by such broker. (Reference: Section 20-312a)

The final point here has to do with *which party does what when a licensee changes brokers or is otherwise terminated*.

As noted, and tested, above (Topic Area I-E), *when a licensee changes brokers, it is the licensee's responsibility to notify the Commission of the license transfer*. However, regarding records, client agreements, and compensation, the following points apply
- *licensees shall immediately turn over to the former broker any and all information and records* obtained during the licensee's employment or affiliation
- *brokers shall give the former licensee, within ten days of the date on which the licensee turns over any and all information and records* in accordance with this section, *or within forty-five days of said termination, whichever is earlier*, a written accounting setting forth all active listing agreements, agency agreements, transactions, commissions and compensation in which the licensee was involved and may yet receive (Reference: Section 20-328-10a)

II-B. Duties to Parties (Expect 1-3 questions from this area)

This Topic Area takes its name directly from the Commission Regulation, Section 20-328-2a, Duties to Parties, which has eight subsections and four sub-subsections.

The presentation below will arrange key testable points to provide better logical groupings and explanations; these will be followed by a few related supplementary regulations that elaborate on these duties and have no other "content home" on this outline.

The primary categories in Duties to Parties can be identified as (1) disclosure of licensee interest in real estate transactions, (2) listing agent duties to sellers/lessors, (3) written approval required for sign placement, (4) buyer-agent duties to buyers/lessees, and (5) handling of offers and counteroffers.

#1—Disclosure of licensee interest in real estate transactions
Although the language in this regulation regarding a licensee's disclosure of personal interest in a real estate transaction does not specify that it be put in writing, it would, in most cases, be wise to make it part of the transaction documentation. A paper trail would help to counter later claims against the licensee of an undisclosed conflict of interest.

A licensee shall not undertake to provide professional services concerning a property where the licensee has a present or contemplated interest *unless such interest is specifically disclosed to all affected parties.* (Reference: Section 20-328-2a(a))

Regarding a listing taken by a licensee, the licensee shall not pursue the acquisition of the property for the licensee personally, any member of the licensee's family, the licensee's firm or any member thereof, or any entity in which the licensee has a substantial ownership interest, *without disclosing to the owner the licensee's interest and relationship to prospective buyers.*

II. Connecticut Laws Governing the Activities of Licensees
(Expect 10 questions from this Outline Section)

In selling or leasing property in which the licensee has any ownership interest, the licensee must disclose this interest to prospective buyers or tenants. (Reference: Section 20-328-2a(b))

#2—Listing agent duties to sellers/lessors

Listing agents have specific duties under this regulation, including those of making diligent efforts in the best interests of the principals. According to the regulation, this means that:

A licensee accepting *an exclusive right to sell* or lease listing or *an exclusive agency* to sell or lease listing *shall make a diligent effort to sell or lease the property listed*.

All dealings concerning property exclusively listed with an agent shall be conducted with the listing agent, and not the seller, owner or lessor.

However, *a licensee may contact the seller, owner, or lessor* of property exclusively listed with an agent *if the listing agent consents* to the contact *or the licensee, after diligent effort, is unable to communicate with the listing agent or a licensee designated* by listing agent *to service the listing in the listing agent's absence.*

In the sale or lease of property exclusively listed with a real estate broker pursuant to an exclusive right to sell or lease listing or an exclusive agency to sell or lease listing, *the broker shall cooperate with other real estate brokers upon mutually agreed upon terms when it is in the best interests of the party or parties for whom the broker is acting*. (References: Section 20-328-2a(c),(f)(1),(h))

#3—Written approval required for sign placement

Agents also have a specific duty under this regulation regarding getting written approval for placing signs on a property for sale or lease. *Though this permission would typically be included in a listing agreement, it must be obtained by any licensee posting signs*.

According to the regulation, this means that:

No signs shall be placed on any property that relate to a real estate transaction *without the written consent of the owner or the lessor*, or their authorized agent.

(Reference: Section 20-328-2a(g))

#4—Buyer-agent duties to buyers/lessees

Buyer-agents have specific duties under this regulation, including those of making diligent efforts in the best interests of the principals. According to the regulation, this means that:

A licensee who agrees to become *an exclusive agent of a prospective buyer* or lessee *shall make a diligent effort to find a property within the prospective buyer's or lessee's specifications*.

All dealings concerning a prospective buyer or lessee who is exclusively represented by an agent shall be conducted with the prospective buyer's or lessee's agent, and not with the prospective buyer or lessee.

II. Connecticut Laws Governing the Activities of Licensees
(Expect 10 questions from this Outline Section)

However, *a licensee may contact a prospective buyer or lessee* who is exclusively represented by an agent *if the agent* representing the prospective buyer or lessee *consents* to the contact *or the licensee, after diligent effort, is unable to communicate with the prospective buyer's or lessee's agent or a licensee designated* by the buyer's or lessee's agent *to service the buyer in the buyer's or lessee's agent's absence*.

(References: Section 20-328-2a(c),(f)(2))

#5—Handling of offers and counteroffers

The **handling of offers** has several important elements. According to this Commission Regulation, these include:

No licensee shall submit to an owner a written offer to purchase or lease real property unless either (1) such offer *contains the essential terms and conditions of the offer, including the manner in which the purchase is to be financed*; or (2) such offer is conditioned upon the later execution of a bond for deed or complete agreement for sale

No licensee shall submit to an owner a written agreement or a bond for deed for the sale of real estate that contains a *mortgage contingency clause* that conditions the prospective buyer's performance on obtaining a mortgage from a third party unless the contingency clause includes at least the
(1) *principal amount of the mortgage* the prospective buyer must obtain;
(2) *time period within which the mortgage commitment must be obtained*; and
(3) *term of years of the mortgage*. (Reference: Section 20-328-2a(d))

The *listing real estate broker shall submit all offers or counter-offers to the seller*, owner, or lessor *as quickly as possible*.
- Unless the listing real estate broker and the seller, owner, or lessor agree otherwise, the listing real estate broker shall not be obligated to continue to market the property after an offer or counter-offer has been accepted.
- *After the acceptance* of an offer or counter-offer, *the listing real estate broker shall advise any other offerors that an offer or counter-offer on the listed property has been accepted*. (Reference: Section 20-328-2a(e)(1))

A *licensee acting as the agent of the buyer or lessee shall present all offers or counter-offers* to the prospective buyer or lessee *as quickly as possible*.
- Unless a licensee acting as the agent of the prospective buyer or lessee and the buyer or lessee agree otherwise, the licensee shall not be obligated to continue to show properties to the prospective buyer or lessee after an offer or counter-offer has been accepted. (Reference: Section 20-328-2a(e)(2))

Please note that this regulation requires agents for BOTH parties to submit <u>ALL</u> offers or counteroffers. Period.

The points above from the regulation regarding Duties to Parties do not attempt to cover a licensee's full range of duties to parties within, or after, a transaction. There are a host of other statutes and regulations regarding the details of other duties, many of which will be addressed in subsequent Topic Areas.

II. Connecticut Laws Governing the Activities of Licensees
(Expect 10 questions from this Outline Section)

However, since this is the first appearance of a transaction-specific Topic Area, it is worth noting that there are numerous key elements regarding Connecticut-specific requirements and guidelines for the handling of documents, funds, and transaction record keeping. Some of these include

- who signs what and when
- who gets copies of what and when
- offers, multiple offers, and counteroffers: procedural requirements and other issues
- if and when the parties need to initial changes
- property description disclosure forms and other disclosures
- providing written notice of the availability of the lists of hazardous waste facilities and local properties on which hunting or shooting sports regularly take place
- if faxes, e-mails, and other electronic document transmissions are legally binding
- proper handling of transaction-related funds
- record keeping aspects, such as which documents must be retained, for how long, and at what point the clock starts ticking

Most of the particulars of contractual elements required to create valid, complete *listing agreements* as well as *buyer agency agreements* and *lessee agreements* will be covered in Topic Area III-B, Agency Agreements. Further, agency disclosure requirements and forms will be found in several Topic Areas in Roman Numeral Content Outline Section III.

While most of the points bulleted above will be addressed on the Salesperson Content Outline, record keeping requirements have only recently been clarified and codified in Connecticut.

Record keeping *details are tested as part of the Broker exam, since it is a broker-level responsibility to maintain the records, but all licensees should be familiar with the requirements to ensure that proper care is taken with particular documents and files throughout, and after, a transaction.*

According to legislation enacted in late 2006, ***required records must be maintained for a MINIMUM of seven (7) years.***

Required records include, but are not limited to, the following documents:

- ***listing agreements as well as buyer or tenant representation agreements***, including extensions, amendments, and applicable disclosures
- purchase contracts, leases, options, written offers and counteroffers
- canceled as well as unused checks, checkbooks, and bank statements for escrow and trust accounts

Finally, ***the required records may be retained in any format, electronic or otherwise, capable of producing an accurate copy in paper format of the original document***.

(Reference: Section 20-325m)

Violation Alert!
It is worth noting here that ***there is at least one Section 20-320 violation land-mine*** in this Topic Area ***that could be grounds for the maximum fine ($2,000) and/or license suspension or***

II. Connecticut Laws Governing the Activities of Licensees
(Expect 10 questions from this Outline Section)

revocation. You could be invited to meet your Real Estate Commissioners in Hartford for
- entering into an exclusive listing agreement or buyer agency agreement *if it provides for an automatic extension of the listing period*, or
- *failing to deliver immediately a copy of above agreements* or related transaction instruments to any party or parties entitled to them   (References: Section 20-320(6),(7))

II-C. Handling of Deposits and other Monies   (Expect 1-3 questions from this area)

This Topic Area concentrates on state regulations that reinforce a licensee's fiduciary duty with transaction-related funds, most often earnest money and similar deposits.

That means that the following issues are central to this area, and to test questions
1. **How deposit/transaction funds are processed**
   - a licensee *shall promptly pay over* all transaction-related funds to the licensee's broker
   - the broker shall *deposit funds* in *an escrow or trust account* in a bank doing business in the State of Connecticut *within three banking days* of the date of the agreement
2. **Who holds deposits, and where**
   - all funds received in the course of a real estate transaction are to be maintained in a broker's *separate escrow or trust account*, which must be distinct from operational or personal accounts
3. **When deposit money can be released, returned, or retained**
   - *transaction funds* held in the escrow or trust account *shall be held pending final legal disposition* of such funds per the instructions of the person legally entitled to them
   - *in the event of disputed funds*, such as damages for breach of contract, a court may order some or all of the transaction funds transferred via certified funds to the court pending resolution and relieve the broker of continued liability as a fiduciary holding the funds
   - *in the event a transaction is not consummated for any reason, the broker has no automatic claim on deposits or escrow funds*
4. **What records need to be retained and for how long**
   - *canceled and unused escrow/trust account checks, checkbooks, and bank statements* must be retained for a <u>*MINIMUM*</u> of *seven (7) years*
   - *the seven-year clock* starts ticking when *the latest* of these events occurs:
     - *expiration* of the listing agreement or buyer or tenant representation agreement
     - *closing* of the transaction
     - *final disbursement* of all transaction funds held in escrow

Also, *the Commission may examine and audit any escrow or trust account <u>whenever</u> it deems such action necessary*. (References: Sections 20-324k; 20-325m; 20-328-7a; and 20-328-8a(b))

The requirements of trust accounts and records are the responsibility of a licensee's broker and not, therefore, appropriate for salesperson exam questions.

However, the following details regarding account interest are worth mentioning here, since all licensees should be familiar with certain basic procedures in order to explain them to members of the public.

II. Connecticut Laws Governing the Activities of Licensees
(Expect 10 questions from this Outline Section)

As you will find in the upcoming Topic Area on the Landlord and Tenant Act (IV-B), ***residential security deposits*** are to be held in an ***interest-bearing account and earn a rate of at least one and one-half percent***. Further, ***accrued interest must be either paid over or credited to the tenant on each annual renewal anniversary date***. (Reference: 47a-21(h)(i))

There is also a provision in the statutes that requires brokers to ***establish interest-bearing escrow or trust accounts and contribute earned interest to a fund that provides mortgage assistance to low and moderate income first time homebuyers***.

Although broker participation is mandatory, ***client funds are not automatically subject to having any interest attached for the mortgage assistance program****; details are best left to those brokers who establish accounts subject to the program's requirements.*

(Reference: Section 8-265f)

Violation Alert!
It is worth noting here that ***there are at least two Section 20-320 violation land-mines*** in this Topic Area ***that could be grounds for the maximum fine ($2,000) and/or license suspension or revocation***. You could be invited to meet your Real Estate Commissioners in Hartford for
- ***failing***, within a reasonable time, ***to account for or remit any moneys coming into the licensee's possession which belongs to others***, or
- ***commingling funds*** of others with the licensee's own, ***or failing to keep funds of others in an escrow or trustee account*** (References: Section 20-320(5),(10))

Further, according to <u>Sec. 20-324k. Brokers to maintain escrow or trust account for certain moneys held. Disputed deposits.</u>, *there is a possibility of jail time* for violators! Sec. 20-324k(e) says:

"*Any broker who willfully violates any provision of this section shall be fined not more than* <u>*one thousand dollars*</u> *or* <u>*imprisoned not more than six months*</u> <u>*or both.*</u>"

So, no fooling around with other people's money!!

II-D. Misrepresentation   (Expect 1-3 questions from this area)

A misrepresentation is considered *"material"* when it *is significant in a party's decision-making process of approving or disproving a purchase; when known or reasonably should have been discovered by a seller, a seller's agent, or even a buyer's agent, material facts must be disclosed*. Failure to do so is, in Connecticut, an actionable violation.

Material facts may include anything *that actually affects a buyer or seller's approval or rejection,* ***even down to types of available financing and date of closing or possession***.

As noted in Topic Area I-A, Section 20-320(1),(2) makes any licensee found ***guilty of making any material misrepresentation***, *or* ***making any false promise*** *of a character likely to influence, persuade, or induce, subject to license suspension, revocation, and/or a fine of* ***no more than $2,000***.

That is all the Connecticut Real Estate License Law notes specifically regarding material

II. Connecticut Laws Governing the Activities of Licensees
(Expect 10 questions from this Outline Section)

misrepresentation. However, *on misrepresentation, there is this*

- *a licensee shall not misrepresent or conceal any material facts* in any transaction
- *no licensee shall misrepresent the actual selling price of real estate to any lender or any other interested party*, either verbally or through the preparation of a false sales contract
- *a real estate broker shall exercise diligence at all times in obtaining and presenting accurate information in the broker's advertising* and representations to the public; the following advertising-related misrepresentations will also be noted, and may be tested, in Topic Area II-F, Advertising,
    - *no broker shall advertise* to sell, buy, exchange, rent or lease the property of another *in a manner indicating the offer* to sell, buy, exchange, rent or lease such property *is being made by a private party* not engaged in the real estate business
    - *no real estate broker shall either advertise without disclosing the broker's name or permit any person associated with the broker to use individual names*, telephone numbers, or mailing addresses, *to the exclusion of the name of such broker*

(References: Section 20-328-5a(a)(b)(c))

A key aspect of the **Residential Property Condition Disclosure Report** bears on **implications of misrepresentation**, and though the Report is the sole subject of Topic Area IV-A-6, the statement regarding misrepresentation is worth including here, especially since it refers to this very Section regarding misrepresentation.

Basically, **providing a good-faith accurate disclosure relieves some liabilities but does not relieve others**. As a required statement in the Report puts it:

"This report in no way relieves a real estate broker of the broker's obligation under the provisions of section 20-328-5a of the Regulations of Connecticut State Agencies *to disclose any material facts. Failure to do so could result in punitive action taken against the broker, such as fines, suspension or revocation of license."* (Reference: Section 20-327b(d)(2)(C))

II-E. Disclosure of Nonmaterial Facts   (Expect 1-2 questions from this area)

Simply put, Connecticut Real Estate License Law has long identified *"psychologically impacted properties"* as those with a potentially stigmatizing history including, but not limited to, being a site where

- an occupant is, or was at any time suspected to be, infected with the human immunodeficiency syndrome (HIV/AIDS)
- there was a real or suspected occurrence of a homicide, suicide, or felony

Amendments passed by the 2004 General Assembly tweaked this area by using the term *nonmaterial fact concerning real property* to replace *psychologically impacted properties*.

- *Nonmaterial fact* provides a neutral categorization for *certain facts about a property's history that are to be treated by licensees as immaterial, such as that the property was the site of a homicide, suicide, other death, felony, or residence for someone with HIV/AIDS or other reportable disease*

II. Connecticut Laws Governing the Activities of Licensees
(Expect 10 questions from this Outline Section)

- It also removes specific reference to HIV/AIDS, substituting instead the "fact that an occupant of real property is or has been infected with a disease on the list of reportable diseases issued by the Commissioner of Public Health." (Reference: Section 20-329cc)

Regardless of the names one uses, it's understandable that some people would be uncomfortable about moving into a property with a history that might have strange effects on their, or their children's, imaginations after dark.

But in Connecticut, a licensee is not automatically responsible for disclosing the historical facts noted above. According to Connecticut Real Estate License Law
- *the existence of any fact or circumstance that may have a psychological impact* on the purchaser or lessee *is not a material fact* that must be disclosed in a real estate transaction
- *no cause of action shall arise* against an owner of real estate, his or her agent, or any agent of the transferee *for the failure to disclose to the transferee that the transferred property was the site of a "nonmaterial fact,"* as defined in section 20-329cc

(Reference: Section 20-329dd)

However, even though licensees are not required to volunteer information about the particulars noted above, *potential buyers or renters who are seriously interested* in the property have *the right to ask for information, in writing,* and get a straight answer.

According to Connecticut Real Estate License Law, the following statements apply
- *If a real estate purchaser or lessee* of real estate in the process of making a bona fide offer *advises an owner or the owner's agent, in writing, that knowledge of a property's history as noted above is important to the decision* to purchase or lease the property, *the owner, through the owner's agent, shall make a written report of any findings*. The report, however, is subject to and must be consistent with applicable laws of privacy.
- *If the owner refuses to disclose such information, the owner's agent shall so advise the purchaser or lessee in writing*. (Reference: Section 20-329ee)

Finally, though, *nondisclosure of material flaws in a property's physical condition* <u>cannot be justified with arguments like</u> "a ghost busted the foundation, so I was not required to either discuss or disclose it."

Rather, the regulations say that *nothing identified as a "nonmaterial fact" above shall alter the legal rights of a purchaser, lessee, seller, or lessor of real estate for regarding disclosures of physical deficiencies* of the transferred property. (Reference: Section 20-329ff)

So, watch carefully for the term ***"nonmaterial facts"*** *in test questions regarding the effect of certain facts on a property's marketability, disclosure requirements, liability for nondisclosure, and acceptable language on forms.*

II. Connecticut Laws Governing the Activities of Licensees
(Expect 10 questions from this Outline Section)

II-F. Advertising (Expect 1-2 questions from this area)

The one or two questions you will see regarding advertising rules will most likely concentrate on one of the following points

- needing the *written consent of an owner to place a sign on a property*; this would typically be included in a listing agreement
- ensuring that *all advertised information is accurate*
- *revealing that the ad was placed by a licensee*, not a private individual
- *including the broker/firm name in all advertising*
- *no licensee shall modify listing information without the express permission of the listing broker*
- *any licensee who lists property listed by a broker with whom the licensee is not affiliated must*
    - *have the listing broker's permission*
    - *update information at least every 72 hours*
    - *make clear in the advertising that the property is not listed with the licensee*
- *Internet advertising* or marketing under a licensee's control *shall have a home page that includes*
    - *the licensee's name and office address* as they appear on the licensee's real estate license
    - *the affiliated broker's name* as it is registered with the Commission
    - *all states in which the licensee is licensed*
    - *the last date on which property information shown on the site was updated*
- *Internet advertising and marketing communications* via e-mail, e-mail discussion groups, bulletin boards, or other means, *must include on the first or last page*
    - *the licensee's name and office address*
    - *the affiliated broker's name* as it is registered with the Commission
    - *all states in which the licensee is licensed*

(References: Sections 20-328-2a(g); 20-328-5a(c),(d),(e),(f))

Though this is not likely to be tested, traditional **"cold calling"** *and similar telemarketing advertisements or solicitations are quite likely illegal due to the statutory restrictions in the relatively recent Sections included in Chapter 743m: Telemarketing, especially Section 42-288a, which also prohibits blocking the outgoing caller ID for telemarketing solicitations.*

The Department of Consumer Protection oversees an in-state "No Sales Solicitation Calls" list; as a licensee, you should investigate this prior to determining phone-bank marketing strategies.

II-G. Commissions and Compensation (Expect 1-2 questions from this area)

Questions in this Topic Area are most likely to concentrate on something included in the following Section of the license law:

> ***Each written agreement that fixes the compensation to be paid to a real estate broker*** for the sale, lease, or purchase of real property ***shall contain the following statement*** in not less than

II. Connecticut Laws Governing the Activities of Licensees
(Expect 10 questions from this Outline Section)

ten-point boldface type or in a manner which otherwise stands out significantly from the text immediately preceding any provision of such agreement relating to broker compensation:

> **"NOTICE: THE AMOUNT OR RATE OF REAL ESTATE BROKER COMPENSATION IS NOT FIXED BY LAW. IT IS SET BY EACH BROKER INDIVIDUALLY AND MAY BE NEGOTIABLE BETWEEN YOU AND THE BROKER."** (Reference: Section 20-325b)

Questions drawn from these statements will concentrate on *written agreements*, *the need for the statement to be prominent*, and the fact that *broker compensation is not set by convention, professional agreement with other brokers, or law*: such arrangements would violate antitrust laws.

The idea of making an antitrust statement very visible is neither new nor unique to Connecticut. Some of the following points, though, regarding commissions and compensation are. And they are more fruitful topics for test questions. They include

- *a licensee shall not accept any compensation in any form from any party without the knowledge and consent of the principal and, sometimes, all parties to a transaction*
- *a licensee shall not make any form of compensation to an unlicensed person who performs transaction-related activities that require a license*
- any *compensation given directly to, and intended for, a particular licensee needs to be signed over to the licensee's broker*, who may then reassign it per any agreement(s) between them
- *brokers must make all licensee compensations through the licensee's broker* unless there is written knowledge and consent of the licensee's broker to do otherwise
- *in the event a transaction is not consummated for any reason, the broker has no automatic claim on deposits or escrow funds*   (Reference: Section 20-328-8a)

Since *matters of money are crucial in business*, the entire regulation supporting the above summaries is given here:

Sec. 20-328-8a. Commissions and compensation.
  (a) *No licensee shall demand compensation unless reasonable cause for payment of compensation exists*.
  (b) *When an owner*, lessor, prospective buyer or lessee *wrongfully fails or is unable to consummate a transaction, the real estate broker has no right to any portion of the money, if any, deposited with the real estate broker even though compensation may have been earned*.
  (c) While engaging in the real estate business, *a licensee shall not accept any commission, rebate, or profit on expenditures made for the licensee's principal without the knowledge and consent of the licensee's principal*.
  (d) A licensee *shall not accept compensation from more than one party in a real estate transaction without notifying all parties to the transaction prior to the closing*.
  (e) *No licensee shall* offer, promise, allow, give, *pay* or rebate, directly or indirectly, any part or share of the licensee's commission or compensation arising or accruing from any real estate transaction *to any person who is engaging in the real estate business and who was not licensed as a real estate broker or real estate salesperson at the time* the real estate broker or real estate salesperson performed the acts or rendered the services for which the

II. Connecticut Laws Governing the Activities of Licensees
(Expect 10 questions from this Outline Section)

licensee offers, promises, allows, gives, pays or rebates such commission or compensation.

(f) *If a licensee receives or is awarded any compensation with respect to any transaction* in which the licensee is engaged on behalf of the real estate broker with whom the licensee is affiliated, *the licensee shall promptly pay over or assign such compensation to such real estate broker.*

(g) *In a cooperative real estate transaction, a real estate broker shall compensate the cooperating real estate broker and shall not compensate* nor offer to compensate, directly or indirectly, *any of the real estate salespersons or brokers employed by or affiliated with the cooperating real estate broker* without the prior express knowledge and consent of the cooperating broker.

In addition, when it comes to the line between compensation and licensed/unlicensed activities, the Commission has issued a policy that states,

- **Licensees should not share commissions with unlicensed persons** acting as assistants, clerical staff, closing secretaries, etc. (Reference: Connecticut Real Estate Commission Policy on Use of Unlicensed Persons by Licensees, 12/5/1996)

Interestingly, Connecticut is a forerunner nationally in protecting the rights of real estate licensees to compensation through statutes authorizing **broker's liens** for almost all real estate transactions, though these liens are generally intended for certain commercial leases.

The regulation that lays out all the particulars is lengthy and dense, but notes that among the other contract elements, the following clause needs to be included in the real estate contract

THE REAL ESTATE BROKER MAY BE ENTITLED TO CERTAIN LIEN RIGHTS PERSUANT TO SECTION 20-325a OF THE CONNECTICUT GENERAL STATUTES

To have full force and effect, a duly executed broker's lien should be recorded according to the guidelines in the statute noted above. (Reference: Section 20-325a)

Although it is doubtful that you will be tested on anything having to do with broker's liens, you should know that they exist and look into the particulars once you become an active licensee. This tip alone may pay you back for many times the price of this book!

II-H. Unlicensed Personal Assistants   (Expect 1-2 questions from this area)

In order to provide guidance to licensees with regard to which activities related to a real estate transaction unlicensed persons can and cannot perform, the Commission established a policy on **activities that can be performed by unlicensed persons**.

The Commission has published the following list as a guideline to help licensees understand which activities they may delegate to those who act as personal assistants, clerical support staff, closing secretaries, and other employees and/or assistants. **These activities include, but are not necessarily limited to, matters such as**

- **answering the phone** and forwarding calls to licensee
- **transmitting listings and changes to a multiple listing service**
- following up on loan commitments after a contract has been negotiated

II. Connecticut Laws Governing the Activities of Licensees
(Expect 10 questions from this Outline Section)

- *assembling documents for closing*
- *securing documents*; i.e., public information from town/city hall, courthouse, sewer district, water district, tax assessor, etc.
- *having keys made* for company listings
- *writing and preparing ads* (with review of licensee), flyers and promotional materials and placing such advertising
- *recording and depositing earnest money* and other trust funds
- *typing contract forms* under a licensee's direction
- monitoring licenses and personnel files
- *computing commission checks*
- *placing signs on property*
- *ordering items* of routine repair as directed by licensees
- *acting as a courier* service to deliver documents, pick up keys, etc.
- *scheduling appointments* for licensees to show listed property
- *measuring property*

The Commission notes that *an unlicensed assistant is not a decision-maker; rather, shall take all direction from the supervising licensee*.

Finally, though it was mentioned in the preceding Topic Area on Compensation, it is worth repeating for emphasis here that the Policy specifically states that *licensees should not share commissions with unlicensed persons* acting as assistants, clerical staff, closing secretaries, etc.

- *The temptation for such unlicensed persons, in such situations, to go beyond what they can do and negotiate or take part in other prohibited activities is greatly increased when their compensation is based on the successful completion of the sale*.

(Reference: Connecticut Real Estate Commission Policy on Use of Unlicensed Persons by Licensees, 12/5/1996)

Violation Alert!
It is worth noting here that *there are TWO "catch-all" Section 20-320 violation land-mines* that are *applicable to EVERY Topic Area* in this Content Outline Section *that could be grounds for the maximum fine ($2,000) and/or license suspension or revocation*. You could be invited to meet your Real Estate Commissioners in Hartford for
- *any act or conduct that constitutes dishonest, fraudulent, or improper dealings*, or
- *a violation of any provision of this chapter or any regulation adopted* under this chapter (i.e., Chapter 392: Real Estate Brokers and Salespersons, which means the entire License Law)

(References: Section 20-320(11),(13))

This ends the presentation of key terms and concepts likely to be either tested or used as distractors in this Content Outline Section.

III. Connecticut Real Estate Agency   (Expect 8 questions from this Outline Section)

SPECIAL NOTE ON THE AGENCY OUTLINE SECTION

It has been at least ten years since the Connecticut Real Estate Commission began transforming common law agency understandings into state-specific distinctions and requirements regarding licensee agency representation relationships and disclosures.

So read the following carefully, since it provides perhaps the pithiest presentation of a tangled set of agency forms and requirements available to date here in Connecticut.

In order to make this material as direct and concise as possible, there are places in the following presentation of regulations where the actual language of the regulations has been "boiled down."

For example, "broker" will be short for the firm's broker of record; "licensee" will be short for all affiliated brokers and salespeople; "agent" will refer to any licensee in an agency relationship with another party.

A review of the source regulation or Commission policy, memorandum, or form should verify that the meaning has not been distorted out of testable range; references are provided for verification purposes.

A 1997 Commissioner's Memorandum on Agency and the 2000 Connecticut Real Estate Commission Policy on Agency provide concise overviews of important agency issues discussed here.

These documents are brief and worth reviewing in their entirety to better grasp some of the fine points of Connecticut Real Estate Agency Law; they can be found in Appendix E.

III-A. Agency: the Representing of a Client vs. Working with a Customer
(Expect 1-2 questions from this area)

In broad, general terms, a **client** is **a party who has entered into an agency representation relationship with a licensee** whereas a **customer** is **a party who has not**, and is therefore not legally represented by a licensee even though a licensee may be working with that party.

In Connecticut, **the law allows licensees to work with a buyer as either a client or a customer**.

According to the Commission Memorandum reproduced in Appendix E, a **"brokerage firm that lists properties cannot refuse to work with a buyer on a customer basis if that buyer does not seek representation and wishes to be shown in-house listed properties."**

The Memorandum notes that **since listing licensees are legally required to make a diligent effort to sell the property, any agent efforts or office policies that exclude working with buyers as customers legally breaches the listing firm's fiduciary obligations to its seller-clients.**

III. Connecticut Real Estate Agency   (Expect 8 questions from this Outline Section)

The following definitions help clarify specific type of agents/agency and the client(s) whom they represent; these terms will receive further treatment in subsequent Topic Areas.

- *"Licensee"* means a real estate broker and/or real estate salesperson;
- *"seller's agent"* or *"agent of the seller"* mean a licensee who acts in a fiduciary capacity for the prospective seller or prospective lessor in a real estate transaction;
- *"buyer's agent"* or *"agent of the buyer"* mean a licensee who acts in a fiduciary capacity for the prospective buyer or prospective lessee in a real estate transaction;
- *"dual agent"* means a licensee who acts in a fiduciary capacity for both the prospective seller or prospective lessor and the prospective buyer or prospective lessee in a real estate transaction;
- *"designated seller agent"* means a licensee designated by the licensee's affiliated broker to solely represent a seller/landlord client; and
- *"designated buyer agent"* means a licensee designated by the licensee's affiliated broker to solely represent a buyer/tenant client.

(References: Sections 20-311(7)(8) and 20-325d-1(c)(d)(e)(f))

A licensee representing a client as an agent puts the client's interests ahead of unrepresented persons (customers) and those represented by other agents; an agent owes the client certain undivided *fiduciary obligations*, such as

- *loyalty*
- *reasonable care*
- *disclosure*
- *obedience to lawful instruction*
- *confidentiality*
- *accountability (accounting)*

Of course, the law also stresses that all licensees are obligated to *treat all parties to a real estate transaction honestly and fairly*, regardless of which, if any, party they may represent.

Nevertheless, *unrepresented parties have the responsibility to protect their own interests* by reading all agreements and documents carefully and consulting appropriate professionals for advice on financing, legal, accounting, and other matters related to the transaction.

A customer who has not contracted *in writing* for agency representation *should NOT assume that legally supportable agency representation* exists based solely on time spent with, or assistance provided by, a licensee.   (Reference: Section 20-325d-2)

> *It is important to mention at this point that **agency disclosures** are critical, and that there are **several specific types of forms** from which licensees must choose, **including one to be given to unrepresented persons**, and specific guidelines for when and to whom they must be provided. These matters will be the subject of Topic Area III-C, Agency Disclosure.*

The Commission Policy on Agency has guidelines for working with buyers as both customers and clients.

The Policy notes that *a licensee may conduct "preliminary activities"* for a buyer before a written buyer representation agreement is entered into, *given that the licensee*

III. Connecticut Real Estate Agency (Expect 8 questions from this Outline Section)

- *asks whether the buyer is currently being represented* by another real estate firm;
- *explains the real estate firm's office policy on* the various *agency, dual agency, designated agency, and customer relationships* that the licensee could potentially have with the buyer; and
- *specifically tells the buyer not to provide confidential information unless and until the buyer and licensee have entered into an agency relationship*

At this point, *the licensee, still without entering into a written buyer agency agreement, may give the buyer* the following information
- *property information*;
- *information on the licensee's firm*; or
- *information on mortgage rates and lending institutions*

However, *the licensee must either have (1) a signed buyer agency agreement*, which makes the buyer a client, *or (2) have given the buyer the Agency Disclosure Notice Given to <u>Unrepresented Persons</u>*, which clarifies that the buyer remains an unrepresented customer, *in order to* take any of the following actions
- *ask the buyer to disclose confidential information* (including information about the buyer's financial status, reasons for purchasing, etc.);
- *express an opinion on or give advice about particular real estate* (note that a licensee representing the seller should be cautious expressing an opinion or giving advice);
- *physically show the buyer in-house listings*;
- *physically show the buyer property listed with another firm*;
- *discuss an offer with the buyer*; or
- *engage in any verbal or written negotiations on the buyer's behalf* concerning the price or any terms or conditions of the purchase

(Reference: Connecticut Real Estate Commission Policy on Agency)

III-B. Agency Agreements (Expect 1-2 questions from this area)

Overview and Definitions
In general, *agency runs from a client to the broker in a brokerage firm and from there to all licensees in that firm*. This means that if the firm has entered into a listing agreement with a seller, then all of the licensees in that firm are agents of that seller, represent that seller, and owe fiduciary duties to that seller.

Likewise, if the firm enters into a buyer agency agreement with a buyer, then all of the licensees in that firm are the agents of the buyer, represent the buyer, and owe fiduciary duties to that buyer. *(See below for how dual agency and designated agency address the conflict of interest inherent in showing in-house properties to an in-house buyer.)*

(Reference: Connecticut Real Estate Commission Policy on Agency)

Connecticut *listing agreements establish an agency representation relationship* between a principal, whether a seller or residential landlord, and a broker/firm *and must meet certain minimum requirements to be in legal compliance*. They must
- *be in writing*
- *properly identify the property* (a street address is acceptable for a listing, though the legal

III. Connecticut Real Estate Agency   (Expect 8 questions from this Outline Section)

- description needs to be in any deed)
- *contain all of the terms and conditions* of the sale, exchange or lease, *including the commission to be paid*
- *include the following statement* regarding compensation arrangements
    - NOTICE: THE AMOUNT OR RATE OF REAL ESTATE BROKER COMPENSATION IS NOT FIXED BY LAW. IT IS SET BY EACH BROKER INDIVIDUALLY AND MAY BE NEGOTIATED BETWEEN YOU AND THE BROKER.
- *state the date on which the listing agreement is entered into*
- *give the listing's expiration date*
- *be signed by the principal or* the principal's appropriately *authorized agent*
- *be signed by the broker or* the broker's *authorized agent*
- *clearly indicate the type of listing*, e.g. exclusive or open
- *identify, if applicable, that the agent will permit non-affiliated licensees to advertise the property* (e.g., Multiple Listing Services, Internet links, etc.) *along with any exceptions* to same
- *include the following statement regarding discriminatory practices*
    - This agreement is subject to the Connecticut General Statutes prohibiting discrimination in commercial and residential real estate transactions (C.G.S. Title 46a, Chapter 814c)   (References: Sections 20-325b; 20-328-4a; and 20-328-6a(a)(1))

Special regulations regarding net listings
"Net listing" means a listing contract in which the broker receives as a commission all excess moneys over and above the minimum sales price agreed upon by the broker and seller; *no licensee shall accept or enter into a net listing*. In cases where the owner or the lessor wishes to list in this manner, the agreed upon fee shall be added and listings made in the usual manner.

(References: Sections 20-328-1a(e) and 20-328-6a(c))

Buyer agency & lessees
Connecticut *buyer and lessee agency agreements*, like their seller/lessor counterparts, also establish an agency representation relationship between a principal, whether a prospective buyer or tenant, and an agent and must meet certain minimum requirements to be in legal compliance. They must

- *be in writing*
- *contain all of the terms and conditions* of the agreement, *including the compensation to be paid*
- *include the following statement* regarding compensation arrangements
    - NOTICE: THE AMOUNT OR RATE OF REAL ESTATE BROKER COMPENSATION IS NOT FIXED BY LAW. IT IS SET BY EACH BROKER INDIVIDUALLY AND MAY BE NEGOTIATED BETWEEN YOU AND THE BROKER.
- *state the date on which the agreement is entered into*
- *state the* agreement's *expiration date*
- *be signed by the prospective buyer or lessee or* a properly authorized *agent*
- *be signed by the broker or* the broker's authorized *agent*
- *include the following statement*

III. Connecticut Real Estate Agency   (Expect 8 questions from this Outline Section)

- This agreement is subject to the Connecticut General Statutes prohibiting discrimination in commercial and residential real estate transactions (C.G.S. Title 46a, Chapter 814c)

(References: Sections 20-325b; 20-328-4a; and 20-328-6a(a)(2))

For all instruments other than listing agreements, buyer agency agreements, or lessee agreements, *the licensee, for the protection of all parties, shall* use the licensee's best efforts to *assure that all contractual commitments regarding real estate transactions* with which the licensee is associated are
- *in writing*,
- *dated*, and
- *express the agreement of the parties*.   (Reference: Section 20-328-6a(b))

Commercial contracts

A licensee attempting to negotiate or negotiating sale, exchange or lease of a commercial real estate transaction shall obtain a listing, buyer, or tenant representation agreement, memorandum, letter, or other writing stating for whom the licensee will act or has acted, signed by the party for whom the licensee will act or has acted in the commercial real estate transaction, the duration of the authorization, and the amount of any compensation payable to the licensee.

(Reference: Section 20-328-6a(d))

Violation Alert!

It is worth noting here that *there are two Section 20-320 violation land-mines* in this Topic Area *that could be grounds for the maximum fine ($2,000) and/or license suspension or revocation.* You could be invited to meet your Real Estate Commissioners in Hartford for
- entering into an exclusive listing agreement or buyer agency agreement *if it provides for an automatic extension of the listing period*, or
- *failing to deliver immediately a copy of above agreements* or related transaction instruments to any party or parties entitled to them   (References: Section 20-320(6),(7))

III-C. Agency Disclosure   (Expect 1-2 questions from this area)

Agency disclosure requirements seem to be as varied as the types of possible customer and client agency relationships.

However, there are a few basic forms that help explain available types of representation for clients and customers. The *most commonly used forms* that present agency descriptions and/or disclosures are either broker-generated or statutorily "fixed"
1. *Company Listing and/or Buyer Agency Agreements*, which generally incorporate Consent to Subagency statements, and sometimes dual/designated agency agreements *(form per Broker)*
2. *Real Estate Agency Disclosure Notice* Given to <u>Unrepresented Persons</u> *(form per Sec. 20-325d-2)*
3. *Dual Agency Consent Agreement (form per Sec. 20-325g)*
4. *Dual Agency/Designated Agency Disclosure Notice and Consent Agreement* Given to <u>Persons Represented by the Same Brokerage Firm</u> *(form per Sec.20-325j-1)*

III. Connecticut Real Estate Agency (Expect 8 questions from this Outline Section)

The regulations concerning which agent provides the applicable disclosure notice, when, and other details are scattered in the statutes and regulations; however, below is a consolidated summary of them.

Seller or lessor's agents shall make a written disclosure of whom the licensee represents in a real estate transaction to prospective purchasers and lessees *at the beginning of the first personal meeting concerning the specific needs of the prospective purchaser or lessee*
- *this requirement applies* to all parties *unless such prospective purchaser or lessee is represented by another licensee*
- any such disclosure shall be (1) *signed by the prospective purchaser or lessee* and (2) *attached to any offer or agreement to purchase or lease* signed by the prospective purchaser or lessee
  - *if the prospective purchaser or lessee refuses to sign* the disclosure, *the agent shall note this refusal on the line indicated* for the prospective party's signature

Buyer or lessee's agents shall disclose such intended representation to the seller or lessor *at the beginning of the first personal meeting* with the seller or lessor *concerning the seller or lessor's real property*
- *this requirement applies* to all parties *unless such seller or lessor is represented by another licensee*
- any such disclosure shall be (1) *signed by the seller, lessor, or their agent* and the prospective buyer/lessee's agent, and (2) *attached to any offer, binder, option, or agreement to purchase or lease*
  - *if the prospective seller, lessor, or their agent refuses to sign* the disclosure, *the agent shall note this refusal on the line indicated* for the prospective party's signature   (References: Sections 20-325d; 20-325d-2; and 20-325d-5)

Fortunately, required disclosure notices *need only be given once* to each prospective seller, lessor, buyer, or lessee by a real estate licensee; also,
- any licensee acting as a cooperating licensee shall be responsible for providing the notice . . . *[if] no cooperating licensee is involved . . . the seller's or buyer's or the dual agent shall be responsible for providing the notice*

(Reference: Section 20-325d-6)

And *at open houses*, disclosure notices *do not have to be given to individuals* attending an open house as long as the following conditions apply
- *the licensee, by sign, poster, pamphlet, or similar means, conspicuously discloses the licensee's agency relationship*, and
- *no personal meeting* concerning the prospective buyer or lessee's specific real estate needs *occurs at the open house*   (Reference: Section 20-325d-7)

Violation Alert!
It is worth noting here that *there are two disclosure-of-representation Section 20-320 violation land-mines* in this Topic Area *that could be grounds for the maximum fine ($2,000) and/or license suspension or revocation*. You could be invited to meet your Real Estate Commissioners in Hartford for
- acting as an agent for more than one party in a transaction *without the knowledge of all parties*

III. Connecticut Real Estate Agency   (Expect 8 questions from this Outline Section)

for whom the licensee acts, or
- *representing or attempting to represent a real estate broker* other than the licensee's named broker *without the express knowledge and consent of the named broker*

(References: Section 20-320(3),(4))

III-D. Subagency Limitations   (Expect 1-2 questions from this area)

Subagency, as a common law concept, is relatively simple: when an agent for a principal authorizes a third party to act cooperatively on behalf of the principal, *the third party*, as an agent of the primary agent, *has been granted subagency* and *is referred to as a subagent*.

SUBAGENCY: A CRITICAL NOTE FOR HISTORICAL CONTEXT

For many, many decades, when brokerage firms took listings and submitted property information to a REALTORS® Association multiple listing service (MLS), common membership of firms and affiliated licensees in the Association meant that all subscribing members were automatically subagents of the seller.

*In turn, most licensees working with buyers were technically working for the sellers, even if they never met, and **NOT** for the buyers, who generally thought the licensee providing all the rides to view listings was, in fact, their trusted representative. And most licensees also thought they were "working for their buyer," even though they were simultaneously very aware that their compensation came from the seller's side of the closing statement.*

To avoid the many genuine and perceived opportunities for misrepresentation subagency invites, and to limit public exploitation and/or lawsuits, most jurisdictions nationwide have legislated specific applications of agency law at various times within the past twenty years.

Some have gone so far as to specifically leave the terms 'subagency/subagent' out of their list of agency relationships in an effort to obliterate any possibility that its very existence would allow an entrenched history of 'automatic' creation to cloud present attempts to restrict its applicability. The concept and basic relationship, though, still survive.

In some other states, like Connecticut, there are now legal restrictions on automatic subagency, as well as provisions allowing and defining relationships such dual agency and designated agency.

The Connecticut Real Estate Commission Policy on Agency (see Appendix D) helps clarify how subagency, dual agency, and designated agency work in practice: each will be taken up in its own Topic Area in this Content Outline Section.

The Connecticut Real Estate Commission Policy on Agency has the following *statement summarizing the practice of subagency in Connecticut:*

Limits on Subagency
In cooperating sales, there is no longer the presumption that the broker working with the buyer is the subagent of the seller. The *primary purpose of this change is to encourage buyer representation.*

III. Connecticut Real Estate Agency (Expect 8 questions from this Outline Section)

Subagency is still allowed, but *for each listing shown, the seller would have to approve the subagency relationship by signing a written consent to subagency*.

The Policy also clarifies that since agency runs to the brokerage firm, *when a seller consents to a cooperating broker acting as a subagent, all of the broker's affiliated licensees, except those specifically appointed as designated agents, are also that seller's subagents*.

(Reference: Connecticut Real Estate Policy on Agency)

The specific regulation that prohibits a broker's creation of subagency without the principal's written consent *also limits the broker's ability to be creative in working around that informed consent.* Further, the broker must use a *subagency consent agreement that informs the principal of the principal's vicarious liability for acts of the subagent*.

No real estate broker shall make any unilateral offer of subagency or *agree to compensate, appoint, employ, cooperate with or otherwise affiliate with a subagent* for the sale or purchase of real property *without the informed written consent of the person whom the real estate broker represents*.

Such written consent shall contain the name and real estate license number of the real estate broker to be appointed as the subagent and *shall contain a statement notifying the person whom the real estate broker represents that the law imposes vicarious liability on the principal for the acts of the subagent*.

(Reference: Section 20-325f)

III-E. Dual Agency (Expect 1-2 questions from this area)

In Connecticut, **"dual agent"** means a licensee who acts in a fiduciary capacity for both the prospective seller or prospective lessor and the prospective buyer or prospective lessee in a real estate transaction.

(Reference: Section 20-325d-1(e))

SPECIAL NOTE REGARDING DUAL AGENCY

Dual agency relationships open especially delicate—and litigious—prospects regarding **licensee conflicts of interest and misrepresentation**, *since a licensee representing both parties has unusual restrictions on every fiduciary duty, most notably loyalty, confidence, and disclosure.*

In general, dual agency imposes obvious **constraints on disclosures of confidential material known about either party**, *and conflicts over "full" representation to each arise easily.*

For example, if a dual agent's keeping the confidence of a seller's motivation from the buyer hurts the buyer's ability to negotiate a lower price, the buyer may feel cheated, perhaps enough to sue.

Some lawyers—and real estate instructors—doubt the basic validity of "dual agency": they argue it is a legal impossibility to act as a true fiduciary for opposing parties.

They might even suggest it would be prudent for each party to engage separate lawyers and simply let the "dual agent" licensee play messenger and handle the transaction paperwork.

III. Connecticut Real Estate Agency   (Expect 8 questions from this Outline Section)

Connecticut's Statutes and Regulations provide practical explanations, guidelines, and forms for dual agency, but you will soon find that even "basic" dual agency is anything but simple.

Connecticut regulations establish the foundation for licensees to engage in dual agency relationships. According to the Commission Policy on Agency, dual agency legislation authorizes guidelines and forms to clarify specifics of disclosure requirements.

Commission-approved **dual agency consent forms or an acceptable statement regarding dual agency in a brokerage firm's agency agreements must be used to obtain a buyer's and seller's (or landlord and tenant's) consent to dual agency**.

For in-house sales, where only one brokerage firm is involved, **the brokerage firm can represent both the buyer and seller as a dual agent, provided that this consent is obtained**. The consent forms provide guidance as to what type of disclosures *cannot* be made in a dual agency relationship.   (Reference: Connecticut Real Estate Commission Policy on Agency)

But, by the regulations adopted in Connecticut and elsewhere, **dual agency restricts basic fiduciary obligations**. According to Connecticut Real Estate License Law
- **the firm shall not be required to, and shall not, disclose to either buyer or seller any personal, financial, or other confidential information** to such other party **without the express written consent** of the party whose information is disclosed
    - **this does not apply to information related to material property defects** known to the firm **and other information the firm is required to disclose by law**
- **the firm may not disclose**
    - **to the buyer** that the seller will accept less than the asking or listed price, unless otherwise instructed to do so in writing by the seller
    - **to the seller** that the buyer can or will pay a price greater than the price submitted in a written offer to the seller, unless otherwise instructed to do so in writing by the buyer
    - **the motivation of the seller or buyer** for selling, buying, or leasing property, unless otherwise instructed in writing by the respective party
    - **that a seller or buyer will agree to financing terms other than those offered**, unless instructed in writing by the respective party

The statutes recognize the delicate nature of a dual agent's dual allegiances, and advise **both parties to seek competent legal and tax advice with regard to transactions**, and with regard to all documents executed in connection with transactions, including a Dual Agency Consent Agreement.
(Reference: Section 20-325g)

Further, regulatory provisions have this to add about understanding dual agency
- **Dual agency** means that **the brokerage firm, and all licensees for the firm that are <u>NOT</u> acting as designated agents**, are dual agents and **act in a fiduciary capacity for both sides of the transaction**. Therefore, **the brokerage firm and its dual agents do not represent either side exclusively**, and **neither side can expect the firm or its dual agents' undivided loyalty**.
    - The brokerage **firm may not disclose to one side what it knows about the other** regarding personal, financial, or confidential information unless otherwise instructed by

III. Connecticut Real Estate Agency (Expect 8 questions from this Outline Section)

the originating party or required by law. ***This includes such information as either party's***
- ***willingness or ability to accept less or pay more***, or
- ***material motivation*** for pursuing the transaction, such as selling due to a pending divorce or bankruptcy, or need to buy to defer capital gains.

(Reference: Dual Agency/Designated Agency Disclosure Notice and Consent Agreement)

Finally, according to Connecticut Real Estate License Law, there shall be a conclusive presumption that a person has given *informed consent to a dual agency relationship* with a real estate broker *if that person executes a written consent* in the promulgated form *prior to executing any contract* or agreement for the purchase, sale or lease of real estate. (Reference: Section 20-325g)

In practice, approach dual agency with caution: this type of agency invites the greatest potential for ***conflict of interest*** of any agency relationship. After all, the firm and all of its licensees have a lot of trouble figuring out how to avoid sharing one party's confidential information with the other party when they know they have a basic fiduciary duty to the other party to disclose it.

III-F. Designated Agency (Expect 1-2 questions from this area)

In Connecticut, a basic understanding of designated agency and types of designated agents begins with the following statutory definitions
- ***designated agency*** means the appointment by a broker of one or more licensees to solely represent a buyer or tenant as a designated buyer's agent and appoint another to represent a seller or landlord as a designated seller's agent in a transaction
    - ***designated seller agent*** means a licensee designated by the licensee's broker to solely represent a named seller or landlord client of the broker during the term of a listing agreement or authorization
    - ***designated buyer agent*** means a licensee designated by the broker to solely represent a named buyer or tenant client of the broker during the term of a buyer representation agreement or authorization (References: Section 20-311(6),(7),(8))

Real estate brokers are allowed to appoint a separate seller agent and separate buyer agent for a dual agency transaction. ***The designated agents are not considered dual agents***.
(Reference: Connecticut Real Estate Commission Policy on Agency)

Designated buyer agents and seller agents
Any <u>broker may appoint one or more designated seller agents as additional agents</u> for a seller or landlord ***or a designated buyer agent as an additional agent*** for a buyer or tenant. ***Such designation may be made <u>with regard to a particular transaction only</u>***.

Upon such designation, the responsibility to satisfy the respective duties as a sellers or landlord's agent or as a buyers or tenant's agent shall be the primary responsibility of the individual so designated, who ***shall not be deemed a dual agent, except in the case of an individual designated to represent both a seller and buyer in the same transaction***. (Reference: Section 20-325i)

III. Connecticut Real Estate Agency (Expect 8 questions from this Outline Section)

Regulatory provisions have this to add about understanding how *single agency can be maintained when an in-house listing and an in-house buyer representation create a legal environment for conflict of interest* by using the option of designated agency

- *designated agency* involves the appointment by the brokerage firm of *one licensee* to solely represent the seller or lessor *as the Designated Seller Agent* and *another licensee* to solely represent the buyer or tenant *as the Designated Buyer Agent*, under which representation the following conditions apply
  - any designated agent is not deemed to be a dual agent, though other agents in the Firm may be
  - *designated agents owe undivided fiduciary duties* to the party for whom they have been appointed
  - *designated agents may use confidential information legally obtained* for their client's benefit; however,
    - *information obtained before the designation is still confidential* and must not be shared with the client
- the <u>brokerage firm</u> involved with designated agents *is <u>still considered a dual agent</u>*

(Reference: Dual Agency/Designated Agency Disclosure Notice and Consent Agreement)

III-G. Confidential Information (Expect 1-2 questions from this area)

Under the common law of agency, *a fiduciary's duty of confidentiality continues beyond the expiration of the agency relationship*.

However, in the course of reviewing and codifying agency relationships and duties for Connecticut's own in-state use, the statutes have added regulatory definition that have punitive teeth for violations.

The regulation governing prohibitions on using or disclosing confidential information is specifically designed to comfort principals regarding an agent's obligation of maintaining the confidentiality of privileged information acquired during a real estate transaction.

According to Connecticut Real Estate License Law, the following statements apply regarding confidential information

- *confidential information* means *facts* concerning a person's assets, liabilities, income, expenses, motivations to purchase, rent, or sell real property, and/or previous offers received or made to purchase or lease real property *that are NOT*
  - *authorized to be disclosed by the client*,
  - *a matter of general knowledge*,
  - *part of a public record*, or
  - *otherwise subject to disclosure* under any other provision of the general statutes or any regulation of Connecticut state agencies *(i.e., material facts)*
- regarding the handling of confidential information, *no licensee shall*
  - *reveal confidential information* concerning a person whom the licensee represented either as an agent, designated buyer agent, or a designated seller agent,
  - *use confidential information* concerning that person *to the person's disadvantage*, or

III. Connecticut Real Estate Agency (Expect 8 questions from this Outline Section)

- *use confidential information* concerning that person *for the licensee's advantage or the advantage of a third party*, *EXCEPT* as required by legal process, as necessary *to defend the licensee or licensee's firm from allegations of wrongful or negligent conduct, or* as necessary *to prevent the commission of a crime*

(Reference: Section 20-325h)

Violation Alert!

It is worth noting here that *the TWO "catch-all" Section 20-320 violation land-mines* are *especially applicable to this Topic Area* and *could be grounds for the maximum fine ($2,000) and/or license suspension or revocation*. You could be invited to meet your Real Estate Commissioners in Hartford for

- *any act or conduct that constitutes dishonest, fraudulent, or improper dealings*, or
- *a violation of any provision of this chapter or any regulation adopted* under this chapter *(i.e., Chapter 392: Real Estate Brokers and Salespersons, which means the entire License Law)*

(References: Section 20-320(11),(13))

III-H. Interference with Agency Relationship (Expect 1-2 questions from this area)

This final Topic Area in the Agency Content Outline Section should serve as a warning that *the Real Estate Commission is serious about ensuring agency relationships proceed undisturbed by improper interference*.

The following particulars define and *prohibit interfering with the agency relationship of another licensee* by taking such actions as

- *counseling a client of another licensee on how to terminate or amend an existing agency contract*,
- *demanding a referral fee* from another licensee without reasonable cause, or
- *threatening to take harmful action against a client* of another licensee because of the agency relationship.

In short, Connecticut Real Estate License Law and Commission policies specifically note that

- *a licensee shall not engage in any practice or take any action that interferes with the agency relationship* of another licensee
- *no licensee shall induce or attempt to induce any party to a contract of sale, lease, listing, or buyer representation for real property to breach or terminate such contract for the purpose of substituting in lieu thereof a new contract with another principal of the licensee* (References: Section 20-328-9a and the Connecticut Real Estate Commission Policy on Interfering with Agency Relationships)

Violation Alert!

Yet again, it is worth noting that *the TWO "catch-all" Section 20-320 violation land-mines* noted at the end of the previous Topic Area have direct application here as well. Watch out!

III. Connecticut Real Estate Agency (Expect 8 questions from this Outline Section)

__This ends the presentation of key terms and concepts likely to be either tested or used as distractors in this Content Outline Section.__

IV. Connecticut-Specific Real Estate Principles and Practices
(Expect 7 questions from this Outline Section)

SPECIAL EXAM NOTE

There are seven Topic Areas in this Roman Numeral Content Area from which you will receive seven scored test questions.

"Seven questions for seven topics" suggests one question per Topic Area.

In reality, though, the Commission identifies some Topic Areas as being worth more emphasis than others for testing, so your version of the test may present two or three questions from a particular Topic and none from certain others. Other test takers, however, will get questions from Topics your test version may have omitted.

And that is why each Topic Area in this book has a range of questions—to indicate its relative importance within its Roman Numeral Content Area.

A closer look at this Content Area, though, shows that since the first Topic Area has six Subtopics, there are actually 12 specific subjects identified for testing in this Content Area.

The simple math of seven questions for twelve subjects means there will be __at least__ five subjects on which you will receive no __scored__ questions.

However, the testing company "pretests" five questions on each exam that do not get counted toward your score, so __you may actually see one question__ from each Topic Area as well as each Subtopic in the first Topic Area.

Since you will not be able to tell the difference between scored and pretest questions, __answer every question as if it counts – it just might!__

IV-A. Connecticut-Specific Real Estate Principles and Practices
(Expect 2-3 questions from this area)

This Topic Area has six subtopics that provide state-specific applications of general principles.

For example, types of multi-party ownership has applications in other states regarding marital property rights, tenancy by the entirety concerns, and many other legal intricacies that do not apply in Connecticut.

And whereas each state has its own preferred methods of handling land records and assessing taxes on property sales, among other details, the Real Estate Commission feels those entering the real estate profession here should know the basics of these issues as they apply specifically to Connecticut real estate matters.

IV. Connecticut-Specific Real Estate Principles and Practices
(Expect 7 questions from this Outline Section)

So, this Topic Area will make state-specific points on these general real estate areas; this overview will attempt to be brief yet comprehensive in treating each of the six subtopics.

1. Co-ownership forms and shares

Broadly speaking, when it comes to residential properties, ***Connecticut recognizes two types of co-ownership: tenancy in common and joint tenancy***, regardless of whether ownership is by two or more unrelated people or a married couple.

> ***Connecticut is not one of the eight or nine community property states***, *which have specific provisions for both spouses regarding marital property,* ***nor does it automatically recognize tenancy by the entirety***, *another form of marital ownership applicable in some states, such as New York. So, you don't need to know about these for the test, though you might in reality if you buy or sell out-of-state property.*

But ***Connecticut does have a state-specific wrinkle in the joint tenancy*** arena. ***Joint tenancy typically involves taking title subject to "the four unities,"*** meaning (1) all names are on the same *title*, (2) title was taken at the same *time*, (3) there is an undivided right of ***possession***, and (4) each party has the same prorated property ***interest***.

In Connecticut, though, joint tenants are specifically allowed to have unequal interests. In short, three parties may buy a property together with one having a 50% interest, a second having 30%, and the third having 20%.

> ***The interests of the grantees under any such conveyance*** *[i.e., deeds that assign ownership to the survivor(s) of multiple owners]* ***may be held by them in equal or unequal shares.***
> (Reference: Section 47-14a)

Further, ***in cases where a married couple divorces while holding property as joint tenants***, unless otherwise provided in the divorce or dissolution documents, ***their ownership interests become tenants in common***, without "survivorship" rights.

> ***Whenever a husband and wife are joint tenants in the same real estate . . . a divorce or dissolution of the marriage . . . severs their interests and converts them into tenants in common as to each other*** but not as to any remaining joint tenant or joint tenants.
> (Reference: Section 47-14g)

2. Adverse possession/prescriptive easement time

This subtopic is simple: In Connecticut, ***the statutory period*** required to have legal standing to apply for and/or acquire either ***title interest through adverse possession*** or an ***easement interest through prescriptive easement is fifteen (15) years***.

In Connecticut, these types of acquisition of property rights are referred to as ***adverse use***, and apply to both possession and easements. As the statutes put it:

IV. Connecticut-Specific Real Estate Principles and Practices
(Expect 7 questions from this Outline Section)

When acquired by adverse use. No person may acquire a right-of-way or any other easement from, in, upon or over the land of another, by the adverse use or enjoyment thereof, unless *the use has been continued uninterrupted for fifteen years*. (Reference: Section 47-37)

There are specific requirements for applying for legal entitlement to adverse use rights, and specific obligations of owners to fend off claims. Refer to the statutes, and work with a lawyer, to ensure you correctly understand and handle your side of an adverse use (adverse possession or prescriptive easement) claim.

Nevertheless, if you suspect someone may make a claim against your property, it is best to legally "interrupt" the use before the fifteen-year mark is reached!

3. Land records and recording

Connecticut is one of a very few states that records land records by municipality, i.e. town or city, and not by county seat. In Connecticut, there are no county seats, just county names.

Though professionals in Connecticut are used to this system, it often seems confusing and disjointed, such as conducting title searches for properties in Mystic.

Since Mystic is not really a town and cannot be researched in some central New London county location, title searches for Mystic require going to the town hall in Groton, Stonington, or Ledyard, depending on the actual address. Similar situations abound.

SPECIAL EXAM NOTE: *The **general exam—not the state**—may include questions that refer to **county courts** holding records – **the county system was abolished in Connecticut a long time ago** in favor of keeping land records and most other official records in the municipality.*

A few points about recording conveyances have to do with the legal status of recorded versus unrecorded conveyances, which ultimately will be left to the lawyers. However, ***in any transaction where lawyers are not involved, tell your new owner to record the deed***.

No conveyance shall be effectual to hold any land against any other person but the grantor and his heirs, ***unless recorded on the records of the town in which the land lies***.
(Reference: Section 47-10(a))

The effective date of title is the recording date; title searches to establish marketable title only have to go back forty (40) years.   (References: Sections 47-33b(e); 47-33c)

Practical note on title searches: *for years the convention for title searches was to go back 60 years, and many "old school" title searchers and lawyers still hold to that standard, so don't be surprised if you hear 60 versus 40 when the subject comes up among your professional colleagues; it is likely to appear as a distractor on test questions, too!*

And, not unlike ***changing your name*** and address information with the Department of Motor Vehicles, in the event an owner of property changes their personal or corporate name, the change ***needs to be logged into the town records within sixty days***.

IV. Connecticut-Specific Real Estate Principles and Practices
(Expect 7 questions from this Outline Section)

Any person, corporation, limited liability company or limited liability partnership owning real estate or having an interest therein whose name has been changed . . . ***shall, within sixty days after the change . . . file with the town clerk of the town in which the real estate is located a certificate . . . giving the name before and after the change*** . . .   (Reference: Section 47-12)

Effective October 1, 2009, Connecticut adopted the ***Uniform Real Property Electronic Recording Act***, which allows, but does not require, town clerks to accept electronic land records for recording.

Provided these records meet the same legal standards for valid contracts, they will have the same legal force and effect of hard-copy submissions for recording.   (Reference: Sections 7-35aa-gg)

4. Real property taxes and assessments

In Connecticut, ***each municipality assesses every property within its borders*** according to state-required time periods, currently ***at least once every five years***. The values are put on what is known as ***the Grand List*** for each town, and is a value ***as of October 1st*** of every year.

The assessment is called a ***mass appraisal*** and is conducted by an appraisal company hired by the municipality to research properties and assign a Fair Market Value (FMV) from which the municipality derives an ***Assessment Value of 70% of the FMV***.

Based on the Assessment Value, the municipality then applies its own municipality-determined mill rate to compute the actual tax due from a particular property.

For testing purposes, the following points are worth noting;

Commencing October 1, 2006, each town shall implement a ***revaluation*** not later than the first day of October that follows, ***by five years***, the October first assessment date on which the town's previous revaluation became effective.   (Reference: Section 12-62(b)(1))

Also, beginning with the first grand list following the implementation of a required ***five-year revaluation*** after October 1, 2005, ***a municipality <u>may</u> require its assessor to adjust property values annually***, basing them on recent—generally within the past twelve months—fair market sales and the value of new construction.

If a municipality gets the approval of its legislative body to implement this ***annual adjustment*** option, the following conditions apply
- ***no mailing of a written notice of assessment increase needs to be made to owners***
- ***the municipality must continue with annual adjustments until the next revaluation***
- ***the annual adjustment is capped at five percent per year***
- ***adjustments may be made by specific geographic areas of the municipality***

(Reference: Sec. 12-62o)

Taxpayer note: since any municipality that implements this option will begin the year after the statutory five-year revaluation, sandwiched between any two statutory revaluations, there will

IV. Connecticut-Specific Real Estate Principles and Practices
(Expect 7 questions from this Outline Section)

be *four annual adjustment periods*, e.g., reval on 10/1/08, adjustments in '09, '10, '11, and '12 *for a total of four,* then a new reval in '13).

With a possible annual increase of five percent (5%), this means **there is a potential total property value increase of twenty percent (21.55% with compounding!) between revals**, without any formal notification requirements! Ouch! Have your clients monitor their tax bills closely for this!

Though the statutes worth student review and testing include Section 12-81, Exemptions, the statutes go on for pages.

The only points worth noting for a beginning real estate licensee are that ***there are veteran-related property tax discounts and/or exemptions on property taxes***. *Check with your town's assessor on this, but qualified veterans are entitled to a tax break.*

(Reference: Section 12-81g)

Although most vets know their rights, if you are working with vets, advise them to look into property tax reductions based on vet status: several of my own family members who served during times of war recorded their discharge papers and got tax breaks on their residences.

In addition, many municipalities also have tax breaks, or exemptions, for limited-income seniors and others with handicaps. Check with your town's assessor on available exemptions, requirements, and procedures for obtaining and maintaining them.

5. Conveyance tax

Conveyance taxes are relatively simple to understand and compute. But they are subject to change, so keep up, even though it is in the professional realm of the closing attorneys to run the numbers and be accountably accurate.

In short, the state taxes the SELLER of residential and unimproved real property .75% of the gross sales price, and the municipality gets an additional .25% of the gross sales price.

The conveyance tax does not apply to conveyances for consideration of less than $2,000, which are few and far between. Also, certain municipalities, like Hartford, Bridgeport, and a few other cities, are allowed a .5% municipal tax. ***Note, too, that the state will tax non-residential conveyances other than unimproved land, e.g., commercial, at 1.25% rather than .75%.***

As far as ***conveyance tax questions on the test*** *go, if it is a computation question, you should be given all the necessary information about the municipality's tax rate, then plug in .75% for the state and run the numbers.* ***Barring a municipality variance, most residential sales will have a combined state and municipal conveyance tax liability of an easy-to-compute 1%.***

In the case of ***residential properties*** that sell for ***over $800,000***, the ***state increases its tax to 1.25% for the portion of the price that is over $800,000***. (Reference: Section 12-494)

IV. Connecticut-Specific Real Estate Principles and Practices
(Expect 7 questions from this Outline Section)

*Leave the computations to the closing agents/lawyers, but do alert your clients, regardless of the property price range, that there are sales taxes due at closing, and that unlike the usual check-out sales tax paid by purchasers, this one is **payable by the seller, and will come to 1% for most properties.***

*For example, a simple scenario of selling a house in Deep River for $290,000 would incur a conveyance tax payment of .75% to the state ($2,175) plus .25% to the town of Deep River ($725) for a **total tax cost to the SELLER** of $2,900.*

6. Residential property condition disclosure

The ***Uniform Property Condition Disclosure Act*** (Public Act No. 95-311) requires the seller of residential property to provide a **Residential Property Condition Disclosure Report *at any time prior to*** the prospective purchaser's ***execution of any binder, contract to purchase, option, or lease containing a purchase option.***

These provisions apply to the transfer of residential real property of four dwelling units or less, including condominiums and coops, made ***with or without the assistance of a licensee***, which means that ***even "For Sale By Owner" property sellers must comply with this disclosure requirement***.

The report specifically states that the *"**seller will be required to credit the purchaser with the sum of $300.00 at closing** if the seller fails to furnish this report as required by this act."*

(Reference: Section 20-327b-1)

Also, ***every agreement to purchase residential real estate for which a written residential condition report is required shall include a requirement that the seller credit the purchaser $300.00 at closing should the seller fail to furnish it.*** (Reference: Section 20-327c)

As you probably remember from your course review of the form, it includes areas to answer and/or explain conditions of basic systems, such as heating, hot water, plumbing, sewage, air conditioning, electrical, drinking water, security, and more. It also catalogues structural issues, like roof condition, foundation type and condition, insulation, and more.

And the form must "include information concerning ***municipal assessments***, including, but not limited to, ***sewer or water charges*** applicable to the property." Such information ***shall include the amount of current and/or any unpaid assessments***, and ***anticipated future assessments***. (Reference: Section 20-327b(d)(1))

The regulations require a *copy* of the report *signed by both the seller and purchaser* to be **attached to any agreement to purchase** the property.

Further, ***the seller must complete the form personally***—the licensee or home inspector cannot fill it out and have the seller sign it!

The report also expressly notes that *"**Connecticut law requires the owner of any dwelling in which <u>children under the age of six</u> reside to <u>abate or manage</u> materials containing toxic levels of lead.**"*

IV. Connecticut-Specific Real Estate Principles and Practices
(Expect 7 questions from this Outline Section)

And it includes a statement that the report *"in no way relieves a real estate broker of his or her obligation . . . to disclose any material facts. Failure to do so could result in punitive action* taken against the broker, such as fines, suspension or revocation of license."

(Reference: Section 20-327b-1)

Certain types of property transfers are exempt from this disclosure regulation; among them are transfers

- *from one or more co-owners solely to one or more of the co-owners*
- *made to the spouse*, mother, father, brother, sister, child, grandparent or grandchild *of the transferor where no consideration is paid*
- *of newly-constructed residential real property for which an implied warranty is provided* under Chapter 827: New Home Warranties
- *made by executors, administrators, trustees, or conservators*
- *by deed in lieu of foreclosure*
- *of property acquired by a judgment* of strict foreclosure or by foreclosure by sale or by a deed in lieu of foreclosure
- *pursuant to an order of the court*   (Reference: Section 20-327b(b))

The Residential Property Condition Disclosure Report is reproduced below for your review.

CONNECTICUT DEPARTMENT OF CONSUMER PROTECTION

RESIDENTIAL PROPERTY CONDITION DISCLOSURE REPORT

Name of Seller(s):
Property Street Address:
Property Municipality: Zip Code:

The Uniform Property Condition Disclosure Act (Connecticut General Statutes Section 20-327b) requires the seller of residential property to provide this disclosure to the prospective purchaser prior to the prospective purchaser's execution of any binder, contract to purchase, option, or lease containing a purchase option. These provisions apply to the transfer of residential real property of four dwelling units or less made with or without the assistance of a licensed broker or salesperson. The seller will be required to credit the purchaser with the sum of $300.00 at closing if the seller fails to furnish this report as required by said act.

[handwritten: $500.00]

Connecticut law requires the owner of any dwelling in which children under the age of 6 reside to abate or manage materials containing toxic levels of lead.

Pursuant to the Uniform Property Condition Disclosure Act, the seller is obligated to answer the following questions and to disclose herein any knowledge of any problem regarding the following:

IV. Connecticut-Specific Real Estate Principles and Practices
(Expect 7 questions from this Outline Section)

YES	NO	UNKN	I.	GENERAL INFORMATION
			1.	How long have you occupied the property? _____ Age of structure _____
☐	☐	☐	2.	Does anybody other than yourself have any right to use any part of your property, or does anybody else claim to own any part of your property? If yes, explain _____
☐	☐	☐	3.	Is the property in a flood hazard area or an inland wetlands area? If yes, explain: _____
☐	☐	☐	4.	Do you have any reason to believe that the municipality in which the subject property is located may impose any assessments for purposes such as sewer installation, sewer improvements, water main installation, water main improvements, sidewalks, or other improvements? If yes, explain: _____
☐	☐	☐	5.	Is the property located in a municipally designated village district, municipally designated historic district, or special tax district, or listed on the National Register of Historic Places? If yes, explain: _____

Special statement: Information concerning village districts and historic districts may be obtained from the municipality's village or historic district commission, if applicable.

YES	NO	UNKN	II.	SYSTEM/UTILITIES
☐	☐	☐	6.	Heating system problems? If yes, explain and list fuel types. _____
			a.	Is there an underground fuel tank? If yes, give age of tank if known, and location. _____
			b.	Are you aware of any problems with the fuel tank? If yes, please explain: _____
☐	☐	☐	7.	Hot water problems? If yes, explain: _____ Type of Hot Water Heater _____ Age _____
☐	☐	☐	8.	Plumbing system problems? If yes, explain: _____
☐	☐	☐	9.	Sewage system problems? If yes, explain: _____
			a.	Type of sewage disposal system (central sewer, septic, cesspool, etc.) _____
			b.	If private (a) Name of service company _____ (b) Date last pumped _____ Frequency _____
			c.	If public (1) Is there a separate charge made for sewer use? Yes _____ No _____ (2) If separate charge, is it a flat amount or metered? _____ (3) If flat amount, please state amount and due dates: _____ (4) Are there any unpaid sewer charges? Yes _____ No _____ If yes, state the amount _____
☐	☐	☐	10.	Air conditioning problems? If yes, explain: _____ Air conditioning type: Central _____ Window _____ Other _____
☐	☐	☐	11.	Electrical system problems? If yes, explain: _____
☐	☐	☐	12	Are you aware of any problem with the well or domestic water quality, quantity, recovery, and/or pressure? If yes, explain: _____ a. Was well water tested for contaminants/volatile organic compounds? If yes, attach a copy of the report. b. Are there any unpaid water charges? If yes, state the amount: _____ c. Is there a separate expense for water usage? If yes, state if flat or metered, give the amount and explain: _____
☐	☐	☐	13.	Electronic security problems? If yes, explain: _____
☐	☐	☐	14	Carbon monoxide or smoke detector problems? If yes, explain: _____
☐	☐	☐	15.	Fire sprinkler system problems? If yes, explain: _____

IV. Connecticut-Specific Real Estate Principles and Practices
(Expect 7 questions from this Outline Section)

YES	NO	UNKN	III.	BUILDING/STRUCTURE IMPROVEMENTS
☐	☐	☐	16.	Foundation/slab problems/settling? If yes, explain: _____
☐	☐	☐	17.	Basement Water/Seepage/Dampness? If yes, explain amount, frequency and location. _____
☐	☐	☐	18.	Sump pump problems? If yes, explain: _____
☐	☐	☐	19.	Roof leaks, problems? If yes, explain _____ Roof type: _____ Age: _____
☐	☐	☐	20.	Interior walls/ceiling problems? If yes, explain: _____
☐	☐	☐	21.	Exterior siding problems? If yes, explain: _____
☐	☐	☐	22.	Floor problems? If yes, explain: _____
☐	☐	☐	23.	Chimney/fireplace/wood or coal stove problems? If yes, explain: _____
☐	☐	☐	24.	Fire/smoke damage? If so, explain: _____
☐	☐	☐	25.	Patio/deck problems? If yes, explain: _____ If made of wood, is wood treated or untreated? _____
☐	☐	☐	26.	Driveway problems? If yes, explain: _____
☐	☐	☐	27.	Termite/insect/rodent/pest infestation problems? If yes, explain: _____
☐	☐	☐	28.	Is house insulated? If yes, type _____ Location _____
☐	☐	☐	29.	Rot and water damage problems? If yes, explain: _____
☐	☐	☐	30.	Water drainage problems? If yes, explain: _____
☐	☐	☐	31.	Are asbestos containing insulation or building materials present? If yes, location _____
☐	☐	☐	32.	Is lead paint present? If yes, location _____
☐	☐	☐	33.	Is lead plumbing present? If yes, location _____
☐	☐	☐	34.	Has test for radon been done? If yes, attach copy of report. State whether a radon control system is in place, or whether a radon control system has been in place in the previous twelve months. If yes, explain. _____
☐	☐	☐	35.	Does the property include any leased items? If yes, explain. (Items to be listed include, but are not limited to: propane fuel tanks, water heaters, major appliance, alarm systems and solar devices.) _____
☐	☐	☐	36.	Is the property subject to any types of land use restrictions, other than those contained within the property's chain of title or that are necessary to comply with state laws or municipal zoning? If yes, explain. _____

The Seller should use this area to further explain any item above. Attach additional pages if necessary and indicate here _____ the number of additional pages attached.

I. Seller's Certification
To the extent of the Seller(s)' knowledge as a property owner, the Seller acknowledges that the information contained above is true and accurate for those areas of the property listed. In the event a real estate broker

IV. Connecticut-Specific Real Estate Principles and Practices
(Expect 7 questions from this Outline Section)

or salesperson is utilized, the Seller authorizes the brokers or salespersons to provide the above information to prospective buyers, selling agents or buyer's agents.

DATE _____ SELLER _____ SELLER _____
                    (Signature)   (Type or Print)
DATE _____ SELLER _____ SELLER _____
                    (Signature)   (Type or Print)

II. Responsibilities of Real Estate Brokers
This report in no way relieves a real estate broker of his or her obligation under the provisions of Section 20-328-5a of the Regulations of Connecticut State Agencies to disclose any material facts. Failure to do so could result in punitive action taken against the broker, such as fines, suspension or revocation of license.

III. Statements Not to Constitute a Warranty
Any representations made by the seller on this report shall not constitute a warranty to the buyer.

IV. Nature of Disclosure Report
This residential disclosure report is not a substitute for inspections, tests, and other methods of determining the physical condition of the property.

V. Information on the Residence of Convicted Felons
Information concerning the residence address of a person convicted of a crime may be available from law enforcement agencies or the Department of Public Safety.

VI. Buyer's Certification
The buyer is urged to carefully inspect the property and, if desired, to have the property inspected by an expert. The buyer understands that there are areas of the property for which the seller has no knowledge and that this disclosure statement does not encompass those areas. The buyer also acknowledges that the buyer has read and received a signed copy of this statement from the seller or seller's agent.

DATE _____ BUYER _____ BUYER _____
                    (Signature)   (Type or Print)
DATE _____ BUYER _____ BUYER _____
                    (Signature)   (Type or Print)

Questions or Comments? Consumer Problems? Call the Department of Consumer Protection at 1-800-842-2649

Special Legislative Update Note: The Residential Property Condition Disclosure Report undergoes periodic updates to incorporate particulars that make it more comprehensive and responsive to potentially material property details. So, in the course of your career, the above form may grow from 36 points to ??? (Reference: Section 20-327b(d)(1)(B),(C))

IV-B. Connecticut Landlord-Tenant Act (Expect 1-2 questions from this area)

The Connecticut Landlord and Tenant Act is found in the Connecticut General Statutes under Title 47a, Landlord and Tenant; the Landlord and Tenant Act is comprised of Sections 47a-1 through 47a-74, otherwise known as Chapters 830-834.

IV. Connecticut-Specific Real Estate Principles and Practices
(Expect 7 questions from this Outline Section)

The Act is lengthy and far more detailed than most real estate licensees need to grasp, unless you become directly involved in property management, in which case you should familiarize yourself with the entire Act.

Of course, knowledge of the Act it is also useful in your personal life if you either live in a rental property or own property that you rent to others.

For the purposes of most licensees, and for testing, the following points are worth knowing:

1—Which rentals are covered by the provisions of the Act?

Generally speaking, the Landlord Tenant Act applies to standard **rentals of residential "dwelling units"** in complexes, apartments in multi-family houses, and single-family residences; the statutes define a "dwelling unit" to include units occupied by "roomers" who share common facilities, such as bathrooms and kitchens.

However, **the Act does NOT apply to** most forms of institutional, medical, educational, fraternal, or **transient housing** such as hotels and motels.

The statutes **MAY apply to motel and hotel rooms** if (1) a renter uses the motel or hotel as a primary residence from the beginning of occupancy, or (2) the occupancy extends past thirty days and constitutes a primary residence, or (3) the occupancy extends past ninety days.

(Reference: Section 47a-2)

2—What statutory particulars apply to leases?

In Connecticut, *a residential rental agreement shall NOT include provisions saying that the tenant agrees to*:
- **accept a cut-off date for late charges that is shorter than the statutory grace period**, which is within nine days after the due date for month-to-month rentals or within four days on week-to-week rentals;
- **pay a heat or utilities surcharge if heat or utilities is included** in the rental agreement;
- **permit the landlord to evict the tenant** *(also known legally as **dispossess**) **without resort to court order**;*
- **seize the tenant's property for rent** *(known legally as **distrain** [verb], and **distraint** or **distress** [noun])*;
- **waive the right to the interest on the security deposit** as provided by law;
- **remove or limit any liability of the landlord arising under law**, or to indemnify the landlord for that liability or the costs connected therewith;
- **waive or forfeit rights or remedies** provided by statute or municipal ordinance **unless such waiver is expressly allowed** by that same statute or ordinance;
- authorize the landlord to automatically prevail legally on a claim arising out of the rental agreement; or
- pay the landlord's attorney's fees in excess of fifteen per cent of any judgment against the tenant in any action in which money damages are awarded.

IV. Connecticut-Specific Real Estate Principles and Practices
(Expect 7 questions from this Outline Section)

Further, if included in a rental agreement, *any of the above provisions is unenforceable*.
(Reference: Section 47a-4)

3—What statutory particulars apply to rent monies?

In Connecticut, the following rules apply to rent monies:
A—Security Deposits:
- *cannot exceed the equivalent of two months' rent*, which may be in addition to the current month's rent
  - *for tenants age sixty-two and over, a landlord cannot demand a security deposit in excess of one month's rent*
    - an existing tenant who reaches the age of sixty-two is entitled to the return of all funds in excess of one month's rent (Reference: Section 47a-21(b))
- *are to be held in an interest-bearing escrow account* and *earn a rate of at least one and one-half percent*
  - *accrued interest* is to be either *paid to the tenant on the anniversary date and annually thereafter* or *credited annually to the next rental payment* due from the tenant (References: Section 47a-21(h),(i))
- *remain the property of the tenant* and *cannot be attached by any creditor of the landlord or the landlord's successors* nor seen as their asset in any legal proceeding or real property transfer (Reference: Section 47a-21(c))
- *are to be returned to the tenant within thirty days* of the termination of tenancy, *less any legitimate damage fees, which must be itemized in writing*; the *returned deposit monies must include all accrued interest*
  - *landlords who violate these requirements are liable to the tenant for twice the value of the total security amount*; if the violation is limited to failing to pay accrued interest, the liability will only be for double the amount of interest due
  (Reference: Section 47a-21(d))

B—Rent Payments, Time Periods, Termination Rights:
- *if rent is paid in cash, the landlord MUST provide the person making the payment with a receipt* stating the amount received, the purpose of the payment, and the date of the payment (Reference: Section 47a-3a)
- *if rent is unpaid when due and the tenant fails to pay within nine days thereafter* (or, for a week-to-week, four days thereafter), *the landlord may terminate the rental agreement in accordance with statutory procedures* for notice to the tenant to quit the premises and subsequent application to the authorities for eviction
  (References: Sections 47a-15a; 47a-23; 47a-23a; 47a-23b)

4—What statutory particulars apply to basic landlord and tenant responsibilities?

In Connecticut, the following rules apply to the responsibilities of each party:
A—Landlord Responsibilities: A landlord shall
- make all repairs and do whatever is necessary to *put and keep the premises in a fit and habitable condition*, except where the premises are intentionally rendered unfit or

IV. Connecticut-Specific Real Estate Principles and Practices
(Expect 7 questions from this Outline Section)

uninhabitable by the tenant, a member of his family or other person on the premises with his consent, in which case such duty shall be the responsibility of the tenant;
- *keep all common areas of the premises in a clean and safe condition*;
- *maintain in good and safe working order and condition all electrical, plumbing, sanitary, heating, ventilating and other facilities and appliances and elevators*, supplied or required to be supplied by him;
- *provide and maintain appropriate receptacles* for the removal of ashes, garbage, rubbish and other waste incidental to the occupancy of the dwelling unit and arrange for their removal; and
- *supply running water and reasonable amounts of hot water at all times and reasonable heat* except if the building which includes the dwelling unit is not required by law to be equipped for that purpose or if the dwelling unit is so constructed that heat or hot water is generated by an installation within the exclusive control of the tenant or supplied by a direct public utility connection.

(Reference: Section 47a-7)

B—Tenant Responsibilities: A tenant shall
- *keep such part of the premises that he occupies and uses as clean and safe as the condition of the premises permit*;
- *remove from his dwelling unit* all ashes, garbage, rubbish and other waste in a clean and safe manner to the place provided by the landlord;
- *keep all plumbing fixtures and appliances in the dwelling unit or used by the tenant as clean as the condition of each such fixture or appliance permits*;
- *use all electrical, plumbing, sanitary, heating, ventilating, air conditioning and other facilities and appliances, including elevators, in the premises in a reasonable manner*;
- *not wilfully or negligently destroy*, deface, damage, impair or remove any part of the premises or permit any other person to do so;
- *conduct himself and require other persons on the premises with his consent to conduct themselves in a manner that will not disturb his neighbors' peaceful enjoyment of the premises* or constitute a nuisance or a serious nuisance; and
- *if a judgment has been entered against a member of the tenant's household for serious nuisance by using the premises for the illegal sale of drugs, not permit such person to resume occupancy of the dwelling unit, except with the consent of the landlord*. (Reference: Section 47a-11)

IV-C. Connecticut Common Interest Ownership Act (Expect 0-1 question from this area)

Connecticut's Common Interest Ownership Act is found in the statutes under Title 47, Land and Land Titles, as Chapter 828 (Sections 47-200 through 47-299). It is based on a model law adopted in numerous other states, and was adopted in 1984 to update and expand laws governing the operation of common interest properties, particularly the guidelines in the Condominium Act of 1976.

The Act defines and codifies for Connecticut many of the generally shared principles regarding condominiums, cooperatives, planned communities, time shares, common elements, and units as well as requirements for declarations and resale of units.

IV. Connecticut-Specific Real Estate Principles and Practices
(Expect 7 questions from this Outline Section)

Since there are no significant differences between the general concepts and definitions of common interest properties and their application in Connecticut, you should see no questions in this area on these basics.

However, there are a few points worth quick note here, even though they are substantially similar to general points on common interest properties:

In a cooperative, a unit owner's interest in a unit and its allocated interests is a real property interest for all purposes, except that ***the real property constituting the cooperative shall be taxed and assessed as a whole and a unit owner's interest shall not be separately taxed***.
(Reference: Section 47-204(a))

A common interest community may be created pursuant to this chapter ***only by recording a declaration executed in the same manner as a deed*** and, in ***a cooperative, by conveying the real property subject to that declaration to the association***. (Reference: Section 47-220(a))

If walls, floors or ceilings are designated as boundaries of a unit, all lath, furring, wallboard, plasterboard, plaster, paneling, tiles, wallpaper, paint, finished flooring and any other materials constituting any part of the finished surfaces thereof are a part of the unit, and all other portions of the walls, floors or ceilings are a part of the common elements.
(Reference: Section 47-221(1))

Any shutters, awnings, window boxes, doorsteps, stoops, porches, balconies, patios and all exterior doors and windows or other fixtures ***designed to serve a single unit, but located outside the unit's boundaries***, are ***limited common elements*** allocated exclusively to that unit.
(Reference: Section 47-221(4))

A legally sufficient description of a unit is one which sets forth the
(1) name of the common interest community,
(2) recording data for the original declaration,
(3) town in which the common interest community is located, and
(4) identifying number of the unit.
These elements provide a legally sufficient description of that unit and all rights, obligations and interests appurtenant to that unit which were created by the declaration or bylaws as amended or restated. (Reference: Section 47-223)

In the ***resale of common interest ownership units, the seller is obligated to provide the buyer with certain documents***, such as the declaration, association rules, and certain financial information related to the association and the unit's obligations to the association.
(References: Sections 47-202; 47-224; and 47-270)

IV-D. Connecticut Fair Housing Laws   (Expect 1-2 questions from this area)

By statutory definition, the *"Fair Housing Act"* means *"Title VIII of the Civil Rights Act of 1968, as Amended,"* also known as the *federal Fair Housing Act*.

IV. Connecticut-Specific Real Estate Principles and Practices
(Expect 7 questions from this Outline Section)

Connecticut's regulations regarding discriminatory housing practices serve to reinforce and amplify federal laws by making them more directly applicable under State law.

As with all Fair Housing issues, the idea is ***do not discriminate***, and if tempted, do not look for legal loopholes or play games with distinctions: the Connecticut Real Estate Commission takes a very dim view of licensees who violate fair housing requirements.

A few points will be pulled out of the statutes for testing that reflect areas where Connecticut's fair housing law, codified primarily in ***Chapter 814c: Human Rights and Opportunities*** of ***Title 46a: Human Rights***, goes beyond federal guidelines (which should be tested on the general exam, not the state-specific portion); so note that

- ***housing for older persons refers either to people fifty-five and older or sixty-two and older, depending on the situation***
- ***protected classes identified in Connecticut law include the following***, some of which are not included in the list of federal protected classes
  - *race*
  - *creed*
  - *color*
  - *national origin*
  - *ancestry*
  - *sex*
  - *marital status*
  - *age*
  - *lawful source of income*
  - *familial status*
    - familial status includes a pregnant woman alone as well as one or more individuals under eighteen living with a parent or legal guardian or in the process of acquiring legal custody or adoption
  - *learning disability or physical or mental disability*
    - mental disability includes mental retardation

(References: Sections 46a-64b and 46a-64c)

According to the statutes, ***discrimination includes***

- ***refusal to permit, at the expense of a person with a physical or mental disability, reasonable modifications of a premises***; if the premises is a rental, the landlord may, where reasonable, condition the modifications on the tenant's agreeing to restore the rental property to its original condition
- ***refusal to make reasonable accommodations*** in rules, policies, practices, or services when such accommodations may be necessary to afford such person equal opportunity to use and enjoy a dwelling
- ***failing in the design and construction of multi-family dwellings*** for first occupancy after March 13, 1991, ***to have them comply with the greatest accommodation*** available under Fair Housing Act or state building code
  - *"covered multi-family dwellings" means buildings consisting of four or more units if such buildings have any elevators, and ground floor units consist of four or more*

IV. Connecticut-Specific Real Estate Principles and Practices
(Expect 7 questions from this Outline Section)

- *refusal to sell or rent* after the making of a bona fide offer, or to refuse to negotiate for the sale or rental of a dwelling, or otherwise make unavailable or deny a dwelling *to a member of a protected class*
- *representing to a member of a protected class that a particular dwelling is not available for inspection, sale, or rental when in fact it is*

State Fair Housing law also stresses that *any person or other entity engaged in residential real-estate-related transactions is prohibited from discriminating against any qualified person* in making such transactions available to them if the discrimination is based on violating their rights as a member of at least one protected class

- *this means that licensees, <u>and the public</u>, are subject to Fair Housing law*

A few definitions that apply in Connecticut Fair Housing Law include
- "dwelling," which means any building, structure, mobile manufactured home park or portion thereof that is occupied as, or designed or intended for occupancy as, a residence by one or more families, and any vacant land offered for sale or lease for the construction or location thereon of any such building, structure, or mobile manufactured home park or portion thereof
    - "mobile manufactured home park," which means a plot of land upon which two or more mobile manufactured homes occupied for residential purposes are located

The *provisions of Fair Housing Law does not apply to* a few housing situations; several of the exceptions noted include
- *the rental of a room or rooms in an owner-occupied single-family dwelling*
- *a unit in a dwelling containing living quarters for no more than two families living independently if one is owner-occupied*
- marital status prohibitions shall not be construed to prohibit *the denial of a dwelling to a man or a woman who are both unrelated by blood and not married to each other*
- *prohibitions based on sex do not apply to rental of sleeping accommodations using shared bathroom facilities* when the accommodations are provided by associations or organizations that rent accommodations for the exclusive use of one sex based on considerations of modesty and privacy

(References: Sections 46a-64b and 46a-64c)

One area where Connecticut goes on record with additional protected classes is sexual orientation. According to the statutes, sexual orientation means having a preference for heterosexuality, homosexuality, or bisexuality.

It is against the law in Connecticut to discriminate in housing based on sexual orientation, although it is not prohibited to deny rental units to unmarried couples.

(References: Sections 46a-81a; 46a-81e; and 46a-64c)

Interestingly, although Connecticut law has defined sexual orientations and protected people from discrimination based on it, it adds this qualification

IV. Connecticut-Specific Real Estate Principles and Practices
(Expect 7 questions from this Outline Section)

- *Nothing in [various sections] shall be deemed or construed to mean the state of Connecticut condones homosexuality or bisexuality or any equivalent lifestyle . . . or to establish sexual orientation as a specific and separate cultural classification in society.* (Reference: Section 46a-81r)

An important component of Connecticut's Fair Housing Law is the Public Accommodations Act (Section 46a-64), which was originally adopted to guarantee full and equal service in places of public accommodation, resort, or amusement.

Connecticut's civil rights law has constantly evolved since then, and is enforced by the **Commission on Human Rights and Opportunities (CHRO)**.

In 1990, Public Act 90-246 separated Fair Housing statutes from public accommodation law and provided for more substantial penalties for violations.

According to Connecticut public accommodation law, it is a violation to
- ***deny any person full and equal accommodations in any place of public accommodation, resort, or amusement*** based on
  - *race*
  - *creed*
  - *color*
  - *national origin*
  - *ancestry*
  - *sex*
  - *marital status*
  - *age*
  - *lawful source of income*
  - *mental retardation*
  - *mental disability or physical disability*, including but not limited to, blindness or deafness
- to discriminate, segregate, or separate based on any of the protected classes above
- for a place of public accommodation, resort, or amusement to
  - *restrict or limit a mother's right to breast-feed her child*
  - *fail or refuse to post a notice in a conspicuous place* that any blind, deaf, or mobility impaired person accompanied by *a guide dog in a harness or orange-colored leash and collar may enter* such premises or facility (References: CHRO Website and Section 46a-64)

Licensees have serious obligations regarding Fair Housing laws and anti-discrimination practices in the course of real estate business.

Connecticut statutes reemphasize federal definitions and prohibitions in real estate transactions concerning blockbusting and steering. Under Connecticut law, these are defined as

IV. Connecticut-Specific Real Estate Principles and Practices
(Expect 7 questions from this Outline Section)

- *"blockbusting"* means to induce or attempt to induce a person to sell or rent a dwelling by representations regarding the entry or prospective entry into the neighborhood of a person or persons of any of the protected classes listed above
- *"steering"* means to restrict or attempt to restrict the choices of a person by word or conduct in connection with seeking, negotiating for, buying, or renting a dwelling so as to perpetuate, or tend to perpetuate, segregated housing patterns, or obstruct choices in a community, neighborhood, or development, regarding any of the protected classes listed above (Reference: Section 20-328-1a)

Further, *the law puts the following requirements on licensee conduct* under Fair Housing and Public Accommodation law when involved in a covered real estate transaction with a member of a protected class

- *a licensee shall neither deny an individual equal professional services nor be a party to any plan or agreement to discriminate* against any member of a protected class
- *a licensee shall not participate in activities constituting blockbusting or steering*
- a licensee shall *place in all listing and buyer agency agreements a statement in the following form*
    - **This agreement is subject to the Connecticut General Statutes prohibiting discrimination in commercial and residential real estate transactions (C.G.S. Title 46a, Chapter 814c)** (Reference: Section 20-328-4a)

A party that believes it has been discriminated against has *180 days from the alleged act of discrimination to file a complaint with CHRO,* which then brings the complaint to the attention of the licensee or other alleged violator to get their side of the story.

CHRO standards state it will investigate the matter within one hundred days of filing and a final administrative disposition will be made within a year of filing unless impracticable. (Reference: Section 46a-64c)

IV-E. Connecticut Lead Paint Laws   (Expect 0-2 questions from this area)

Lead paint is a well-known health hazard, and Connecticut has reinforced federal laws with regulations regarding the abatement of lead in dwellings. *Most of these regulations are promulgated and overseen by the Department of Public Health (DPH).*

There is not much for real estate licensees to know regarding lead paint regulations, since they concentrate mostly on the obligation of physicians to report blood lead levels in children above a minimum standard or else are specific to lead abatement professionals.

There is potential trouble in the event a seller misrepresents the property's lead-hazard condition: the listing agent may still be liable for having accepted the seller's self-reporting without performing a due diligence review and confirmation of the seller's statements.

However, the following statutes are worth noting regarding residential properties.

IV. Connecticut-Specific Real Estate Principles and Practices
(Expect 7 questions from this Outline Section)

The owner of any dwelling in which the paint, plaster or other materials contain toxic levels of lead and *in which children under the age of six reside, shall abate or manage such dangerous materials* consistent with regulations adopted pursuant to this section.

(Reference: Section 19a-111c)

Paint on the accessible surfaces of a tenement house shall not be cracked, chipped, blistered, flaking, loose, or peeling so as to *constitute a health hazard.* (Reference: 47a-54f)

IV-F. Connecticut Disclosure of Off-Site Conditions Law
(Expect 0-1 questions from this area)

Among the many disclosures that must be provided in the course of a real estate transaction, *there is one related to hazardous waste sites* and *one related to sport hunting and shooting*.

According to the statutes, *a seller has to notify a purchaser that a list of hazardous waste sites is available from the municipal clerk*. According to the "Act Concerning Disclosure of Certain Conditions in Connection with the Sale of Real Estate (2002)," *neither the seller nor the licensee has any obligation to either disclose specific waste facilities or compile the list*.

Basically it states if the seller of a one-to-four family residential property provides *a written notice of the availability of a list of hazardous waste facilities* either *before or upon entering into a sales contract*, the seller and transaction-involved licensees will have satisfied any duty to disclose these facilities. *The list itself does not have to be included, just referenced.*

(Reference: Section 20-327f)

The following additional points help clarify the process of determining what constitutes hazardous waste and how the lists are prepared and maintained.

"Hazardous waste" means any *waste material which may pose a present or potential hazard to human health or the environment* when improperly disposed of, treated, stored, transported, or otherwise managed . . . *but does not include scrap tires*.

"Hazardous waste facility" means *land and appurtenances or structures used to dispose, treat, store, or recover hazardous waste.* (Reference: Section 22a-115)

The *Commissioner of Environmental Protection* shall maintain a hazardous waste disposal site inventory and provide for a method of recording the status of sites therein.

The inventory shall include all sites listed on the report entitled "An Inventory of Hazardous Waste Sites in Connecticut and recommendations for Continuing Action."

(Reference: Section 22a-133c)

The Commissioner of Environmental Protection *shall provide the clerk of each municipality in the state with a list of all hazardous waste facilities located within such municipality. . . . Each such list shall be updated by the Commissioner at least quarterly*.

IV. Connecticut-Specific Real Estate Principles and Practices
(Expect 7 questions from this Outline Section)

Each municipal clerk shall maintain a copy of the list provided pursuant to subsection (a) of this section, as updated, *and shall post a notice of the availability of the list* in the area where the municipal land records are kept. (Reference: Section 22a-134f)

Effective July 1, 2007, the same seller's written notification *"that a list of local properties upon which hunting or shooting sports regularly take place may be available at the office of the town clerk,"* relieves the seller and licensee of any disclosure duties regarding these sites. (Reference: Section 20-327g)

Interestingly, it is the option of property owners to volunteer information to the town clerk about whether sport hunting occurs on their land (see Section 7-32k), though permits to hunt, especially deer in season, are typically required when an owner gives consent to another to use the property.

The text of Section 20-327g shows it goes well beyond gun clubs to encompass all hunting on private property, such as using a hunting bow or rifle to shoot deer "out behind the house" whenever they are in season.

After all, a prospective neighbor might like to know that every fall there's a chance of a stray arrow hitting their garage, or worse. Reporting, though, is voluntary on the part of the property owner where such hunting occurs.

IV-G. Connecticut Uniform Electronic Transactions Act (Expect 0-1 questions from this area)

In 2000, the federal government passed the *Electronic Signatures in Global and National Commerce Act (ESIGN)*, which defines and covers the legal force of electronic signatures in interstate and international commerce.

There was also a model law made available in 1999 for state adaptations that governs the legal validity of electronic records and signatures, *Uniform Electronic Transactions Act (UETA)*.

The *Connecticut Uniform Electronic Transactions Act (CUETA)* is an adaptation of UETA that was signed into law in 2002; it specifically conforms to the requirements of ESIGN.

The provisions of CUETA governing the legal effect, validity, or enforceability of electronic records or signatures, and of contracts formed or performed with the use of such records or signatures, conform to the requirements of the Electronic Signatures in Global and National Commerce Act. (Reference: Section 1-286)

Essentially, CUETA asserts that most electronic documents have legal validity and force.
- *A record or signature may not be denied* legal effect or enforceability *solely because the record or signature is in electronic form.*
- *A contract may not be denied* legal effect or enforceability *solely because an electronic record was used in the formation of the contract.*
- If a law requires a record to be in writing, *an electronic record satisfies the law.*
- If a law requires a signature, *an electronic signature satisfies the law.*
- In a proceeding, *evidence of a record or signature may not be excluded solely because such record or signature is in electronic form.* (References: Sections 1-272 and 1-278)

IV. Connecticut-Specific Real Estate Principles and Practices
(Expect 7 questions from this Outline Section)

Certain documents, however, *must be furnished in hard copy*, including
- *notice of cancellation or termination of a utility service*
- *notice of default, acceleration, foreclosure, or eviction* of a *primary residence*
- *notice of cancellation or termination of life and/or health insurance or benefits*
- *notice of product recall* or material failure
- *documents intended to accompany hazardous or toxic materials*

(Reference: Section 1-268(c)(2))

Also, there are conditions that define sending and receiving records as well as circumstances under which they are considered not sent or received.

An electronic record is sent when it:
- *is addressed properly or otherwise directed properly to an information processing system that the recipient has designated* or uses for the purpose of receiving electronic records or information of the type sent *and from which the recipient is able to retrieve the electronic record*;
- *is in a form capable of being processed by such system*; and
- *enters an information processing system outside the control of the sender* or of a person that sent the electronic record on behalf of the sender *or enters a region of the information processing system designated or used by the recipient that is under the control of the recipient.*

An electronic record is received when it:
- *enters an information processing system that the recipient has designated* or uses for the purpose of receiving electronic records or information of the type sent and from which the recipient is able to retrieve the electronic record; and
- *is in a form capable of being processed by such system*, further
- *an electronic record is received even if no individual is aware of its receipt.*

(References: Sections 1-280(a),(b),(e))

It is presumed that an electronic record is not sent to or received by a consumer if the sender of the electronic record is aware that the consumer
- *did not receive the electronic record*, or
- *did not receive it in a manner allowing the record to be opened and read* by the consumer. (Reference: Section 1-284(b))

Record retention may also be managed electronically for both electronic transactions and paper documents, like checks, that have been put into electronic form.

If a law requires that a record be retained, the requirement is satisfied by retaining an electronic record of the information in the record that:
- *accurately reflects the information set forth in the record* after it was first generated in its final form as an electronic record or otherwise; and
- *remains accessible for later reference*. (Reference: Section 1-277(a))

IV. Connecticut-Specific Real Estate Principles and Practices
(Expect 7 questions from this Outline Section)

If a law requires a record to be presented or retained in its original form, or provides consequences if the record is not presented or retained in its original form, *such law is satisfied by an electronic record* retained in accordance with subsection (a) of this section.

(Reference: Section 1-277(d))

If a law requires retention of a check, the requirement is satisfied by retention of an electronic record of the information on the front and back of the check in accordance with subsection (a) of this section.

(Reference: Section 1-277(e))

Finally, a few definitions related to electronic transactions include
- *"Electronic"* means relating to technology having electrical, digital, magnetic, wireless, optical or electromagnetic capabilities or similar capabilities
- *"Electronic record"* means a record created, generated, sent, communicated, received or stored by electronic means, *including, but not limited to, facsimiles, electronic mail, telexes, and Internet messaging (IMs)*.
- *"Electronic signature"* means an electronic sound, symbol or process attached to or logically associated with a record and executed or adopted by a person with the intent to sign the record.
- *"Information"* means data, text, images, sounds, codes, computer programs, software, databases or the like.
- *"Information processing system"* means an electronic system for creating, generating, sending, receiving, storing, displaying or processing information.
- *"Transaction"* means an action or set of actions occurring between two or more persons relating to the conduct of business, consumer, commercial, charitable or governmental affairs.

(References: Sections 1-267(5),(7),(8),(10),(11),(16))

This ends the presentation of key terms and concepts likely to be either tested or used as distractors in this Content Outline Section.

THE SAMPLE EXAMS BEGIN AFTER THE FOLLOWING "TEST TIPS."

Transition Page Between Exam Prep and Sample Exams

A Few Test-Taking Tips

The exam-prep power of each question will be multiplied as much as four-fold if you make sure you know the meaning of the wrong answers, or distractors, as well as the correct one.

   Distractors are generally written using
- terms and concepts from the same category as the correct answer
- common misconceptions, misunderstandings, or mistakes
- information that is incomplete, overly complete, or correct for a different, closely-related reason

So remember – when reading the questions, and especially when reviewing your answers, pay special attention to the distractors: *Many of them will be used as the "real" answers on the real exam!*

Some of the points made regarding math questions earlier in this book are true for all questions, such as
- "Mark" any question you need to spend time on, leaving its answer choices blank, then come back to it – something in another question may loosen your mental log-jam
- Leave no question unanswered when you consider yourself finished with the test:
   - *Pure guessing gives you 1 out of 4 odds*
- However, you should be able to rule out at least a few of the answer choices, and then be able to make a better-odds guess at whatever's left
- You get to miss questions and still pass – and you get to miss a lot of them (just over 20 on the General and almost 10 on the State)!

   Finally, remember these Math-Specific points as you go into the General test
- If you miss only the math questions, you would still score over 90% on the test
- Most of the seven (7) questions on the test are not particularly complicated
- Those that are simply require you to take a deep breath and think a little harder
- Expect the questions themselves to provide the numbers and information necessary to do the math

Also note that PSI uses the numbers 1-4 rather than the letters A-D for its multiple-choice options – do NOT mistakenly think it is the first number in math choices. *And since PSI uses numbers, so will the sample exam questions in this book.*

After completing and scoring the following questions, remember that even if your scores are strong, you should review all of the questions to make sure you also understand the terms and concepts presented in the distractors.

Now get out that scratch paper and begin reading and answering the following questions. Good Luck!

Appendix A: Sample PSI General Real Estate Exam

1. Which of the following statements BEST defines real property?
    1. Land and the air space above it.
    2. Land and its improvements and all included ownership rights.
    3. Property that has been surveyed and identified by a full legal description.
    4. All of the rights to land and improvements as identified in a property deed.

2. Residents of an area with wells that go dry during severe droughts arranged with the municipality to provide city water to each property. This work is MOST likely to be funded through a
    1. special assessment.
    2. general assessment.
    3. municipal bond for improvements.
    4. grant from the Environmental Protection Agency.

3. Which of the following events will terminate an agency relationship?
    1. Any arrest of the agent.
    2. Bankruptcy of the principal.
    3. Transfer of ownership of the real estate firm.
    4. Violent disagreement between the principal and the agent.

4. A homeowner hires a carpenter to build a back deck and then refuses to pay. The carpenter is entitled to take which of the following actions?
    1. Remove the deck.
    2. Levy a special assessment.
    3. Place a mechanic's lien on the property.
    4. Petition the courts for a partition sale and recover the amount due from the proceeds.

5. When applied to a real estate sales contract, the term "rescission" is MOST likely to indicate that the contract has been
    1. assigned.
    2. recorded.
    3. notarized.
    4. terminated.

6. In the preparation of a competitive market analysis (CMA) or appraisal, which of the following situations is MOST likely to be interpreted as a stigmatizing property condition?
    1. Substandard construction.
    2. The presence of radon gas.
    3. Undiscovered termite infestation.
    4. A history of a major crime on the site.

7. Property managers are often granted a wide range of job-related authority to act on behalf of their principal. This is known as which of the following types of agency?
    1. Special.
    2. General.
    3. Universal.
    4. Subagency.

Appendix A: Sample PSI General Real Estate Exam

8. A property deed indicates that the easternmost boundary includes a fifteen-foot right of way allowing owners farther from the main road the right to cross the property. The property across which the others are allowed to pass is known as a
   1. subdivided parcel.
   2. landlocked parcel.
   3. servient tenement.
   4. dominant tenement.

9. A prospective buyer has offered $127,800 for a condominium that appraises at $122,500 and has made a deposit of $5,000. If the buyer arranges a first mortgage of 85% of the appraised value and asks the owner for seller-financing on the difference, how much will that be?
   1. $18,375.
   2. $18,420.
   3. $18,675.
   4. None of the above.

10. Which of the following terms identifies an element that is essential to creating a valid real estate sales contract?
    1. Recording.
    2. Legal purpose.
    3. Title insurance.
    4. Notarized signatures.

11. A couple with a modest combined income and strong employment history is having difficulty qualifying for a conventional loan to purchase a home due to their income and limited cash. Which of the following sources of real estate funding is MOST likely to meet their needs?
    1. Seller financing.
    2. Private investment groups.
    3. The secondary mortgage market.
    4. The Government National Mortgage Association (GNMA/"Ginnie Mae").

12. When preparing a competitive market analysis (CMA), an amenity worth $5,000 in a comparable property is BEST handled in which of the following ways?
    1. It is added to the subject property's estimated base value.
    2. It is subtracted from the comparable property's sales price.
    3. It is disregarded if it represents less than five percent of the comparable's value.
    4. It is averaged over the number of comparables used and added to the subject property.

13. The type of legal description that refers to a point of beginning, may refer to monuments, and uses distances and directions to come back to the point of beginning is
    1. lot and block.
    2. metes and bounds.
    3. vertical land description.
    4. government rectangular system.

Appendix A: Sample PSI General Real Estate Exam

14. A licensee acting as a buyer's broker is preparing an offer for a buyer, who asks the licensee if there are any tax benefits to arranging seller-financing instead of going to a conventional lender. Which of the following statements represents the licensee's BEST response to this question?
    1. "Seller-financing may be better for the seller than for you."
    2. "I would have to look more closely at the other variables before I can give you an accurate answer."
    3. "The tax consequences of different kinds of financing do not vary greatly enough to worry about it."
    4. "Make your best offer and include a contingency allowing you to review your options with a tax accountant or tax attorney."

15. Which of the following types of buyer-broker agreements provides the licensee with the GREATEST assurance of receiving compensation if the buyer purchases a property?
    1. Nonexclusive agency.
    2. Open buyer agency.
    3. Exclusive-agency buyer agency.
    4. Exclusive buyer agency.

16. Which of the following types of listing agreements allows a seller to contract with multiple licensees and only compensate the one that produces the buyer?
    1. Net.
    2. Open.
    3. Exclusive agency.
    4. Exclusive right-to-sell.

17. Which of the following ownership interests applies to parties who own real property as tenants in common?
    1. The ownership interests must be equal.
    2. The ownership interests may be conveyed separately.
    3. The last surviving owner gets title to the property in severalty.
    4. The ownership interests may not be transferred by will or intestate distribution.

18. Which of the following terms identifies the clause that allows a lender to call the entire remaining loan balance due in the event of buyer default?
    1. Novation.
    2. Entitlement.
    3. Acceleration.
    4. Hypothecation.

19. A buyer arranges for a $90,000 mortgage loan with an annual interest rate of 8% and a fixed monthly payment of $745. If the first loan payment is due 30 days after the loan origination date, how much of that payment will represent principal? (Use a 360-day year and 30-day months.)
    1. $125.
    2. $145.
    3. $600.
    4. None of the above.

Appendix A: Sample PSI General Real Estate Exam

20. A homeowner without any liens on the property arranges for a loan that provides a series of small monthly payments to the owner rather than a single large payment that must be paid back in installments. This arrangement is BEST identified as which of the following types of loans?
    1. Blanket.
    2. Open end.
    3. Home equity.
    4. Reverse annuity.

21. Shortly after taking a property listing, the listing licensee is approached by a family member who asks the licensee to prepare an offer at a significantly reduced price. Under the common law of agency, the licensee MUST
    1. refuse to prepare or present this offer.
    2. attempt to get the relative to match the list price.
    3. discuss the potential conflict with an attorney prior to proceeding.
    4. disclose the family relationship with the potential buyer to the seller.

22. A licensee showing some properties to a client-buyer only selects properties in areas where the owners are of the same general age, sex, and ethnic background as the client-buyer. According to federal Fair Housing law, this conduct would be an example of an illegal practice known as
    1. steering.
    2. redlining.
    3. panic peddling.
    4. property stigmatization.

23. A residential property owner wants to buy a vacant lot next to the property to build a garage and small guest house. The lot has a recent appraisal of $10,000, but the property owner is prepared to pay more than that, if necessary, to be able to expand. Which of the following terms BEST identifies the amount the owner is willing to pay?
    1. Market price.
    2. Market value.
    3. Assessed value.
    4. Actual cash value.

24. A property owner clears brush along a property line that borders an unimproved, wooded lot and puts a fence three feet inside the neighboring property. This fence is an example of
    1. a lien.
    2. a license.
    3. an encumbrance.
    4. an encroachment.

25. Which of the following terms identifies a property owner who has entered into an agency relationship with a licensee?
    1. Proxy.
    2. Vendee.
    3. Principal.
    4. Fiduciary.

Appendix A: Sample PSI General Real Estate Exam

26. A couple asks their buyer agent which way to take title so that a surviving spouse will inherit the other person's interest even without a will and the agent says, "Joint tenancy with the right of survivorship is the way you want to go." In this situation, the agent's response is BEST described as
    1. sound advice.
    2. misrepresentation.
    3. illegal practice of law.
    4. valid only in community property states.

27. As used in property management, the term "constructive eviction" is BEST understood to mean that a
    1. landlord is building a case against a tenant for eviction.
    2. court has made public its decision to support an eviction request.
    3. property has been sold and the tenant has been paid to vacate the premises.
    4. tenant has left a property after a landlord has allowed it to become uninhabitable.

28. An express agency relationship is MOST likely to be created in which of the following situations?
    1. A potential buyer asks a licensee at an open house if the licensee has other similar properties.
    2. A property owner asks a friend who is a licensee to list a property and signs an open listing agreement.
    3. A licensee canvasses a neighborhood for prospective sellers and gets a request for a listing presentation.
    4. A coworker of a licensee's spouse calls the licensee and asks for information on the local housing market.

29. During an appraisal of a residential property, an appraiser estimates the cost of rebuilding the subject property so that it is identical to its current size and condition. This is an example of which of the following appraisal principles?
    1. Balance.
    2. Conformity.
    3. Substitution.
    4. Anticipation.

30. An appraiser determines that a subject thirty-year-old residence has a replacement cost of $185,000 and is on a parcel of land worth $47,000. The structure's accrued depreciation from physical deterioration and functional obsolescence is estimated at approximately 40%. Given this information, which of the following BEST represents the property's value?
    1. $139,200.
    2. $158,000.
    3. $232,200.
    4. None of the above.

31. Which of the following statements BEST defines what is meant by the term "material defect"?
    1. Any condition that may change a principal's mind about buying or selling.
    2. Any property defect that would cost more than 10% of the sales price to correct.
    3. All conditions that add to a property's overall structural deterioration or depreciation in value.
    4. All factors that the seller would prefer prospective buyers not to know about the seller's motivation.

193

Appendix A: Sample PSI General Real Estate Exam

32. A buyer-broker agreement is MOST likely to create which of the following types of agency relationships?
    1. Dual.
    2. Single.
    3. General.
    4. Universal.

33. Which of the following government powers provides for the transfer of ownership of real property from an owner to the State in the event the property owner dies without a will or known heirs?
    1. Escheat.
    2. Taxation.
    3. Police power.
    4. Eminent domain.

34. Which of the following statements BEST defines what a "time is of the essence" clause means in a real estate sales contract?
    1. The contract provisions must be met in a timely fashion.
    2. The contract is subject to cancellation if any time requirement is not met.
    3. Any party that breaches the conditions of the clause is liable for liquidated damages.
    4. The conditions of the clause must be satisfied within forty-eight hours of acceptance or the contact becomes void.

35. The BEST statement about the relationship between a property mortgage and a promissory note is that the mortgage
    1. provides evidence of who made the loan to the property owner while the note identifies the face value of the loan.
    2. provides the details of the installment payments required for the loan while the note creates the legal liability for the repayment.
    3. creates a property lien as security for the note, which gives the details of both the amount of the debt and the terms of repayment.
    4. creates a public record of a property's indebtedness based on the note, which identifies the property location and credit history of the property owner.

36. Which of the following situations BEST exemplifies an implied agency relationship?
    1. A new licensee becomes affiliated with a firm and begins hosting open houses.
    2. A seller expresses an interest in finding a similar property in a neighboring town and the listing licensee brings the seller to see some in-house listings.
    3. A prospective buyer becomes quite friendly with the listing licensee during an open house and agrees to see other listings even after declining to sign a representation agreement during that meeting.
    4. A licensee who has been going to a particular physician for over five years is hosting an open house and the physician comes in and talks with the licensee at length about property details and the neighborhood.

Appendix A: Sample PSI General Real Estate Exam

37. Which of the following documents creates and identifies the extent of authority for a property manager acting on behalf of an owner?
    1. License law.
    2. Local zoning laws.
    3. Management agreement.
    4. Federal and state civil rights statutes.

38. The use of which of the following construction materials is specifically banned by federal law?
    1. Oil-based paint.
    2. Lead-based paint.
    3. Fiberglass insulation.
    4. Styrofoam insulation.

39. According to the statute of frauds, in order for real estate sales contracts to be enforceable in court they MUST be
    1. recorded.
    2. witnessed.
    3. in writing.
    4. between competent parties.

40. According to the Truth-in-Lending Act (Regulation Z), which of the following statements in an advertisement for real estate financing MUST include specific disclosures?
    1. "Flexible repayment schedule!"
    2. "Affordable financing available!"
    3. "Low interest for qualified applicants!"
    4. "Yours with just thirty-six easy payments!"

41. The provisions of the Americans with Disabilities Act (ADA) are MOST likely to apply to owners of which of the following types of property?
    1. Condominiums.
    2. Time-share properties.
    3. Single-family residences.
    4. Multiplex movie theaters.

42. A property sold for $227,500 with a 5% commission paid by the seller for brokerage services. The selling company retained 60% of the commission and the buyer's agent received 55% of the compensation paid to the buyer's company. In this situation, the buyer's company netted how much on this sale?
    1. $1,993.25.
    2. $2,047.50.
    3. $2,502.50.
    4. None of the above.

Appendix A: Sample PSI General Real Estate Exam

43. Which of the following situations BEST characterizes a property suffering from external (economic) obsolescence?
    1. A car dealership is located downwind of a new hog farm.
    2. A house loses value due to leaking gutters and old wiring.
    3. A school building is discovered to have asbestos problems.
    4. A shopping center has an anchor tenant that goes bankrupt.

44. During an open house, a listing licensee receives three offers, one of which is substantially less advantageous to the seller than the other two. According to the common law of agency, the licensee MUST present
    1. all offers.
    2. the offers the seller asks to see.
    3. each offer until the seller accepts one.
    4. only the two that are clearly best for the principal.

45. A listing licensee discovers the listed property has a history of faulty plumbing that has never been adequately corrected. The licensee's responsibility regarding this information is that the licensee MUST
    1. include a reference to the plumbing in all advertising.
    2. disclose it only if asked directly by a prospective buyer.
    3. discuss it with the seller and disclose it to prospective buyers.
    4. treat it as confidential and disclose it only with the permission of the seller.

46. A CORRECT statement about mortgage insurance premiums charged for Federal Housing Authority (FHA) loans is that they
    1. may be included in the total loan amount.
    2. may be paid in single annual installments.
    3. must be returned after the loan balance drops by 10%.
    4. must be paid by the seller for buyers meeting FHA low-income standards.

47. A developer approaches a municipality with a plan to purchase an available lot in a growing neighborhood if they will allow it to be used for a combination laundry and convenience store. Which of the following characteristics of value is MOST apparent in this developer's plan?
    1. Utility.
    2. Scarcity.
    3. Demand.
    4. Transferability.

48. The Sherman Antitrust Act specifically prohibits which of the following activities in the course of a real estate transaction?
    1. Usury.
    2. Price-fixing.
    3. Refusal to return earnest monies.
    4. Failure to disclose property defects.

Appendix A: Sample PSI General Real Estate Exam

49. What type of a contract is a real estate option contract?
    1. Void.
    2. Implied.
    3. Bilateral.
    4. Unilateral.

50. A prospective buyer and an agent prepare an offer. The seller reviews the offer and accepts it with the added provision that the earnest money will be forfeited by the buyer if the buyer backs out for any reason. Which of the following statements about this situation is CORRECT?
    1. There is a binding contract on the property.
    2. The prospective buyer is obligated to the terms but the seller is not.
    3. The seller has legally rejected the original offer and replaced it with a counteroffer.
    4. The provision about the earnest money is not an essential part of a valid contract and violates the statute of frauds.

51. Which of the following interests in real property does a prospective buyer receive once an offer to purchase becomes a binding offer?
    1. Possession.
    2. Ownership.
    3. Equitable title.
    4. Right to encumber.

52. A licensee takes an "as-is" listing on a residential property downhill from an abandoned industrial site. The licensee finds a buyer for the property who discovers after closing that residual industrial waste has been leaching into the house's water supply for several years. In this situation, which of the following parties is MOST likely to have liability for the expense of correcting this problem?
    1. The new owner only.
    2. The industrial property's owner only.
    3. The former residence owner and the licensee only.
    4. The industrial property owner, the former and the current residence owners, and the licensee.

53. When a deed or a lien is placed in the public records in order to make them available to anyone searching the records, this is known as
    1. recording a lis pendens.
    2. recording a satisfaction piece.
    3. providing actual notice.
    4. providing constructive notice.

54. Which of the following statements represents a PRIMARY purpose of the Fair Credit Reporting Act?
    1. To help borrowers make informed credit decisions.
    2. To protect the public against inaccurate credit reports.
    3. To prohibit discrimination in consumer credit transactions.
    4. To require lenders to provide meaningful cost-of-credit information.

Appendix A: Sample PSI General Real Estate Exam

55. Which of the following terms identifies the ownership of real property that is complete and has no restrictions on its use or transfer?
    1. Fee simple.
    2. Abstract of title.
    3. Severalty ownership.
    4. Prior appropriation doctrine.

56. A municipal mass appraisal has assigned a property a fair market value of $306,750. If the municipality has a mill rate of 16.86 and assesses property at 70% of FMV, the annual taxes on this property would be which of the following amounts? (Round to the nearest dollar.)
    1. $1,220.
    2. $2,440.
    3. $3,486.
    4. None of the above.

57. Which of the following general property conditions is MOST likely to be categorized as material?
    1. A small attic.
    2. A cracked foundation.
    3. An exterior in need of paint.
    4. An outdated set of kitchen appliances.

58. Under federal Fair Housing Act requirements, a property manager of a residential multi-unit property may legally refuse to approve which of the following situations?
    1. Allowing a handicapped person to make any accessibility modifications to unit.
    2. Allowing a handicapped person to keep a support animal based on a written no-pet policy that is enforced for all units.
    3. Renting a unit in a property exclusively occupied by persons over sixty-five to a single parent with an infant child.
    4. Renting a unit in a low-rent property to someone whose income is considerably above that of the other tenants.

59. According to the common law of agency, a licensee has which of the following obligations to an individual that prefers to remain a customer rather than become a client?
    1. Confidentiality.
    2. Courtesy and patience.
    3. Honesty and fair dealing.
    4. Only those agreed to in writing.

60. The name of the colorless, odorless gas often found in residential properties that represents an environmental health hazard associated with promoting lung cancer is
    1. radon.
    2. methane.
    3. asbestos.
    4. carbon monoxide.

Appendix A: Sample PSI General Real Estate Exam

61. A developer has purchased a 17.3 acre property and intends to subdivide the property into as many building lots as possible. If each lot must be at least 12,500 square feet, and the developer must dedicate a total of 1.7 acres for roads and a subdivision recreation area, what is the MAXIMUM number of lots that can be created on this property?
    1. 44.
    2. 48.
    3. 54.
    4. None of the above.

62. Which of the following appraisal methods would be the MOST appropriate one to use in the valuation of a twenty-year-old post office?
    1. Cost.
    2. Income.
    3. Capitalization.
    4. Direct sales comparison (market data).

63. Access ramps to government buildings, grab-bars in public rest rooms, and a row of pay phones with several placed lower than the others are examples of compliance with which of the following federal laws?
    1. Regulation Z.
    2. Federal Fair Housing Act.
    3. Uniform Commercial Code.
    4. Americans with Disabilities Act.

64. A person who owns a house in severalty dies intestate. This person's spouse has also passed away, and one of their three children ran away from home and has not been heard from in over twenty years. Which of the following statements about the transfer of this property is CORRECT?
    1. The property will escheat to the state since the owner died intestate.
    2. The two known children will receive a life estate interest in the property.
    3. The three children will be named as joint tenants with right of survivorship.
    4. The missing child represents a cloud on the title for future property transfers.

65. A lender is MOST likely to require a borrower to pay for private mortgage insurance in which of the following situations?
    1. The buyer has a history of bankruptcies.
    2. The property is in an area known for hurricanes.
    3. The lender foreclosed on the property's past owner.
    4. The loan amount is for 90% of the property's value.

66. An unmarried carpenter bought a building lot and erected a two-story home and lived there for three years before selling it for a large profit. According to IRS regulations, what is the MAXIMUM amount of any profit that would be exempt from capital gains tax?
    1. $125,000.
    2. $250,000.
    3. $500,000.
    4. None since the carpenter is a professional builder.

Appendix A: Sample PSI General Real Estate Exam

67. A CORRECT statement about compensation arrangements in real estate agency employment contracts is that they are
    1. determined by application of state regulations.
    2. adjusted periodically by the closest Board of Realtors.
    3. established by negotiation between the seller and the agent.
    4. subject to change if the local housing market fluctuates dramatically during the agreement period.

68. A lead-based paint disclosure notice MUST be included with a
    1. lease for any property open to the public.
    2. lease for office space for more than 15 employees.
    3. listing agreement for the sale of any historic property.
    4. sales contract for a residential property built before 1978.

69. Which of the following situations BEST exemplifies what is meant by "conversion of funds"?
    1. Using client funds as a source for temporary personal loans.
    2. Depositing an earnest money check in an office trust account.
    3. Disbursing office funds from an operating account to cover routine expenses.
    4. Transferring money from an account at a listing office to one at the selling office.

70. A property owner lists a residence and specifically avoids telling the listing licensee about a leaking roof. The licensee notices water stains in a closet ceiling, but considers them old and never discusses them with either the owner or the buyer. The property is sold without disclosing this condition and the buyer sues for damages based on material misrepresentation. Do the seller and/or the licensee have any liability? Why or why not?
    1. Neither one is liable because the buyer has the obligation to have the property inspected.
    2. The seller is the only liable party because the licensee was never told about the problem.
    3. The seller and the licensee are both liable because the licensee is responsible for the actions of a principal.
    4. The seller and the licensee are both liable because it is reasonable that the licensee should have discovered this condition.

71. According to the common law of agency, which of the following statements about the fiduciary obligation of confidentiality is CORRECT when an agent represents a principal in a real estate transaction?
    1. It outlasts the termination of the agency relationship.
    2. It must be defined in writing to be legally valid and enforceable.
    3. It is comparable to lawyer/client privilege and cannot be violated.
    4. It applies primarily to information about the principal's finances and motivation.

72. Property taxes for the calendar year are $2,700, payable on December 31, for a property closing on June 15th of the tax year. Which of the following amounts is MOST likely to appear on the settlement statement for prorated taxes? (Use a 360-day year and 30-day months.)
    1. $1,237.50.
    2. $1,350.00.
    3. $1,462.50.
    4. None of the above.

Appendix A: Sample PSI General Real Estate Exam

73. Which of the following statements made in a property advertisement is MOST likely to be characterized as puffing?
    1. "Motivated seller!"
    2. "Seller-financing available!"
    3. "New home with plenty of amenities!"
    4. "Best view of the mountains in town!"

74. Which of the following statements BEST defines what is meant by "appraised value"?
    1. An estimate of value.
    2. A statement of value.
    3. The most recent determination of market value.
    4. The assessment value of a property adjusted for current conditions.

75. A property owner built a house on a 7,500 square foot lot several years prior to the enactment of new zoning that requires at least 20,000 square feet for residential properties in that area. A CORRECT statement about this situation is that the
    1. property represents a nonconforming use and nothing must be done.
    2. municipality must grant a variance to this property and others like it.
    3. title will have a cloud on it that must be removed prior to any future sale.
    4. owner must purchase additional neighboring property to be in compliance.

76. Which of the following documents is used to transfer ownership of personal property that is included in the sale of real estate?
    1. A title.
    2. A bill of sale.
    3. A quitclaim deed.
    4. An original sales receipt.

77. The Truth in Lending Act is a part of which of the following federal laws?
    1. Regulation Z.
    2. Uniform Commercial Code.
    3. Equal Credit Opportunity Act.
    4. Consumer Credit Protection Act.

78. A property owner who is selling a commercial building at a considerable profit wants to legally avoid paying capital gains on the sale for as long as possible. The seller is MOST likely to achieve this objective by
    1. providing seller-financing to the new owner.
    2. creating a sale-leaseback arrangement with the new owner.
    3. reinvesting the money according to the terms of a 1031 exchange.
    4. getting legal representation and filing for bankruptcy protection immediately after closing.

Appendix A: Sample PSI General Real Estate Exam

79. A newly licensed real estate licensee has entered into an independent contractor agreement with a firm's primary broker to work as a salesperson. Under this type of relationship, the firm is MOST likely to be responsible for paying which of the following licensee expenses?
   1. Health benefits.
   2. License renewal fees.
   3. Continuing education course costs.
   4. Office space rent and telephone charges.

80. When acting in a fiduciary capacity for a seller in a real estate transaction, a licensee MUST
   1. be loyal to the seller's interests.
   2. obey all instructions of the seller.
   3. represent no other party in the transaction.
   4. disclose only those facts the seller wants known.

This is the end of the General portion of the exam.

Please check your work closely before scoring your answers.

The Connecticut State-Specific Exam begins on the next page.

Appendix B: Sample Connecticut General Statutes & Regulations State-Specific Real Estate Exam

1. A CORRECT statement about a licensee's obligation toward a former brokerage firm when the licensee changes firms is that the licensee
   1. has the option to take active listings to the new firm.
   2. must wait to transfer until all pending commissions have been paid or risk losing them.
   3. must maintain as confidential all information acquired while with the former brokerage.
   4. shall immediately turn over to the former firm all information and records gathered while there.

2. In Connecticut, listing agreements MUST contain which of the following elements in order to comply with Connecticut Real Estate License Law requirements?
   1. Listing price, brokerage compensation arrangements, and expiration date.
   2. Brokerage compensation arrangements, expiration date, and full legal description.
   3. Listing price, property condition disclosure statement, and signatures of all parties concerned.
   4. Property condition disclosure statement, full legal description, and signatures of all parties concerned.

3. A licensee is approached at a party by an enthusiastic new attorney in town who asks the licensee to put the attorney's new firm on their referral list. The attorney adds that as a start-up incentive, licensees will receive a $500 gift certificate after every closing involving a buyer they referred to the office. A CORRECT statement about this situation is that it represents
   1. an acceptable and well-established business practice for new businesses.
   2. an instance where the licensee's broker must authorize the arrangement.
   3. a violation of license law and regulations for both the licensee and the attorney.
   4. a violation of license law and regulations only if the licensee fails to disclose the compensation.

4. Which of the following actions by a licensee represents a violation of Connecticut Real Estate License Law?
   1. Leaving an earnest money check with an office assistant.
   2. Taking continuing education courses in excess of renewal requirements.
   3. Changing broker affiliation more than twice within a twelve-month period.
   4. Paying an unlicensed assistant who sits open houses on a commission basis.

5. In order to bring a suit for an easement by prescription in Connecticut, the person seeking the easement must have had uninterrupted use of the property for a MINIMUM of how many years?
   1. 10
   2. 15
   3. 20
   4. 25

Appendix B: Sample Connecticut General Statutes & Regulations State-Specific Real Estate Exam

6. Connecticut's Real Estate Guaranty Fund provides which of the following protections for consumers in a real estate transaction?
   1. Up to $25,000 per consumer in damages caused by a licensee.
   2. Up to $25,000 per transaction in damages caused by a licensee.
   3. Refund of commissions if a brokerage firm violated compensation guidelines.
   4. Refund of closing costs for some transactions funded by certain state housing authorities.

7. In the event a seller who is required to provide a Residential Property Condition Disclosure Report fails to do so, the seller MUST
   1. credit the buyer $300 at the closing.
   2. waive the right to sell the property in "as is" condition.
   3. pay for any home inspection ordered by prospective buyers.
   4. put not less than $1,000 in an escrow account for repairs within the first year after the sale.

8. In Connecticut, under which of the following circumstances MUST a licensee ask a seller to disclose that a residential property is on the market due to a recent suicide having occurred there?
   1. Always.
   2. If the event occurred within the past year.
   3. If the prospective purchaser puts the request in writing.
   4. Whenever the licensee is acting as a dual agent in a transaction.

9. Which of the following Connecticut agency relationships creates the GREATEST risk for a licensee to violate Connecticut Real Estate License Law due to a conflict of interest to the parties of a transaction?
   1. Subagency.
   2. Seller agency.
   3. Buyer agency.
   4. Disclosed dual agency.

10. A licensee working as an independent contractor for a broker is found guilty of embezzling client funds. According to Connecticut Real Estate License Law, does the broker have any liability for the licensee's acts? Why or why not?
    1. No; independent contractor status shields brokers from responsibility for licensee infractions.
    2. No; a licensee's actions do not involve the broker unless the broker was a direct participant in misdeeds.
    3. Yes; agency runs to the brokerage firm, not the licensee, so the broker incurs liability for licensee behavior.
    4. Yes; a broker is responsible for the acts of licensees in any situation once the independent contractor agreement has been executed.

Appendix B: Sample Connecticut General Statutes & Regulations
State-Specific Real Estate Exam

11. According to Connecticut Real Estate License Law, a CORRECT statement about a listing agent's obligation regarding multiple, simultaneous offers on a property is that the licensee is required to
    1. submit all offers to the owner.
    2. submit only the offer that is most advantageous to the owner.
    3. discuss the matter with the owner and submit those the owner requests.
    4. review them for contingencies and unacceptable requests for seller concessions.

12. Just prior to closing on a residential property, the listing licensee discovers the plumbing is acting up and there appears to be termite activity. Connecticut Real Estate License Law requires the licensee to take which of the following actions with this information?
    1. Not disclose it because of a seller agent's fiduciary duty of loyalty to the principal.
    2. Not disclose it because of a seller agent's fiduciary duty of confidentiality for the principal.
    3. Disclose it only if the buyer or the buyer's representative asks.
    4. Disclose it since it represents known defects that may be material to the buyer's decision to proceed.

13. A licensee talks with a friend at a class reunion and finds the friend listed a property a few months ago with a popular agent that the friend has begun to find unsatisfactory. The friend says the agent is too busy with other listings to show the property very often, and has only held one open house. The friend asks the licensee how to get out of the listing and the licensee suggests putting the agent on notice that if there isn't a workable offer within 30 days, the listing will be cancelled based on nonperformance. A CORRECT statement about this advice is that it
    1. is reasonable business advice since a principal is entitled to cancel agreements if dissatisfied.
    2. violates Connecticut Real Estate License Law provisions on interfering with agency relationships.
    3. represents a breach of professional ethics unless the licensee followed up with a letter and copied the listing agent.
    4. is acceptable advice between friends and creates no licensee liability for unfair business practices unless the licensee later tries to list the property.

14. A licensee receives an earnest money check on a property listed by another firm. In this case, the licensee is required to take which of the following actions with the check?
    1. Keep it with the paperwork until closing.
    2. Turn it over to the listing broker promptly.
    3. Turn it over to the licensee's broker promptly.
    4. Deposit it in the licensee's business account within 48 hours.

Appendix B: Sample Connecticut General Statutes & Regulations
State-Specific Real Estate Exam

15. Which of the following statements about designated agency in Connecticut is CORRECT?
    1. If a designated agent is at an office meeting, the agent's property cannot be discussed.
    2. A broker can appoint more than one licensee to act as a designated seller or buyer agent in a transaction.
    3. A broker must ensure that clerical staff does not work for designated agents representing opposing parties.
    4. A licensee appointed to act as a designated agent cannot be appointed to work for both parties in a transaction since designated agents cannot also be dual agents.

16. Under Connecticut Fair Housing Law, which of the following individual characteristics has protected class status?
    1. Religious choice.
    2. Sexual orientation.
    3. Employment history.
    4. Educational achievement.

17. According to Connecticut Real Estate License Law, when a licensee changes from one brokerage firm to another, which of the following parties must register the change with the Connecticut Real Estate Commission?
    1. The licensee.
    2. The new broker.
    3. The former broker.
    4. No one; notification is automatic upon license renewal.

18. A listing licensee shares the following confidential information with a prospective buyer: "The property owner is having financial problems and must sell, not only quickly, but perhaps even well below list price." According to Connecticut Real Estate License Law, under which of the following circumstances would this be legal?
    1. The information is related to a recorded tax lien.
    2. The owner has granted consent to disclose this information.
    3. The licensee has a disclosed dual agency with the buyer and seller.
    4. The buyer's offering price is known by the licensee to be acceptable to the owner.

19. According to the provisions of Connecticut's Landlord and Tenant Act, all of the following statements regarding tenant security deposits are correct EXCEPT that they
    1. may be kept in any passbook savings account.
    2. remain the property of the tenant throughout the rental period.
    3. cannot exceed the equivalent of two months' rent for tenants under sixty-two.
    4. shall be returned to the tenant within thirty days of termination of the tenancy.

Appendix B: Sample Connecticut General Statutes & Regulations State-Specific Real Estate Exam

20. According to Connecticut Real Estate License Law, which of the following conditions MUST be met in order for a licensee to accept a finder's fee from a friend for simply locating a buyer for the friend's unlisted property?
    1. The licensee must not be related to the buyer.
    2. The property must be located in Connecticut.
    3. The fee must be paid through the licensee's broker.
    4. The seller must not pay more than 10 percent of the sale price.

21. A licensee showing properties to a client-buyer only selects properties in neighborhoods where the owners are of the same ethnic background as the client-buyer. According to Connecticut Fair Housing law, this conduct would be an example of an illegal practice known as
    1. steering.
    2. redlining.
    3. blockbusting.
    4. material misrepresentation.

22. In Connecticut, when a seller agrees to allow a cooperating broker to act as a subagent of the listing broker, which of the following statements is CORRECT?
    1. The seller must be given a list of all licensees affiliated with the cooperating broker.
    2. The seller must receive a statement regarding the seller's vicarious liability for subagent acts.
    3. The listing broker must ensure that all designated agents prepare a summary of confidential information at the end of the transaction.
    4. The listing broker must review all documents prepared by any licensees acting as subagents before they are submitted to the seller.

23. A licensee has a relative who wishes to purchase a rental duplex. In the event the licensee presents an offer to purchase on behalf of the relative, the licensee MUST make which of the following disclosures?
    1. No disclosure is required.
    2. The licensee's licensing status only.
    3. The licensee's employing broker's name only.
    4. The licensee's status as a licensee representing a relative.

24. Which of the following individuals MUST hold a Connecticut real estate license?
    1. An out-of-state licensee who is interested in buying property in Connecticut.
    2. Anyone involved with Internet advertising of property located in Connecticut.
    3. A person who owns more than four properties that are available for sale at the same time.
    4. A licensee's salaried assistant who hosts open houses and prequalifies prospects for the licensee.

Appendix B: Sample Connecticut General Statutes & Regulations State-Specific Real Estate Exam

25. An unrepresented potential buyer enters a real estate office to ask about some properties listed with that company and begins to discuss them with a licensee. The licensee gets prequalifying information from the prospect in order to focus their search, selects several appropriate properties, and then goes out with the potential buyer to show them. In Connecticut, the above licensee is required to provide the potential buyer with the appropriate agency disclosure and/or representation form(s) NO LATER THAN which of the following times?
    1. When beginning to discuss specific property needs.
    2. Before beginning the prequalification or leaving the office.
    3. Prior to entering and touring the first of the listed properties.
    4. While discussing and preparing a written offer to purchase.

26. According to the Connecticut General Statutes regarding co-ownership of property under a joint tenancy relationship, which of "the four unities" common to joint tenancy does NOT have to be equal in Connecticut?
    1. Title, meaning all parties are named on the same deed.
    2. Time, meaning title was taken by all parties at the same time.
    3. Interest, meaning all parties have the same percentage interest in the property.
    4. Possession, meaning all parties have an undivided right of property possession.

27. According to the laws governing advertisements placed by licensees in Connecticut, a CORRECT statement about an ad that reads, "Gorgeous executive house on lake with all amenities; Gated Community; $325,000; Call 555-3366" is that it violates
    1. no federal or state regulation or guideline.
    2. Regulation Z's financial disclosure guidelines.
    3. the Fair Housing Act by promoting steering of prospects.
    4. Connecticut Real Estate License Law by omitting the name of the real estate company.

28. A licensee lists a property that the owner confides has major plumbing defects. The licensee advertises it as a "handyman special" and sells it with an "as is" clause. Neither the licensee nor the owner discloses the plumbing problems when asked about what repairs are required, saying instead that any prospective buyer is free to have the property inspected. According to Connecticut Real Estate License Law, has the licensee violated any agency relationship requirements? Why or why not?
    1. No; the licensee has not discouraged buyers from performing their own due diligence.
    2. No; the licensee has appropriately adhered to the fiduciary obligation of confidentiality.
    3. Yes; the licensee's refusal to answer property condition questions is both dishonest and misleading.
    4. Yes; the licensee's advertising requires the owner to provide a thorough property inspection report.

Appendix B: Sample Connecticut General Statutes & Regulations State-Specific Real Estate Exam

29. The Connecticut Real Estate Commission may impose which of the following penalties on a licensee who violates a provision of Connecticut Real Estate laws and regulations?
    1. Fines only.
    2. Fines and license revocation only.
    3. License suspension or revocation.
    4. License suspension and online offender registration.

30. According to Connecticut General Statutes governing lead paint in residential properties, which of the following statements is CORRECT?
    1. An owner of any residence in which a child under six lives must abate any lead paint in the dwelling.
    2. Lead paint that has been covered by three or more coats of oil-based or latex paint is considered encapsulated.
    3. Any residence with measurable amounts of lead paint must be brought into compliance or be refused a certificate of occupancy.
    4. All properties built before 1978 must be tested for lead paint levels during any home inspection made while the property is listed for sale.

This is the end of the exam.

Please check your work closely before scoring your answers.

Appendix C: Sample General Real Estate Exam Answer Key and Diagnostics Chart for Analyzing Strengths/Weaknesses

Sample Exam Answer Key & Diagnostic Chart.
Total the Number You Answered Correctly in Each Section and Compare with the Total for that Section. Math questions, Section X, are further indicated with an *.

#	Key	Sec	#	Key	Sec	#	Key	Sec	#	Key	Sec
1.	2	I-A	21.	4	V-B	41.	4	XI-D	61.	3	X-A*
2.	1	II-A	22.	1	IX-B	42.	2	X-D*	62.	1	III-B
3.	2	V-E	23.	1	III-A	43.	1	III-B	63.	4	IX-B
4.	3	II-D	24.	4	I-C	44.	1	VII-F	64.	4	VIII-A
5.	4	VII-I	25.	3	V-A	45.	3	VI-C	65.	4	IV-A
6.	4	III-C	26.	3	IX-F	46.	1	IV-D	66.	2	VIII-F
7.	2	V-A	27.	4	XI-A	47.	1	III-A	67.	3	IX-E
8.	3	I-C	28.	2	V-B	48.	2	IX-H	68.	4	VI-A
9.	3	X-C*	29.	3	III-B	49.	4	VII-A	69.	1	IX-A
10.	2	VII-A	30.	2	X-E*	50.	3	VII-F	70.	4	VI-C
11.	1	IV-C	31.	1	VI-D	51.	3	VII-E	71.	1	V-C
12.	2	III-C	32.	2	V-A	52.	4	VI-C	72.	1	X-D*
13.	2	I-B	33.	1	II-A	53.	4	VIII-C	73.	4	IX-C
14.	4	IX-F	34.	2	VII-E	54.	2	IV-F	74.	1	III-B
15.	4	VII-D	35.	3	IV-E	55.	1	I-D	75.	1	II-B
16.	2	VII-B	36.	2	V-B	56.	4	X-B*	76.	2	VIII-D
17.	2	I-D	37.	3	XI-A	57.	2	VI-D	77.	4	IX-C
18.	3	IV-E	38.	2	II-C	58.	3	IX-B	78.	3	XI-D
19.	2	X-F*	39.	3	VII-A	59.	3	V-D	79.	4	IX-D
20.	4	IV-B	40.	4	IX-C	60.	1	VI-E	80.	1	V-C

Diagnostic Chart for Outline Area Strength/Weakness Assessment

Outline Area	# Correct	# on Test	% Score
Section I	_____	6	_____
Section II	_____	5	_____
Section III	_____	8	_____
Section IV	_____	7	_____
Section V	_____	10	_____
Section VI	_____	7	_____
Section VII	_____	10	_____
Section VIII	_____	4	_____
Section IX	_____	12	_____
Section X	_____	7	_____
Section XI	_____	4	_____
Totals:	_____	**80**	_____

When reviewing your answers, pay special attention to the distractors: If you understand them, too, you will be that much more prepared to recognize them as the CORRECT answer on a "live" test question!

Appendix D: Sample Connecticut Real Estate Exam Answer Key and Diagnostics Chart for Analyzing Strengths/Weaknesses

Sample Exam Answer Key & Diagnostic Chart.
Total the Number You Answered Correctly in Each Section and Compare with the Total for that Section.

#	Key	Sec	#	Key	Sec	#	Key	Sec
1.	4	II-A	11.	1	II-B	21.	1	IV-D
2.	1	III-B	12.	4	II-D	22.	2	III-D
3.	3	I-A	13.	2	III-H	23.	4	II-B
4.	4	II-H	14.	3	II-C	24.	4	I-B
5.	2	IV-A-2	15.	2	III-F	25.	1	III-C
6.	2	I-F	16.	2	IV-D	26.	3	IV-A-1
7.	1	IV-A-6	17.	1	I-E	27.	4	II-F
8.	3	II-E	18.	2	III-G	28.	3	III-A
9.	4	III-E	19.	1	IV-B	29.	3	I-G
10.	3	II-A	20.	3	II-G	30.	1	IV-E

Diagnostic Chart for Outline Area Strength/Weakness Assessment

Outline Area	# Correct	# on Test	% Score
Section I	_____	5	_____
Section II	_____	10	_____
Section III	_____	8	_____
Section IV	_____	7	_____
Totals:	_____	**30**	_____

When reviewing your answers, pay special attention to the distractors: If you understand them, too, you will be that much more prepared to recognize them as the CORRECT answer on a "live" test question!

Appendix E: Statutes, Commission Regulations, and Policies (SCRAP)—Commission Interpretations and Statutory Forms

Statutes, Commission Regulations, and Policies (SCRAP) that Guide Licensee/Buyer Relationships, especially (1) Buyer as Client and (2) Buyer and Seller as Clients (Dual and Designated Agency)

Even though common sense should—and often does—prevail in both the practice of real estate and on test questions, there are **Statutes, Commission Regulations, and Policies (SCRAP)** that need to be reviewed to reinforce good common sense, and to prepare for test questions.

As previously noted, a ***client*** is ***a party who has entered into an agency representation relationship with a licensee*** whereas a ***customer*** is ***a party who has not***, and is therefore not legally represented by a licensee even though a licensee may be working with that party.

Simply put, though a licensee owes a client specific fiduciary obligations, ***a licensee owes a customer honesty and fair dealing***, which includes ***disclosure of material defects.***

> *The Connecticut General Statutes and Real Estate Commission Regulations and Policies have a host of laws and guidelines and special forms to make these matters more complicated in these lawsuit-hungry times.*
>
> *The good news is that most test questions on how to treat customers will be almost intuitive, since they cover topics of honesty, fair dealing, and disclosure of material defects.*
>
> *The bad news is that some of the questions on working with customers will be grounded in particulars of SCRAP.*
>
> *So, these have to be presented here to ensure you are familiar with the language they use, since key phrases are likely to appear as* **the "best" answer, i.e., the one that gets you credit***!*

Everything you read in the shaded boxes below is source material from SCRAP, most of which was summarized and discussed above.

> ***It is important to be familiar with the source materials included here*** *so you can ask yourself what the law would support in a particular situation, both in your practice and in scenarios presented on the test.*
>
> *The author regrets that SCRAP can be lengthy and wants the record to reflect that he did not originate any of it and is sorry that it adds length to this review.*
>
> *That said, you would do well to review all shaded boxes carefully as they represent the bedrock of legal interpretations regarding agency relationships and breaches thereof.*

Please note: *Occasionally there are formatting differences between the actual source material and its presentation here, such as indentations, breaks, numbering, bullets, bold type, italics, ellipses, etc. This is done in the interest of making the material more readable and does NOT include text changes beyond author clarifications, which are identified by being within brackets.*

Appendix E: Statutes, Commission Regulations, and Policies (SCRAP)—Commission Interpretations and Statutory Forms

The first piece of SCRAP is a Commission Memorandum from 1997 asserting the Commission's position that any brokerage company that takes listings must also remain open to working with buyers as customers, among other things.

SCRAP 1: Connecticut Real Estate Commission Memorandum—10/31/1997

MEMORANDUM FOR ALL REAL ESTATE LICENSEES:

I am writing on behalf of the Department of Consumer Protection and the Real Estate Commission to provide you with non-regulatory guidance concerning an emerging issue arising from the new agency law, the question of how brokers can work with buyers. We are providing this guidance to advise you of how you can avoid inadvertent misconduct in a new area.

A common misconception about the new law is that licensees can now only work with buyers as clients. This is not the case. As before, brokers and their salespeople can still work with a buyer in one of two ways:

A broker can work with a buyer as a client.
In this case, the broker and all salespersons working for the broker represent the buyer.
  If this arrangement is pursued, the law requires the broker to enter into a written buyer agency agreement with the buyer before [proceeding;] the broker is still permitted to represent the seller as a client as well as the buyer if both the buyer and seller give their informed consent to dual agency.

A broker can work with the buyer as a customer.
In this case, the broker and all the salespersons working for the broker represent the seller.
  A broker represents a seller by either
    entering into a written listing agreement with the seller, or by
    cooperating with another broker who has entered into a listing agreement with the seller _**and**_
      obtaining the seller's written consent to subagency

The Department and the Commission are concerned that **brokerage firms that take listings may institute office policies that exclude working with a buyer as a customer.**

**This is not permitted**, because a broker representing a seller through an exclusive listing has a fiduciary legal duty to the seller to make a diligent effort to sell the listed property. Part of that duty involves introducing potential buyers to the listed property.

It is the view of this Department that a broker cannot legally refuse to show an in-house listed property to a potential buyer because the buyer would not enter into an agency relationship with that broker.

In summary, the new agency law allows brokers to work with buyers on either a client or a customer basis.

A brokerage firm that lists properties cannot refuse to work with a buyer on a customer basis if that buyer does not seek representation and wishes to only be shown in-house listed properties.

Mark A. Shiffrin
Commissioner
October 31, 1997

Appendix E: Statutes, Commission Regulations, and Policies (SCRAP)—Commission Interpretations and Statutory Forms

*So, **the Commission clearly prohibits firms that list properties from refusing to work with buyers as customers**, since doing so would be a **breach of fiduciary duties to sellers**.*

Another piece of SCRAP is the Commission's Policy on Agency, which is a crucial source for interpreting and applying the numerous statutory and regulatory agency requirements. Though key elements have already been discussed in applicable sections above, it is worth looking closely at this Policy to ensure you grasp additional details as well as "the big picture," especially regarding points specific to working with buyers that do not elect to become a licensee's client.

*Since so many juicy questions can be squeezed out of it, **skip over it at your peril!***

SCRAP 2: The Connecticut Real Estate Commission Policy on Agency—1/6/2000
[Six+ Pages, 15 'Policy Points']

SUMMARY

Two significant new agency laws were enacted in 1996 (Public Act 96-159) and 1999 (Public Act 99-229) that affect real estate brokerage practices. Taken together, these new laws essentially do the following four things:

(i) ***Limit Subagency.*** In cooperating sales, there is no longer the presumption that the broker working with the buyer is the subagent of the seller. The primary purpose of this change is to encourage buyer representation. Subagency is still allowed, but for each listing shown, the seller would have to approve the subagency relationship by signing a written consent to subagency.

(ii) ***Allow Dual Agency.*** Provides for dual agency consent forms to be used to obtain a buyer's and seller's (or landlord and tenant's) consent to dual agency. For in-house sales, where only one brokerage firm is involved, the brokerage firm can represent both the buyer and seller as a dual agent, provided that this consent is obtained. The consent forms provide guidance as to what type of disclosures cannot be made in a dual agency relationship.

(iii) ***Allow Designated Agency.*** Real estate brokers are now allowed to appoint a separate seller agent and separate buyer agent for a dual agency transaction. The designated agents are not considered dual agents.

(iv) ***Protect confidential client information.*** Requires preservation of confidential information at any time during or after an agency relationship.

OVERVIEW

POLICY POINT 1:
AGENCY DOCUMENTS
[adapted from Table 1 in the Regs]

Agency documents are understood to include
   Agency Representation Agreements
      Listing Agreement *[form created/adopted by Brokerage firm]*
      Buyer Agency Agreement (must contain statement about possibility of dual agency for in-house sales) *[form created/adopted by Brokerage firm]*
      Seller Consent to Subagency *[form created/adopted by Brokerage firm]*

Appendix E: Statutes, Commission Regulations, and Policies (SCRAP)—Commission Interpretations and Statutory Forms

Agency Disclosure Notice Given to Unrepresented Parties *[form per Regulations, Sec. 20-325d-2]*
Dual Agency Consent Agreement *[form per Statutes, Sec. 20-325g]*, and
Dual Agency/Designated Agency Disclosure Notice and Consent Agreement *[form per Regulations, Sec. 20-325j-1]*

POLICY POINT 2:
AGENCY IN PRACTICE
[adapted from Table 2 in the Regs]

A: When the Brokerage Firm Represents Seller:

Enter into written Listing Agreement
Before showing property to a Buyer, determine if Buyer is represented by a brokerage firm
- If not, but would like to be represented by your firm, enter into a written Buyer Agency Agreement
- If the Buyer does not want representation, give the buyer an Agency Disclosure Notice for Unrepresented Persons at the time of first personal meeting concerning Buyer's needs, then proceed as the Seller's Agent

If the Buyer is represented by another brokerage firm, proceed as a Seller's Agent
If the Buyer is represented by your firm, ensure that BOTH buyer and seller have signed either the Dual Agency Consent Agreement OR the Dual Agency/Designated Agency Disclosure Notice and Consent Agreement
- if BOTH haven't signed, stop until they do;
- if they signed the latter form, have the responsible broker designate agents
- if they signed the former, proceed as a Dual Agent

B: When the Brokerage Firm Represents the Buyer:

Enter into written Buyer Agency Agreement
Before showing property to a Buyer, determine if Seller is represented by a brokerage firm
- If not, give the Seller an Agency Disclosure Notice for Unrepresented Persons at the time of first personal meeting and proceed as the Buyer's Agent
- If the Seller is represented by another brokerage firm, proceed as a Buyer's Agent
- If the Seller is represented by your brokerage firm, go back to A-4 OR proceed as a Buyer's Agent

C: When the Brokerage Firm is Working with Buyer as a Customer:

Determine whether Buyer seeks representation
- If yes, go back up to B-1 and proceed from there
- If not, determine if Buyer/Customer wants to see an in-house listing
  - If so, proceed as Seller's Agent
  - If not, and Buyer/Customer wants to see another brokerage firm's listing, determine if Seller agrees to Licensee acting as Seller's Subagent
    - If Seller agrees, get written consent to subagency, then go to A-3; the written consent must contain a statement that the law imposes vicarious liability on the Seller for acts of the subagent as well as the subagent Broker's name and licensee number

Appendix E: Statutes, Commission Regulations, and Policies (SCRAP)—Commission Interpretations and Statutory Forms

POLICY POINT 3:
AGENCY RUNS TO THE BROKERAGE FIRM, NOT INDIVIDUAL LICENSEES.

In general, agency runs from a client to the broker in a brokerage firm and all salespersons in that brokerage firm.

This means that if the brokerage firm has entered into a listing agreement with a seller, then all of the brokers and salespersons in that firm are agents of that seller, represent that seller, and owe fiduciary duties to that seller.

Likewise, if the brokerage firm enters into a buyer agency agreement with a buyer, then all of the brokers and salespersons in that firm are the agents of the buyer, represent that buyer, and owe fiduciary duties to that buyer.

Further, once a seller consents to a cooperating broker acting as a subagent, all licensees affiliated with that broker are that seller's subagent for the listed property.

The only exception to this is in the case of the appointment of designated agents, as outlined in [Policy Point] 10.

WORKING WITH BUYERS

POLICY POINT 4:
THE LAW ALLOWS LICENSEES TO WORK WITH A BUYER AS EITHER A CLIENT OR CUSTOMER.

The law does not require that a licensee enter into an agency relationship with a buyer as a client, in order for the licensee to provide services to the buyer.

A licensee can work with a buyer without representing the buyer in one of two ways.

> *(A licensee can also provide some services to a buyer that the licensee intends to potentially represent before a buyer agency agreement is entered into, as outlined in [Policy Point] 5).*

First, the broker can be the buyer's agent as long as the buyer agrees with this. If a licensee represents a buyer, the law requires that a written buyer agency agreement be entered into before the licensee negotiates on behalf of the buyer *(see [Policy Point] 5 for further detail on what constitutes negotiating and the timing).*

Second, a licensee can work with a buyer as a customer, meaning that the licensee does not represent the buyer.

The licensee can show the buyer in-house listings, in which cases the licensee is the agent of the seller.

The licensee can also show the buyer another firm's listing by being the subagent of the seller, after obtaining the seller's written consent to subagency.

Note that a licensee is not legally entitled to enforce a compensation arrangement when working with

Appendix E: Statutes, Commission Regulations, and Policies (SCRAP)—Commission Interpretations and Statutory Forms

a buyer on another firm's listings <u>unless</u> the licensee's firm enters into a buyer representation agreement with the buyer <u>or</u> obtains the seller's written permission to act as a subagent.

<u>A licensee can also work with the buyer without being the buyer's agent for in-house sales and subsequently represent the buyer for another company's listings.</u>

<u>Once the licensee becomes the buyer's agent, the licensee would then be either a dual agent or designated agent for any in-house sales with that buyer.</u>

The steps involved in working with a buyer as a client and as a customer are outlined in more detail in [Policy Point] 2.

Office policy may be more restrictive than what the law allows.

Real estate firms that have chosen to work with buyers only as buyer agents must advise buyers that it is their *policy* (not the law) to only work with buyers as buyer agents.

POLICY POINT 5:
A LICENSEE MAY CONDUCT PRELIMINARY ACTIVITIES <u>FOR A BUYER</u> BEFORE A WRITTEN BUYER REPRESENTATION AGREEMENT IS ENTERED INTO, GIVEN THE FOLLOWING GUIDELINES ARE MET.

a. **Before** a licensee works with the buyer, the licensee should:
    (i) ask whether the buyer is currently being represented by another real estate firm.
    (ii) explain the real estate firm's office policy on the various agency, dual agency, designated agency, and customer relationships that the licensee could potentially have with the buyer; and
    (iii) specifically tell the buyer not to provide confidential information unless and until the buyer and licensee have entered into an agency relationship.

b. The licensee **can do** the following for a buyer, *without entering into a written buyer agency agreement*:
    (i) give the buyer property information;
    (ii) give the buyer information on the licensee's firm; or
    (iii) give the buyer information on mortgage rates and lending institutions.

c. The licensee **cannot do** the following for a buyer, **unless** either (1) a written buyer agency agreement is entered into, **or** (2) the licensee is going to represent the seller and has presented the buyer with the form Agency Disclosure Notice (given to Unrepresented Persons) stating that the licensee represents the seller (and for cooperating sales, obtains the seller's consent to subagency):
    (i) ask the buyer to disclose confidential information (including information about the buyer's financial status, reasons for purchasing, etc.);
    (ii) express an opinion on or give advice about particular real estate (note that a licensee representing the seller should be cautious expressing an opinion or giving advice);
    (iii) physically show the buyer in-house listings;
    (iv) physically show the buyer property listed with another firm; or
    (v) discuss an offer with the buyer; or
    (vi) engage in any verbal or written negotiations on the buyer's behalf concerning the price or any terms or conditions of the purchase.

Appendix E: Statutes, Commission Regulations, and Policies (SCRAP)—Commission Interpretations and Statutory Forms

POLICY POINT 6:
BUYER-BROKERS MUST ACCURATELY EXPLAIN COMPENSATION ARRANGEMENTS WITH BUYER.

A broker entering into a buyer brokerage agreement with a buyer must explain the provisions of the agreement which detail the compensation arrangement.

A broker cannot advertise or represent that buyers can be represented with no liability to pay a fee or commission (unless in fact the buyer has no obligation to pay compensation in any circumstances under the agreement).

POLICY POINT 7:
A LICENSEE IS NOT REQUIRED TO REPRESENT BUYERS THAT COME INTO OPEN HOUSES.

A licensee is not legally required to enter into an agency relationship with buyers who come to the licensee's open house.

The licensee can work with the buyer as the seller's agent.

The form **Agency Disclosure Notice (given to Unrepresented Persons)** need not be given to prospective buyers, provided there is a sign or pamphlet disclosing the licensee's agency relationship <u>and the specific real estate needs of the prospective buyer are not discussed.</u>

If the licensee and buyer both desire, a buyer agency agreement can be entered into.

REPRESENTING BOTH BUYERS AND SELLERS

POLICY POINT 8:
THE POSSIBILITY OF DUAL AGENCY MUST BE STATED IN AGENCY AGREMENTS.

If a brokerage firm represents both buyers and sellers, that firm's agency agreements must contain a statement, as set forth in the licensing regulations, that the potential exists for a broker to be a dual agent.

POLICY POINT 9:
DUAL AGENCY IS ALLOWED, IF BOTH PARTIES GIVE THEIR INFORMED CONSENT.

Dual agency is permitted if both the buyer and seller give their informed consent to it.

One way that this consent can be obtained is by using the Dual Agency/Designated Agency Disclosure Notice and Consent Agreement.

Buyer and Seller must sign the form, having checked that they "do" consent do dual agency. Another way to obtain this consent is to use the Dual Agency Consent Agreement.

Both Buyer and Seller must sign the form. Details on the timing of the execution of these forms are set in [Policy Point] 10.

Appendix E: Statutes, Commission Regulations, and Policies (SCRAP)—Commission Interpretations and Statutory Forms

POLICY POINT 10:
NOTICE OF, AND INFORMED CONSENT TO, DUAL AGENCY
CAN BE OBTAINED BY USING <u>EITHER</u>
THE DUAL AGENCY/DESIGNATED AGENCY NOTICE AND CONSENT FORM <u>OR</u>
(2) THE DUAL AGENCY CONSENT AGREEMENT.

Either the Dual Agency/Designated Agency Disclosure Notice and Consent Agreement *or* the Dual Agency Consent Agreement *may* be generically signed by the seller at the time a listing agreement is entered into, identifying the buyer as "all buyers that the licensee now represents or may represent in the future."

> Similarly, either form *may* be generically signed by the buyer at the time the buyer agency agreement is entered into, identifying the seller as "all sellers that the licensee now represents or may represent in the future" and the property as "all property currently listed with the licensee or listed with the licensee in the future."

> <u>Before a specific buyer-client makes an offer on a specific seller-client's property, both the buyer and seller **must** execute a specific Dual Agency/Designated Agency Disclosure Notice and Consent Agreement *or* Dual Agency Consent Agreement listing the proper parties and property.</u>

Practical Note: for a transaction where designated agents will be appointed, the Dual Agency/Designated Agency Notice and Consent Form should be used to obtain dual agency consent.

POLICY POINT 11:
DESIGNATED AGENCY IS ALLOWED, IF
BOTH PARTIES GIVE THEIR INFORMED CONSENT.

In the case of dual agency, if all parties agree, the Brokerage Firm can appoint one or more licensees to solely represent the Buyer as a Designated Buyer's Agent and one or more licensees to solely represent the Seller as a Designated Seller's Agent in a specific transaction.

These designated agents would not be deemed to be dual agents, although the brokerage firm and other licensees within the firm would still be considered dual agents.

POLICY POINT 12:
DESIGNATED AGENCY IS NOT AN OPTION FOR
ONLY ONE PARTY/CLIENT IN A TRANSACTION.

The designated agency option is not available to only one party to a transaction.

In other words, a brokerage firm can not designate a designated agent to solely represent the Buyer, and not use designated agency for the Seller in a specific transaction.

Appendix E: Statutes, Commission Regulations, and Policies (SCRAP)—Commission Interpretations and Statutory Forms

POLICY POINT 13:
NOTICE OF AND INFORMED CONSENT TO DESIGNATED AGENCY CAN BE OBTAINED BY USING THE DUAL AGENCY/DESIGNATED AGENCY NOTICE AND CONSENT FORM.

For designated agency to occur, the law requires that both the buyer and seller be given notice and give their informed consent.

These two requirements can be met by using the Dual Agency/Designated Agency Disclosure Notice and Consent Agreement.

The designated agents must be listed on the form, having been appointed by the Brokerage Firm.

Additionally, Buyer and Seller must sign the form, having checked that they "have" agreed to the appointment of designated agents.

This portion of the form would be filled out when the dual agency portion is, with the timing being the same.

APPLICATION

POLICY POINT 14:
APPLICATION TO LEASING TRANSACTIONS.

All of the above applies to leasing transactions, except the limitation on subagency.

In a lease transaction (but not a lease-purchase-option transaction), licensees working with a tenant may be a subagent of the landlord, without obtaining a written Subagency Consent document.

POLICY POINT 15:
APPLICATION TO COMMERCIAL PROPERTY.

All of the above applies to both residential and commercial property transactions.

There are three critical *agency forms* that are either in the statutes themselves or delegated by statute to the Real Estate Regulations, which are promulgated by the Real Estate Commission.

1. **Real Estate Agency Disclosure Notice Given to <u>Unrepresented Persons</u> (Regulations: Sec. 20-325d-2)**
2. **Dual Agency Consent Agreement (Statute: Sec. 20-325g)**
3. **Dual Agency/Designated Agency Disclosure Notice and Consent Agreement Given to <u>Persons Represented by the Same Brokerage Firm</u> (Regulations: Sec. 20-325j-1)**

The first shaded box features the Regulation that lays out not only the specific language this disclosure must use, but clarifies that a written disclosure of existing agency relationship is NOT required if the prospective buyer or seller, as the case may be, is represented by another broker.

Appendix E: Statutes, Commission Regulations, and Policies (SCRAP)—Commission Interpretations and Statutory Forms

So, licensees representing either a seller or a buyer are required to provide this form <u>ONLY to unrepresented persons.</u>

> <u>**SCRAP 3a (legal authority):** Sec. 20-325d-2. Agency Disclosure.</u> (a) A real estate broker or real estate salesperson, when acting as a seller's agent, shall make a written disclosure of whom the brokerage firm and its agents represent to prospective buyers or lessees, unless such prospective buyer or lessee is represented by another real estate broker. A real estate broker or real estate salesperson, when acting as a buyer's agent, shall make a written disclosure of whom the brokerage firm and its agents represent to prospective sellers or lessors, unless such prospective seller or lessor is represented by another real estate broker. The disclosure shall be in the following form:

> **SCRAP 3b (form): REAL ESTATE AGENCY DISCLOSURE NOTICE GIVEN TO <u>UNREPRESENTED PERSONS</u>**
> *(Regulations: Sec. 20-325d-2)*

REAL ESTATE AGENCY DISCLOSURE NOTICE
GIVEN TO <u>UNREPRESENTED PERSONS</u>

This is not a contract. Connecticut law requires that you be given this notice disclosing whom the real estate licensee represents. The purpose of such disclosure is to enable you to make informed choices about your relationship with real estate licensees.

GIVEN TO: _____ (UNREPRESENTED PERSON/PERSONS)
ON _____ (DATE)
OUR FIRM _____ REPRESENTS   ☐ SELLER ☐ LANDLORD
                                     ☐ BUYER   ☐ TENANT

UNREPRESENTED PERSON(S)'S RIGHTS AND RESPONSIBILITIES

- The broker and salespersons (referred to as agents or licensees) in this transaction owe the other party to this transaction undivided fiduciary obligations, such as: loyalty, reasonable care, disclosure, and obedience to lawful instruction, confidentiality and accountability. The agent(s) must put the other party's interest first and negotiate for the best terms and conditions for them, <u>not for you</u>.
- All real estate agents, whether representing you or not, are obligated by law to treat all parties to a real estate transaction honestly and fairly.
- You have the responsibility to protect your own interests. Carefully read all agreements to make sure they accurately reflect your understanding. If you need additional advice for legal, tax, insurance or other such matters, it is your responsibility to consult a professional in those areas.
- Whether you are a buyer, seller, tenant, or landlord, you can choose to have the advice, assistance and representation of your own real estate brokerage firm and its agents. Do not assume that a real estate brokerage firm or its agents are representing you or are acting on your behalf <u>unless you have contracted in writing</u> with that real estate brokerage firm.

ACKNOWLEDGMENT OF UNREPRESENTED PERSON(S)*   **ACKNOWLEDGEMENT OF AGENT**

_____   _____
Signature(s)   Signature

_____   _____
Print Name(s)   Print Name
Date: _____   Date: _____

*To be signed by the buyer/tenant when the agent represents the seller/landlord, or
 To be signed by the seller/landlord when the agent represents the buyer/tenant

Appendix E: Statutes, Commission Regulations, and Policies (SCRAP)—Commission Interpretations and Statutory Forms

It is important to note the language of this disclosure form clearly states these points, each of which you should be prepared to stress to unrepresented people when you give them the form:

- ➤ *the form is not a contract*, signing it merely represents an acknowledgement that legally required disclosures have been made
- ➤ *the licensee already owes fiduciary obligations to another party*, and must put that party's interests first
- ➤ *the licensee must treat the unrepresented party honestly and fairly* despite their interests being treated as subordinate to those of the licensee's client
- ➤ *the unrepresented party is solely responsible for protecting their interests* by reading documents carefully and seeking professional advice if confused
- ➤ *the unrepresented party* is entitled to choose representation by another licensee, but **must contract in writing to be assured of an agency relationship with that licensee/firm**

The **Dual Agency Consent Agreement** below is codified in the Connecticut General Statutes: it is not a brokerage-specific document.

Review it closely, since there are numerous particulars that can be used for test questions!

Also note the statutory language below that provides for conclusive presumption of informed consent to dual agency when a party uses the form to indicate their written consent.

> **SCRAP 4a (legal authority for the form below): Sec. 20-325g. Dual agency consent agreements. Conclusive presumption of informed consent.** There shall be a conclusive presumption that a person has given informed consent to a dual agency relationship with a real estate broker if that person executes a written consent in the following form prior to executing any contract or agreement for the purchase, sale or lease of real estate: *[the form above follows this in the law]*

To keep the form on a single page, it will begin at the top of the next page!

Appendix E: Statutes, Commission Regulations, and Policies (SCRAP)—Commission Interpretations and Statutory Forms

SCRAP 4b (form): DUAL AGENCY CONSENT AGREEMENT *(Statute: Sec. 20-325g)*

DUAL AGENCY CONSENT AGREEMENT

Property Address: _____
Seller(s) or Landlord(s): _____
Buyer(s) or Tenant(s): _____

This Dual Agency Consent Agreement is an addendum to and make part of (check all that apply):
    ( ) Listing Agreement dated _____ between brokerage firm and seller or landlord.
    ( ) Buyer or tenant agency agreement dated _____ between brokerage firm and buyer or tenant.

(2) **Seller and buyer** (or landlord and tenant, as the case may be) hereby **acknowledge and agree** that _____ (name of brokerage firm) **is representing both buyer and seller** (or landlord and tenant, as the case may be) in the purchase and sale (or lease) of the above referenced property **and** that **brokerage firm has been and is now the agent of both seller and buyer** (or landlord and tenant, as the case may be). Seller and buyer (or landlord and tenant, as the case may be) have both consented to and hereby confirm their consent to this dual representation.

(3) Seller and buyer (or landlord and tenant, as the case may be) agree:

    The brokerage firm shall not be required to and shall not disclose to either buyer or seller (or landlord or tenant, as the case may be) any personal, financial or other confidential information to such other party without the express written consent of the party whose information is disclosed, other than information related to material property defects which are known to the brokerage firm and other information the brokerage firm is required to disclose by law.

    The brokerage firm may not disclose:

    to the buyer that the seller (landlord) will accept less than the asking or listed price, unless otherwise instructed to do so in writing by the seller (landlord);

    to the seller (landlord) that the buyer (tenant) can or will pay a price greater than the price submitted in a written offer to the seller (landlord), unless otherwise instructed to do so in writing by the buyer (tenant);

    the motivation of the seller or buyer (or landlord or tenant, as the case may be) for selling, buying or leasing property, unless otherwise instructed in writing by the respective party; or

    that a seller or buyer will agree to financing terms other than those offered, unless instructed in writing by the respective party.

Property information available through the multiple listing service or otherwise, including listed and sold properties, which has been requested by either the seller or the buyer (or landlord or tenant, as the case may be) shall be disclosed to both seller and buyer (or landlord and tenant, as the case may be).

Both parties are advised to seek competent legal and tax advice with regard to this transaction, and with regard to all documents executed in connection with this transaction, including this Dual Agency Consent Agreement.

I have read and understand the above agreement.

Buyer (Landlord)	Seller (Tenant)	Brokerage Firm
		(Authorized Representative)
		(Company Name)
Date	Date	Date

Appendix E: Statutes, Commission Regulations, and Policies (SCRAP)—Commission Interpretations and Statutory Forms

The third and final form for review here is the Dual Agency/Designated Agency Disclosure form that can be found in the Connecticut Real Estate Commission Regulations. Unfortunately, it is too long for a single page – so here goes!

SCRAP 5 (form): DUAL AGENCY/DESIGNATED AGENCY DISCLOSURE NOTICE AND CONSENT AGREEMENT GIVEN TO PERSONS REPRESENTED BY THE SAME BROKERAGE FIRM
(Regulations: Sec. 20-325j-1)

Dual Agency / Designated Agency
Disclosure Notice and Consent Agreement
Given to **Persons Represented by the Same Brokerage Firm**

Brokerage Firm: _____
Property Address: _____
Buyer (Tenant): _____
Seller (Landlord): _____

The Brokerage Firm has entered into a **written agency relationship** with both Buyer and Seller (or Tenant and Landlord). Buyer (Tenant) is now interested in buying (leasing) Seller's (Landlord's) Property.

    If this transaction proceeds, Brokerage Firm will be a **dual agent,** since Brokerage Firm represents both parties.

    Connecticut law allows Brokerage Firm to be a dual agent, but *only after both Buyer and Seller* (or Tenant and Landlord) *understand what dual agency is and consent to it.*

Connecticut law also allows Brokerage Firms that are dual agents to appoint individual **designated agents** within their firm to solely represent Buyer and Seller (or Tenant and Landlord);

    Again, this *designation can only be made after both Buyer and Seller* (or Tenant and Landlord) *understand what designated agency is and consent to it.*

Both Buyer and Seller (or Tenant and Landlord) are free to seek legal and tax advice with regard to this transaction, and with regard to all documents signed in connection with this transaction.

Understanding Dual Agency

Dual Agency means that the Brokerage Firm, and all the brokers and salespersons for the firm (unless designated agency is chosen) act in a fiduciary capacity for both Buyer and Seller (or Tenant and Landlord).

In Dual Agency, the Brokerage Firm does not represent either the Buyer or Seller (or Tenant or Landlord) exclusively, and *the parties can not expect the Brokerage Firm's undivided loyalty*.

The Brokerage Firm may not disclose to either the Buyer or Seller (or Tenant or Landlord) any personal, financial, or confidential information to the other party except as authorized by either party or required by law.

Appendix E: Statutes, Commission Regulations, and Policies (SCRAP)—Commission Interpretations and Statutory Forms

The Brokerage Firm may not disclose, unless otherwise instructed by the respective party:
- --- to Buyer (Tenant) that Seller (Landlord) will accept less than the asking or listed price
- --- to the Seller (Landlord) that the Buyer (Tenant) can pay a price greater than the price submitted in a written offer to the Seller, unless otherwise instructed to do so in writing by the Buyer (Tenant);
- --- the motivation of either Buyer or Seller (or Tenant or Landlord) for selling, buying, leasing the Property; and that
- --- that Buyer or Seller will agree to financing terms other than those offered.

Dual Agency Consent
Buyer and Seller (or Landlord and Tenant) understand dual agency and consent to Brokerage Firm acting as a dual agent in this transaction.

Understanding Designated Agency

Designated Agency means the appointment by the Brokerage Firm of one broker or salesperson (referred to as agent) affiliated with or employed by the Brokerage Firm to solely represent Buyer (Tenant) as a Designated Buyer's Agent and appoint another to solely represent Seller (Landlord) as a Designated Seller's Agent in this transaction.

A Designated Buyer's Agent and Designated Seller's Agent owe the party for whom they have been appointed undivided fiduciary obligations, such as loyalty, reasonable care, disclosure, obedience to lawful instruction, confidentiality and accountability. **The Designated Agent is not deemed to be a Dual Agent,** and thus does not owe fiduciary duties to the other party. A designated agent may use confidential information obtained about the other party while a designated agent for the benefit of the party for whom they have been appointed, however, information obtained before the designation is still confidential. In the case of Designated Agency, Brokerage Firm is still considered a Dual Agent.

Appointment of Designated Agents
Buyer and Seller (or Landlord and Tenant) understand designated agency and have agreed to the appointment of designated agents.

If designated agency has been agreed to, the following designated agents have been appointed:

_____ has been designated to solely represent Buyer (Tenant) as a Designated Buyer Agent.
_____ has been designated to solely represent Seller (Landlord) as a Designated Seller Agent.

Appointing broker/authorized agent: _____ Date: _____

Acknowledgement of Buyer (Tenant)   **Acknowledgement of Seller (Landlord)**

_____ _____
Signature(s)   Date   Signature(s)   Date
_____ _____
Print Name(s)   Print Name(s)

The ***Dual Agency/Designated Agency Disclosure and Consent Agreement*** is authorized by the Connecticut General Statutes and promulgated in the Connecticut Real Estate Commission Regulations.

Like the other two forms above, it is not a brokerage-specific document.

Review it closely, since there are numerous points that it raises for test questions!

Notes

Made in the USA
Middletown, DE
12 January 2016